Critical Vehicles

The MIT Press
Cambridge, Massachusetts
London, England

Krzysztof Wodiczko

Critical Vehicles

Writings,
Projects,
Interviews

This book was set in Frutiger by Graphic Composition Inc., Athens, Georgia
Printed and bound in the United States of America.

Library of Congress Cataloging-in-Publication Data
Wodiczko, Krzysztof.
    Critical vehicles : writings, projects, interviews / Krzysztof Wodiczko.
        p.   cm.
    Includes bibliographical references.
    ISBN 0-262-73122-3 (pbk. : alk. paper)
    1. Wodiczko, Krzysztof.   I. Title.
    N7255.P63W64   1998
    709'.2—dc21   98-11709
                                                                          CIP

for Irena Wodiczko

Contents

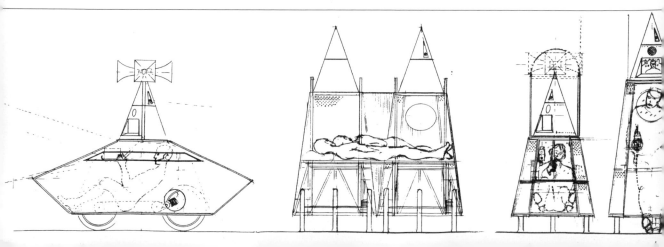

Acknowledgments   Art practice has always been far more familiar territory for me than writing. I wish to extend my gratitude to Roger Conover, editor at the MIT Press, whose encouragement, intellectual companionship, and moral support have allowed me to navigate safely through this foreign textual passage.

Matthew Abbate of the MIT Press has gently and thoughtfully edited all the texts in this book and has done so with sensitivity and respect for their critical intentions, foreign intonations, and artistic determination.

Jean Wilcox, with her tact, wit, and elegance, has transformed this book into a carefully conceived graphic design vehicle well equipped to carry my ideas and projects.

The editorial assistance of Brian Wallis contributed substantially to the choice, clarification, and final arrangement of texts in this book while protectecting most of them from my excessive revisions.

I would like to thank Sherry Buckberrough for her generosity in attending to my textual displacement. She has critically reviewed many texts and essays in this book and has offered numerous and pointed suggestions that greatly added to its intellectual clarity.

Warren Niesłuchowski, who is my fellow nomad, has significantly contributed to this project with his editorial expertise, philosophizing imagination, as well as excellent translation and retranslation of Polish and French transcripts and texts.

Special acknowledgment must be extended to Marie-Anne Sichère, who edited the first collection of my writings titled *Art public, art critique: Textes, propos et documents,* published in French by the École Nationale Supérieure des Beaux-Arts in 1995. The integrity and *esprit* of that book have paved the way for this publication.

The Department of Architecture and the Center for Advanced Visual Studies of MIT's School of Architecture and Planning have provided me with generous research facilities and resources. Such support has enabled me not only to combine teaching with art, but also to establish the Interrogative Design Group, where with the help of my research assistant Adam Whiton and of Sung Ho Kim, Warren Sack, Joshua Smith, Michael Rakowitz, and others, I have developed the most recent projects presented in this book.

I wish to extend my gratitude to Ian de Gruchy, Rosalyn Deutsche, Bruce Ferguson, David Lurie, Yves Michaud, William J. Mitchell, Andrzej Turowski, and above all Leslie Sharpe for their committed support, intellectual presence, artistic advice, and collaboration on various projects presented in this book.

I wish to thank Jagoda Przybylak for her critical and imaginative input, and for her participation and assistance in the development and realization of immigrant instruments.

I would also like to thank Dennis Adams, François Alacocque, Stanford Anderson, Stuart Anthony, Janusz Bąkowski, Marek Bartelik, Steve Benton, Terry Berkowitz, Jody Berland, Karl Beveridge, Tony Bishop, Iwona Blazwick, Manuel Borja-Villel, Wiesław Borowski, Saskia Bos, Peter Boswell, Alan Brody, Andreas Broeckman, Hal Bromm, Johnny Carson, Melvin Charney, Stanisław Cichowicz, Anthony Clementi, Papo Colo, Carol Conde, Kenneth Coutts-Smith, Douglas Crimp, Jean-François Delaine, Jérôme Delormas, Chris Dercon, Tom Eccles, Johnnie Eisen, John Fekete, Jerry Fergusson, Tom Finkelpearl, Yona Fischer, Hal Foster, Elżbieta Góral, Madeleine Grynsztejn, Ingo Gunther, Hans Haacke, Kathy Halbreich, David Hannah, Dick Hebdige, Ydessa Hendeles, Jeanette Ingberman, Jaromir Jedliński, Emilia Kabakov, Ilya Kabakov, Gary Kennedy, Inga Khavkina, Katy Kline, Jerzy Kosiński, Barbara Kruger, Wojciech Krukowski, Francis Lacloche, Ewa Lajer-Burcharth, Ed Levine, Najwa Makhoul, Jean-Hubert Martin, John Massey, Derek May, John Bentley Mays, Declan McGonagle, Jill Medvedow, Ewa Mikina, Andrea Miller-Keller, France Morin, Rachel Mosès, Stéphane Mosès, John Murray, Beverly Naidus, Joshua Nonstein, Beata Nowacka, Adam Obtułowicz, Kyong Park, Józef Patkowski, Patricia Philips, Otto Piene, Patrica Pirreda, Helaine Posner, John Rajchman, Mark Rakatansky, Grai St. Clair Rice, Wellington (Duke) Reiter, Bruce Robbins, Anda Rottenberg, Jean-Christophe Royoux, Piotr Rypson, Ludwig Scharfe, Joseph M. Schwartz, Allan Sekula, Maurine Sherlock, Milada Ślizińska, Neil Smith, Abigail Solomon-Godeau, Jean-Louis Sonzogni, Ryszard Stanisławski, Sally Stein, Jerzy Stypułkowski, Adam Szymczyk, Jean-François Taddei, Stella Tarnay, Francesc Torres, Marcia Tucker, Michael Udow, Andrzej Wajda, Jeff Wall, Ian Wallace, Steven White, Haftor Yngvason, and the many other persons who have offered me a generous hand at my various intellectual and artistic border-crossings and checkpoints.

I would like to extend my special gratitude to Vanessa Brown of the National Temple Recycling Center, Philadelphia, Pierre and Benjamin of Tompkins Square Park, New York, Robert of "Dinkinsville," New York, to the members of WECAN Redemption Center, New York, as well as to all other users, consultants, researchers, operators, participants, production assistants, and coordinators of my projections, vehicles, and instruments.

x For their photographic documentation of my projects, I would like to thank Roland Aellig, François Alacocque, Janusz Bąkowski, Paul Berizzi, Tom Collicott, M. Grafferied, Ya'acov Harlap, Thomas Hömer, Antti Kuivalainen, Larry Lamé, Jagoda Przybylak, John Ranard, Philipp Scholz Rittermann, Dieter Schwerdtle, Ian Smith-Rubenzahl, Lee Stalsworth, Jerzy Stypułkowski, Jerzy Surwiłło, Elżbieta Tejchman, Reinhard Truckenmüller, Chris Wainwright, and Werner Zellien.

I wish to thank Gabrielle Maubrie and the Galerie Gabrielle Maubrie in Paris for their inspiring commitment in generating and coordinating my projects and for contagious ethical energy so generously offered at every stage of the development and presentation of these works.

I would like to thank Galeria Foksal, Warsaw, for their invaluable archival assistance in providing photographs and documents of my earlier vehicles and instruments.

Lastly I would like to extend my special thanks to Mary Sabatino, Cecile Panzieri, and Kelley Bush of Galerie Lelong of New York. Without their indispensable professional assistance, human advice, and empathy with my artistic nomadology, many of the projects presented in this book would not have been realized. I would also like to thank Galerie Lelong for their help in the time- and mind-consuming process of gathering and assembling visual and textual material necessary to the presentation of my work in this publication.

Why Critical Vehicles?

This book is a selection of the textual documentation and writings that accompany nearly thirty years of my artistic and design work. They were written in many different geocultural contexts, socio-economic regimes, and migratory circumstances. Some of those writings have been translated and retranslated from their original languages. The section "Destinations" consists of general theoretical statements and arguments important in situating my work and thinking within an artistic and intellectual tradition and in the turbulent social and cultural dynamics of our time. "Projections," "Vehicles," and "Instruments" include project descriptions, and in some cases the supporting ethical and political argumentation for them. "Questions" elaborates on many issues presented in the previous sections, clarifying, in a conversational mode, the constantly changing terrain on which the projects operate.

Since the time of the earliest projects presented in this book, I have emigrated and immigrated twice, from Poland to Canada in the 1970s, and from Canada to the United States in the 1980s. Those allegiances have provided a shifting base of operations, augmented by temporary residencies in Australia (1981) and France (1992–93). From those bases and residencies I have launched nearly seventy public projections throughout the world, and introduced my vehicles and instruments in more than a dozen cities in a half-dozen countries. At present I have two bases, the first in New York, which serves as an ongoing source of contact with the city and the rest of world; the second in Cambridge, at the Massachusetts Institute of Technology, where I established the Interrogative Design Group at the Center for Advanced Visual Studies, in sympathetic complicity with researchers at the MIT Media Lab, and teach in the Visual Arts Program of the Department of Architecture.

One could look at my artistic biography and conclude that I am a nomad. Even were I to see myself this way, I would emphasize that, contrary to popular opinion, nomads are not detached from their terrain, but in fact try continuously to affix themselves to it, and must know the characteristics of the terrain well in order to be able to do so. In many instances, they know it better than native residents. After saying this, I must admit that I may indeed be a nomad, since the meaning of each of my projects is strongly grounded in its specific terrain, which in each case I have attempted to approach with an attitude of usefulness, and to leave with a judgmental contribution. This survival tactic is similar to the one used by all those who are displaced and who assume the tricky mission and function of magician, storyteller, critic, and soothsayer.

Looking back nearly thirty years to the beginning of my artistic work in Poland, it is striking even to me how much the focus of my concern has always been the vehicle. In those early projects, documented here in considerable detail, vehicles served as a means of enacting (and warning against) the oppressiveness of a psycho-social machine. The subjects of that oppression were themselves often unaware of the extent to which they were an active component—a vital cog or gear—in that machine. Only under the clinical conditions of such an autocratic system could one fully understand the symptomatic dependency and incapacitation of the individual—who was free to enjoy the imaginary free-agency a society like the Poland of the early '70s provided—even in our own various nonautocracies, which ironically now include present-day Poland itself. Similarly, the French aristocrat-philosopher Alexis de Tocqueville, in his *Democracy in America,* had already recognized the tell-tale signs of trouble in the American democracy of the 1830s, there the result of habits learned in the recently overthrown feudal order. Although I do not share his incurable skepticism toward democracy, one must admire the profundity of his analysis of the contradictions between freedom and equality and of his warnings against the resulting psycho-social traps in a liberal democratic machine.

It was only after leaving '70s liberal-autocratic Poland, and with the increasing distance and time and recollection of that experience in the context of Canada, United States, and France, that I truly recognized the Tocquevillian traps in my previous life in Poland. I want to make it clear that I am not chasing, here in a democratic context, phantoms of existential survival under autocratic oppression, nor do I see the present as a replication of brainwashing by an authoritarian propaganda apparatus. Rather I attempt to detect and trace conditions of life under the illusion or delusion of freedom—the hypocritical life we lead when we take refuge in the machine of a political or cultural system while closing one eye to the implications of our own passivity or, frankly speaking, complicity. Life must not be a refuge from full ethical responsibility nor indulgence in the pseudo-existentialism of one's own depoliticization in an attempt to preserve one's dignity and keep one's hands clean, whether in an autocratic, welfare, or liberal jungle state. The danger lies in allowing oneself to live in something Andrzej Turowski called *ideosis*—the commonsense life of well-calculated choices for navigating through the system by claiming a critical or independent perspective on it. If democracy is to be a machine of hope, it must retain one strange characteristic—its wheels and cogs will need to be lubri-

cated not with oil but with sand. This will disrupt its symmetry and legitimacy and keep the machine in a kind of ethical turbulence. In order to remain open, this machine as an organism must be properly disorganized, and this interference will provide the *encore un effort* (yet another effort) of which Derrida, citing Sade's revolutionary exhortation, speaks when describing the necessity of democracy *à venir,* always to come, but always with a future (*avenir*). Democracy is ill, silently suffering, and we must heal it, make it whole, of the wounds from hundreds of years of forced muteness and invisibility imposed on so many of its subjects. My work attempts to heal the numbness that threatens the health of democratic process by pinching and disrupting it, waking it up, and inserting the voice, experiences, and presence of those others who have been silenced, alienated, and marginalized.

The situation in a coffee shop in Warsaw packed with depoliticized pseudo-existentialists intoxicated by the strong coffee and clouds of cigarette smoke strangely resembled the smoky Canada Council cultural bar in Toronto filled with liberal bureaucratized artists and aestheticized bureaucrats. I found an analogous situation in the Parisian cafes, where a sophisticated culture of cultural administration inhabited the incapacitated souls of the artistic *fonctionnaires* and where the difference between the artist and the administrator became as hazy as the smoke swirling around their heads. (Yet, ironically, it is thanks to the program of *commandes publiques* of the French Ministry of Culture that I have received the greatest and most continued level of support for my critical projects.)

On United States territory, the academic artistic left, together with the left-liberal and Marxist intelligentsia, has found refuge in the educational apparatus, teaching the complexity of world problems or development and a critical approach to the operation of socio-economic and cultural machines, while at the same time staying more or less detached from the social terrain—and thereby from the possibility of a true challenge to both the overall system and their own disciplines.

Just as psychology studied the pathologies to be found in a hospital setting in order to understand "normal" psychic phenomena occurring outside, so the pathologies of life under authoritarian regimes should lead us on to investigate the "normal" phenomena outside, whether in the bureaucratic welfare state, the liberal jungle of capitalism, or the newly emerging versions of free enterprise in former socialist states (for which no Tocqueville of postdespotic Eastern capitalist democracy has yet been found).

In the North American phase of my work, the public projections emerged within the Canadian context as a phenomenological investigation of our symptomatic relationship to the bureaucratic architecturalization of the body and the disciplinary "bodification" of architecture. My study of these phenomena, and the resulting night projections, were undoubtedly influenced by the Polish nightmare I had recently left, where humans had become petrified and the monuments had come to life. In the context of jungle capitalism, along the streets and parks of New York City, a more horrifying version of such a nightmare inspired my *Homeless Projections,* leading ultimately to the *Homeless Vehicle* projects. Here, too, the petrified homeless, dying of their wounds or of malnutrition, were advocating the benefits of American freedom in front of monuments of Washington and Lafayette, thus revivifying and reanimating these former dead.

The continuing redesign and reactualization of my original *Vehicle* did not stop in the xenophobic France or Europe of 1992, where welfare democracy, incapable of liberating itself from its Enlightenment illusions, reenacted nineteenth-century nationalistic madness. Encouraged by my experimental *Poliscar* project, an attempt to provide a network of media equipment to the marginalized strata of the urban population, I developed a series of special performative instruments that added yet another, completely new task to their capabilities, one that was not only critical but offered a proactive capacity to heal social and psychological wounds. The *Alien Staff* and the *Mouthpiece* (*Porte-Parole*), a combination of transitional objects and communicative artifices, were a response and ironic counterpoint to Claude Lefort's assertion that "the distinctive modern feature of totalitarianism is that it combines a radically artificialist ideal with a radically organicist ideal. The image of the body comes to be combined with the image of the machine." By mirroring this operation of the authoritarian machine, the instruments provide prosthetic devices, countermachines that empower the wearer, in cyborgian fashion, to survive and transform the conditions of his or her social existence.

The newest equipment for strangers, the *Ægis,* further reinforces the psychological and psycho- and socio-therapeutic functions, with all the narrative capabilities such design implies, without abandoning the cross-cultural, phenomenological, political, and ethical mission of the earlier projects. There is something like an updated generation of new wings for the angel of history emerging here, the Angel who herself is a vehicle that questions its forward

progress, but who can neither afford to, nor wishes to, stop. She moves ahead while critically looking back, in equal measure scrutinizing her present circumstances while skeptically, if not cynically, projecting the future, in hopes of not finding there the present.

Arriving at this point also brings with it the general ethical problem of living protected by the illusion of our own freedom machine, and specifically the role of art in waking us from our numb sleep. If the vehicles constructed in Poland were analytic and metaphorical intuitions translating those imaginary conditions of life into art, the projections, to some degree, and the *Homeless Vehicles* and instruments to a far greater one, went further by constituting an actual intervention in life. They combined methods of critical analysis with the existential metaphor of ideological performance inherent in the Polish case, but acquired an instrumentality to assure the possibility of performing certain urgent and emergent tasks necessary to survival: articulating and disrupting the misperception of *evicts* (evicted persons); providing emergency aid; exposing the unacceptability of their neediness and the scandalous conditions that created those needs; above and beyond this, creating communicative vehicles to open a dialogue between the homeless operator and the nonhomeless, and then to convey homelessness across the economic and social boundaries that divide the city.

I borrowed my "original" vehicle from the Muzeum Sztuki in Łódź to review the parade of all of its later mutations and transformations. This ride was smoother than the original, since the twenty-six-year distance from the time of the first vehicle's conception helped me see its meaning with greater clarity. Having used, or perhaps abused, the metaphoric machine in this way, I shall return it to the museum collection to which it legally belongs and let visitors (and the readers of this book) interpret the project in their own ways.

But before I return this equipment to its historic past and your contemporary interpretations, I would like to offer a last tip: if you wish to interpret this "dialecticycle" or "peripateticycle" as analog equipment embodying the creative process in general (that process being propelled by a mode of back-and-forth, reflective and progressive thinking), the key questions still remain the same for the intellectual and the artist, no matter how creative: How close are we all to the ground? How much contact do we have with the social terrain when pacing or enjoying that creative freedom? To what degree is our creative life-machine under the control of our ethical consciousness? And to what

degree is this machine simply a component of a much larger apparatus, whether centrally controlled in authoritarian ways, operated at arm's length by a liberal system, or run by the law of *capitalisme sauvage*?

The word *vehicle* is associated with the concept of a carrier. In some dictionaries, it is described as "a person or a thing" used as a medium "to convey ideas or emotions." It is commonly understood as a means of transmission, display, and expression. The term *critical* suggests judgment, an act of pointing out shortcomings, defects, or error. It implies indispensability and an alarming or dangerous situation, as well as risk-taking. It denotes a point or state in which a change of properties or characteristics takes place—a turning point or crisis that may demand an urgent response or action. A critical vehicle is, therefore, a medium; a person or a thing acting as a carrier for displaying or transporting vital ingredients and agents. It is set to operate as a turning point in collective or singular consciousness. It transmits those ideas and emotions that are indispensable to the comprehension of the urgency and complexity of a situation. In short, the critical vehicle is an "ambitious" and "responsible" medium—a person or piece of equipment—that attempts to convey ideas and emotions in the hope of transporting to each human terrain a vital judgment toward a vital change.

It is my hope that the projects and associated writings presented in this book constitute a collection of such judgmental vehicles. Each of them was specifically developed to operate on a particular, often shaky, psycho-social terrain. More recent projects were conceived to cross both internal and external boundaries between those terrains. Of course, none of these vehicles alone can fulfill all the critical expectations and communicative functions. Each of them takes on a concrete set of tasks that are most appropriate, or least appropriate from an established point of view, to its time and circumstances.

Some of the writings refer to projects that adopted a form of mobile instrument and mechanized equipment, the objective of which was to reinforce the operation of a communicative economy of persons who themselves are the major critical vehicles of the present: the alienated inhabitants of our cities, and in particular contemporary urban nomads, immigrants—vehicles of hope and change. The other group of projects, the public projections conceived in the 1980s, slide and more recently video and audio events, were an attempt to appropriate, adopt, or pervert the operation of existing and overpresent official vehicles, the ideological machines designed to perpetuate the victorious heri-

tage—public monuments. Those media projects employ the tactics and technique of projection to convert such celebratory structures, uncritical grand suspects and witnesses of the glorious past, into self-critical and critical vehicles.

There is a possibility, perhaps the only reasonable one, of understanding my "original" vehicle as a negative metaphor, as a machine that must be abandoned, or rather from which one must step down and continue one's movement on foot. This book represents the moment of stepping down from those vehicles. But before doing so, one must prepare and arm oneself with the necessary experience and equipment. And if we were to pursue that option seriously, new equipment would have to be designed for all those strangers, and the locals, too, brave enough to cover ground on foot. Behind this suggestion there is perhaps a more general call to a postprogressive, interrogative design, leading to "productivism" of a new kind. It would bring critical methods and new, perhaps difficult to accept but vital, functional programs to the design of tactical equipment. The important elements of this equipment would be: footwear designed to negotiate the terrain; voice and vision empowerment through prosthetic implements; an alternative-perception provider, a kind of post-multicultural kaleidoscope; a memory-recollecting device; a self-examination mirror to reflect one's own position in present time; and a critical-imagination projector-announcer of the vision of the future. The most recent projects (new versions of *Alien Staff, Mouthpiece,* and *Ægis*) are early steps toward this critical goal.

This book, as a textual and, to some degree, pictorial medium, can itself be seen as a theoretical and descriptive vehicle. But "vehicle," in its dictionary definition, also implies "a substance which functions as a binder or solvent for active ingredients and reagents." Each of the ingredients of this book, whether the theoretical texts or the writings referring to particular projects, and, of course, the projects themselves, was conceived to spark a reaction of vital discontent inspiring new visions, counterpoints, and actions. I would thus like to use this vehicle not only as a conveyor of my ideas and feelings, but as an ongoing written invitation for readers to become critical "reagents" ("a substance used to bring about a chemical reaction in another substance")—sustaining in this way a cultural chain reaction in our democratic laboratory.

New York—Cambridge
Summer 1998

one **Destinations**

Designing for the City of Strangers (1997)

The messiah interrupts history.
—Walter Benjamin, "Theses on the Philosophy of History" (1940)

City of the Victors

According to Walter Benjamin, the fact that things "go on" is a catastrophe. The city is a monumental stage for things to "go on" because it perpetuates both a spatial relationship between its inhabitants and its symbolic structures and a psycho-social relationship among its dwellers. These two perpetuations must be perturbed to wake up the city and to save it from the bad dreams of the present, the nightmares of the past, and the catastrophes of the future. I would like to propose the possibility of a design practice that would interrupt these processes and could eventually help to heal the city's wounded psycho-social relations and its catastrophic reality.

Theorist Stéphane Mosès, in analyzing Benjamin's theological-political model of history, focuses on his concept of the *history of the victors,* which operates as a past "transmitted to us through a hermeneutical *tradition* that selects events, preserving some and rejecting others, at times determining their interpretation." It can easily afford to forget the catastrophes it has caused. I recognize this kind of history as the foundation or cement that stabilizes the continuity of the "legitimate" and "familiar" city. The history of the victors, the official presence of the official past, constitutes the *official city.* This official city is a lived tradition that celebrates, in everyday life, "the triumph of the strongest and the disappearance of the weakest."[1] Such a history (as represented in textbooks, national literature, films, and public monuments) cherishes a notion of progress that, according to Benjamin, is inevitably linked to a legacy of destruction.

The history of a nation or city, like every synchronic narrative, collaborates with the *history of catastrophe* by celebrating the lineage of "our" progressive and victorious traditions. To avoid future catastrophes, daily disclosures of the often-hidden destructiveness of the present must be linked to critical recollections of past disasters. This sort of critical approach to history has been—and continues to be—an intuitive and interruptive survival practice of every immigrant.

"The inertia that perpetuates past injustices can only be broken by the eruption of something radically new; unpredictable," says Stéphane Mosès, building on Benjamin's analysis. The history of the victors must be confronted and interrupted by the *memory of the nameless* or the *tradition of the vanquished.*

In staging such an interruption and bringing these traditions to light, the stranger—the vanquished of today—functions as a prophet or messenger. Each time the experience of a stranger is shared and understood, the city revives and returns to its conscious life as a democratic hope for us all. To heal one voiceless stranger, then, is to heal the entire city.

City of the Vanquished

Tremors and aftershocks caused by the end of the Cold War are being felt across the planet. As the old and stable ideological front lines have vanished, a new war has begun, no longer cold and seemingly bloodless, but often hot, like fire, and openly bloody. Refugees are fleeing new religious wars, new chauvinisms, and new nationalisms. For many, the end of the Cold War has been the end of their world, their identity, their community, and the beginning of a new diaspora.

With the official account of the population of refugees soon to reach 40,000,000, the United Nations has called the last quarter-century the "Migration Era." The influx of immigrants to the United States has now reached the historic levels of the nineteenth-century immigration wave. By the year 2010, foreign-born residents and citizens will probably outnumber U.S.-born inhabitants in most American cities. By then, these cities will undoubtedly be the sites of the greatest challenges and hopes for democracy in the United States.

Historically, the city has always been a hope for the displaced. And today, as it was in the past, our cities are worth nothing and will be condemned to destruction if they cannot open themselves to strangers. Look back at Sodom and Gomorrah! Tens of millions of these strangers now traverse and transgress frontiers and borders that are simultaneously internal and external, geopolitical and psycho-social, ethical and spiritual, private and public. Identities and communities are disintegrating, multiplying, crossing, shifting, and reconfiguring, sparking fear and violence among those who feel invaded by others, who import speechless pain.

Immigrant Utopia

As part of the second largest wave of immigration in U.S. history, these wanderers will be confronted by the multitude of divided and competing groups of both U.S.- and foreign-born residents. But unlike the immigrants of the first wave, these new refugees enter cities that are already fully built, with their architectural, ideological, and monumental theaters in place. It is up to these newcomers, then, to transform and unbuild the cities by inserting their presence, their performances, and their histories into the collective memories and democratic discourses of the city itself. The city is reconceived with each new immigrant, assuming that an open communication exists between the immigrant and all others. Too often, however, such openings exist only as wounds, a result of the wars that created the need for these large-scale migrations in the first place, or as a kind of psychosomatic symptom of the fundamentally asymmetrical nature of this passage, for immigrants do not have the rights enjoyed by citizens. But within each immigrant lives an entire city, often richer, more complex, and more hopeful than the public one—the city to come.

This Benjaminian utopia is, according to Stéphane Mosès, "a hope lived in the mode of the present." To survive, the immigrant must establish a utopia, a "no-place" that is located in the present time, not hidden behind the horizon of some idealized future. Why should the immigrant just add to the perpetuated misery of past immigrant experience? Why should this degrading experience, now taken for granted as part of the romantic patrimony, be endlessly imposed on every future immigrant, who must wear it like a pillory of American identity? No! The "no-place" should be a "No!-place." And once formulated in the immigrant's mind, it must be projected onto both the future and the past. The No!-place is an unacceptable place, the site of "my personal experience that I refuse to accept for today, for tomorrow, and forever, for myself, my children, for everyone, immigrants and nonimmigrants alike." "My utopia," says the immigrant, "proposes a vision of hope in which the society of tomorrow houses no place for the perpetuation of the kind of experience I am forced to live through today, the kind of misery that your immigrant parents and grandparents were forced to accept yesterday." The immigrant's No!-place is at once a vision, a criticism, and a resistance.

Cultivation of the tradition of the nameless has a self-defensive function as well: to survive, the stranger must guard against the fate of nomads, who, first deprived by the victors of their history (and even the right to have a history), were later forced to function as merely geographic subjects. As the French philosophers Gilles Deleuze and Félix Guattari teach us, "The defeat of the nomads was such, so complete, that history is one with the triumph of States."[2] Just as we have been told that nomads "invented nothing," so we have presumed that migrants and immigrants have nothing to contribute to public discourse.

But the most questionable question, "Where are you from?," should never replace "In what way can your past and present experience contribute to everybody's well-being today and tomorrow?"

The infusion of the tradition of the vanquished (a critical-visionary history) into the history of the victors (a catastrophic-progress history) can be made by strangers thanks to their *political intuition of the present*. Such an intuition realizes the danger of repeating yesterday's injustices today and tomorrow. Every day a new history needs to be written, one that will retrieve the tradition of the vanquished. This new history, what Nietzsche would call a "critical history," is announced by the stranger and can help to sustain the agonistic democratic process. As philosopher Simon Critchley points out, "Democracy is the form of society committed to the political equality of all its citizens and the ethical inequality of myself faced with the Other. . . . Thus the rational order of the *polis* is justified by a philosophical language which criticizes the *polis* in the name of what it excludes or marginalizes, the pre-rational one-for-the-other of ethics."[3] In other words, democracy can be kept alive by an ongoing recognition, exposition, and legalization of the strangers' "illegitimate" experience, their "illegible" past, and their "illegal" present.

Transitional Artifice

As psychoanalytic theorist Julia Kristeva writes, "Your speech has no past and will have no power over the future of the group: why should one listen to it? . . . One will listen to you only in absent-minded, amused fashion, and one will forget you in order to go on with serious matters. The foreigner's speech can bank only on its bare rhetorical strength, and the inherent desires he or she has invested in it." Unfortunately, this perception by the nonstranger also conforms to the symptomatic condition of the stranger: "Settled within himself, the foreigner has no self. Barely an empty confidence, valueless, which focuses his possibilities of being constantly other, according to others' wishes and to circumstances. I do what *they* want *me* to, but it is not "me"—"me" is elsewhere, "me" belongs to no one, "me" does not belong to "me," . . . does "me" exist?"[4] As Kristeva's statement suggests, strangers need to gain confidence in the possibility of communicating their own experiences, and they need to be able to communicate this confidence as well. The stranger must learn to take his or her own experience seriously. To gain this confidence, however, the stranger must find a communicative form for the experience, then establish a playful distance from it.

Conversely, the nonstranger, or "local," must gain a playful distance from his or her own fear of the stranger to establish a healthy curiosity that will foster communication and closer contact. The presence of a stranger evokes in the nonstranger a well-hidden secret: the recognition of one's own strangeness. The stranger is unfamiliar and uncanny (*unheimlich* in German, or "unhomely"). The uncanny, Freud says, is everything that "ought to have remained hidden but has come to light." Kristeva claims that the ideal situation would be one in which the nonstranger recognized his or her own uncanny strangeness. As she says, "The foreigner is within me, hence we are all foreigners. If I am a foreigner, there are no foreigners." In search of an antixenophobic society, Kristeva notes Freud's stress on "those [esthetic] works in which the uncanny effect is abolished because of the very fact that the entire world of the narrative is fictitious. Such are fairy tales, in which the generalized artifice spares us any possible comparison between sign, imagination, and material reality. As a consequence, artifice neutralizes uncanniness and makes all returns of the repressed plausible, acceptable, and pleasurable."[5]

In sum, the state of being a stranger accumulates as an experience with no form, no language, no expression, and no right to be communicated, and thus becomes a dangerous psychic symptom. This stranger-ness is a strangely familiar, secret, and uncanny condition that we all share and that, when repressed in the ideological caves of our subjectivity, can sometimes explode in the face of an actual stranger. Between the speechless pain of the actual stranger and the sequestered fear of one's own strangeness lies the real frontier to be challenged. Can art operate as a revelatory, expressive, and interrogative passage through such a frontier? Can it be an inspiration, provocation, and opening act for a new form of communication in a nonxenophobic community? If the stranger is a prophet who interrupts history, today's artists and designers should help the prophet by designing special equipment for such an intervention.

The Prophet's Prosthesis

Such equipment would be the result of "interrogative design," a critical articulation of what is most questionable and unacceptable in the present: the stranger's pain in survival. The oldest and most common reference to this kind of articulation and design is the bandage. A bandage covers and treats a wound while at the same time exposing its presence. Its presence signifies both the experience of pain and the hope of recovery. Is it possible to develop this concept further? Could we invent a bandage that would communicate,

---

Allemagne : extrémisme

Un Polonais de 19 ans a eu la langue sectionnée, vendredi à Berlin, par des agresseurs qu'il a identifié comme des extrémistes de droite, a indiqué hier la police. Par ailleurs, à Francfort-sur-l'Oder, deux demandeurs d'asile ont été blessés, samedi soir, à l'issue d'une bagarre entre des réfugiés et des Allemands.

(Libération)

A nineteen-year-old Pole had his tongue cut out on Friday in Berlin by assailants identified as right-wing extremists, police reported yesterday.

Elsewhere, in Frankfurt-an-der-Oder [on the Polish border], two asylum seekers were wounded on Saturday night, while trying to escape a melee between refugees and Germans.

Libération (Paris), winter 1992

interrogate, and articulate the circumstances and the experience of the injury? Could such a transformed bandage address the ills of the outside world as perceived by the wounded? To see the world as seen by the wound!

In the complexity of the contemporary urban context, this equipment becomes a device for communication and mediation—design as tactical media, its purpose being to treat not only the individual human suffering but also the external society that produced the wound. Could this device create new conditions that would soon render the need for it obsolete? Or, if needed, could it become a prosthesis, a (semi)permanent extension of the body (politic)? Such design requires thinking both clinically (therapeutically) and critically.

Over the centuries and millennia, the memory and tradition of the nameless developed certain *tactical* features against the *strategic* character of the history of the victors. Those features, according to Benjamin, have a profoundly "interactive" character based on "nonlinearity, radical negativity," performativity, and "arrest of time." The tactics of this tradition consist of storytelling, magic, miracle, humor, and entertainment (refer back to Freud). This is a "discontinuous tradition while continuity is that of the victor."[6] The tradition of the vanquished brings something new and unknown to the understanding of lived time, transposing subjective experience from the personal sphere to the historical.

Even in those societies that are most open, inviting, and attentive to the displaced, the psychological needs of immigrants are far less recognized than those of children, for instance. But like children, immigrants must develop their autonomous identities in the process of psychic development, independent of internal and external conditions or personal cultures. And they must do so in an experimental, creative, and playful way, in an atmosphere of internal and external trust. Yet, unlike children, they cannot expect the necessary protective space, normally provided by parents or society, for such experiment and play. On the one hand, then, immigrants are treated as hopeless and voiceless, incapable infants or defiant children. On the other hand, they are expected to be super-adults, self-motivated entrepreneurs, and fully independent individuals capable of facing a harsh new world. At the same time, the locals are treated as infants by the immigrants, who believe that the hostile or "naive" native residents do not understand the "sophistication" of the newcomers. The immigrants expect the locals to be super-adults and to extend themselves in special ways to understand foreign customs, ideas, and experiences. Both locals and aliens must refuse to be infantilized or expected to be super-adults.

11   This situation demands a new artifice that would serve both needs: inspiring playful distance and playful contact, as well as reinforcing the stranger's confidence in communicating the experience of alienation. To defuse xenophobic paranoias, one important function of this psycho-social artifice would be to neutralize the uncanniness evoked by the presence of a stranger. To do this, such an artifice should take the form of a special kind of equipment designed to function as a "fictitious narrative," one that nonetheless preserves and disseminates an emotional understanding of a painful and unacceptable reality.

On the other hand, if this psycho-social artifice is to be of any use to the stranger, it would have to function as, in D. W. Winnicott's terms, a "transitional object" or "transitional phenomenon," or, in extreme cases, as a transitional prosthesis. For the immigrant, such equipment would have to be perceived as neither internal nor external but belonging to a "[third zone] of experience in the potential space between the individual and the environment." This space "depends on experience which leads to trust. It can be looked upon as sacred to the individual in that it is here that the individual experiences creative living."[7]

The zones, spaces, and objects that immigrants invent are the territories of play, distance, irony, and humor: the uncanny in the locals' terrain, where the familiar and the unfamiliar wrestle with each other and where the lost land argues and jokes in a mother tongue with the promised land, speaking in the newly acquired language of a new critical history and a new vision of hope. The new kind of "transitional object" must be created here, where the zones of experience of the newcomer and the local can be encouraged, overlapped, and shared. But it is the immigrant who must introduce such an object first. The immigrant is the one who, in order to survive, must learn how to be both provocative and tactful.

Left alone with such newly designed equipment, the immigrant could create a space where he or she could accept, shape, even enjoy the complexity and originality of his or her own strange and often painful experiences. Bringing the instrument into the open would create the sacred and ethical space of the "third zone." This space exists not only between the stranger and the nonstranger but also between the inner and outer worlds of the stranger; between the stranger, the nonstranger, and the "third person" (who may or may not be a stranger, and who represents the point of view of "we," of the larger society as a whole); and, lastly, as in the case of the *Alien Staff,* between prerecorded speech and improvised live speech, contained and "broadcast" by the instrument and performed by the stranger.

In this way, the newly designed equipment could inspire a birth of a new community, even a temporary and momentary rebirth of democratic public space based on the agonistic speech acts and discourses that Hannah Arendt supported, enacted in a place that allows for the "unleashing of passions." Georges Bataille called such a place "sacred." This space will be constituted through the use of the Immigrant Instruments, which, in this way, will become "sacred objects." It will be constituted on the site of the newcomer, who is the stake of the society to come and the new mentality to be born.

The Return of the Said
To summarize, the interruption of the victors by the nameless can only happen through the design and implementation of a new psycho-cultural artifice—transitional object, which, on the one hand, will help the stranger to open up and come forward and, on the other hand, will encourage the nonstranger and other strangers to bring themselves closer to the stranger's experience and presence. This will inspire the new discourse in which the strangeness can be shared across all social boundaries.

In doing so, such new equipment will provide both the means and the field of play, where the speechless can creatively articulate their "saying," interrupting the flow of the "said." Armed with the new equipment, strangers will hopefully gain new rhetorical power to wrestle with the power of the "said." The interactive character of the encounter with the "said," the irony and humor of this unsolicited performance, will help to articulate, expose, and eventually disseminate the image of their unstable identity as well as the complex world of their multiplicity and their internal antagonisms, all overlapping in the process of becoming. Despite all of the power thus gained, the stranger, speaking from the bottom of the experience of the vanquished, will not resemble the victor in speech. As Emmanuel Levinas would say, the stranger, during the performance, will appear as the "said," but this time as the "justifiable said," since the traces of the original "saying" will remain the sole basis of his or her speech act.[8]

The stranger equipped with the immigrant instrument will be able to speak back to all of those strangers or nonstrangers who would like to cast the stranger in some preconceived mold of an individual or collective identity. The strangers and their doubles—the instruments—could disagree with each other or with anybody who wants to fuse the strangers into a particular culture or community. The use of the immigrant instruments, while encouraging trust, can displace any preconceptions of communion and commonality, protecting the stranger's right to exist as a unique singular human being and the right to announce or denounce his or her affiliations and associations.

The summary of the main points for the design of a new equipment for strangers:

Proposition 1: Strangers in their relation to the self and to the nonstranger (as well as to other strangers) need a thing-in-between, an equipment-artifice that will open up discussion and allow them to reveal and to share (communicate) their experiences, identities, visions, and unique strangenesses.

Proposition 2: Such equipment (communicative instrument) is an emergency need in today's migratory era, and the first user of the instrument must be the immigrant, followed by other foreigners, and then all of those native locals who are so profoundly estranged, infantilized, silenced, and excluded that they resemble the immigrant, even if they did not experience crossing the "proper" geopolitical borders.

Proposition 3: Such equipment, which I call the Immigrant Instrument, must offer healing powers to its users, overcoming the ever-present fear of one's own strangeness, as well as communicating the strangeness with playfulness, confidence, and power. For this purpose, the Instrument must operate as a psychological container (the confident companion) and as a social opening (displayed-presenter), the stranger's speaking double.

Proposition 4: The Immigrant Instrument must bring the interlocutor closer to the stranger. To achieve this goal, the Instrument must first take attention away from its user and bring the focus on itself as a "bizarre," "magical," "strange," or "curious" object, cliché, totem, attribute, technological gadget, or prosthetic device. In the second stage of its operation, the Instrument will expose, at a close distance, the stranger as speech-act virtuoso, who, armed with and empowered by the new media technology and ancient instrumental know-how, will be able to entertain and announce her or his critical and prophetic presence. Achieving such goals, the Instrument will increase the user's communicative abilities despite all psychic, linguistic, and cultural barriers in the context of the present-day xenophobia.

Proposition 5: The Immigrant Instrument must operate both as a transitional object (Winnicott) and as a communicative artifice (Kristeva).

Proposition 6: The Immigrant Instrument must function as an artifice, inspiring playful distance and playful contact. The foreigners must learn to take their own experience seriously; to see, however, that one's own often painful experience requires the ability to establish a playful distance from it. Conversely, to establish a communicative contact with the stranger, the nonstranger must gain equally playful distance from his or her fear of the stranger.

Proposition 7: The situation of today's immigrant (who is both a psychic and a social symptom) requires an instrument that would help its operator to become both the patient and the doctor. Self-healing must be combined with healing others, being healed while healing, making whole, and articulating and curing wounded psycho-social relations.

The Immigrant Instrument must aid the stranger in making the transition to nonstrangeness while assisting the local in recognizing his or her own strangeness. This will contribute, as Kristeva would like, to the formation of a communicative cross-stratum based on shared multiplicity of identities in an unstable process of becoming a community or, better, a community of becoming, the only commonality of which will be its communicated uncanny strangeness.

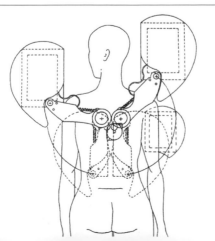

15   **Notes**

1. Stéphane Mosès, "The Theological-Political Model of History," *History and Memory* 1 (Tel Aviv University, 1989), pp. 11, 13.

2. Gilles Deleuze and Félix Guattari, *Nomadology: The War Machine,* trans. Brian Massumi (New York: Semiotext(e), 1986), p. 73.

3. Simon Critchley, *The Ethics of Deconstruction: Derrida and Levinas* (Oxford: Blackwell, 1992), pp. 235, 239.

4. Julia Kristeva, *Strangers to Ourselves,* trans. Leon S. Roudiez (New York: Columbia University Press, 1991), pp. 20–21, 8.

5. Sigmund Freud, "The Uncanny," in *The Standard Edition of the Complete Psychological Works of Sigmund Freud* (London: Hogarth Press, 1955), vol. 17, p. 225; Kristeva, *Strangers to Ourselves,* pp. 192, 187.

6. See the discussion of Benjamin in Mosès, "The Theological-Political Model of History."

7. D. W. Winnicott, *Playing and Reality* (London: Tavistock, 1971), p. 103.

8. For an elaboration of the Levinasian concepts of "saying" and "the said," see the chapter "A Levinasian Politics of Ethical Difference," in Critchley, *The Ethics of Deconstruction,* pp. 229–236.

Fragments of this previously unpublished essay were delivered as parts of lectures for Harvard University, the Public Art Fund Lectures at the Cooper Union, New York, the Institute of Contemporary Arts, London, and the Institute of Contemporary Art, Boston.

Interrogative Design (1994)

Interrogative: 1. Of, pertaining to, or of the nature of questioning; having the form or force of a question. 2. Of a word or form employed in asking questions.

Design as a research proposal and implementation can be called interrogative when it takes a risk, explores, articulates, and responds to the questionable conditions of life in today's world, and does so in a questioning manner. Interrogative design questions the very world of needs of which it is born. It must respond with a double urgency to such a world. First, it should function as an emergency aid in the process of survival, resistance, and the healing of social, psychological, and physical wounds. Second, it needs to increase and sustain the high level of ethical alertness that creates, in the words of Benjamin, a state of emergency understood not as an exception but as an everyday ethical condition, an ongoing motivation for critical judgment toward the present and past to secure a vision for a better future.

Instead of deconstructing itself, design should deconstruct life. Design should unmask and uncover our singular and plural lives, our lived experience, and a history of this experience from the panopticon of our subjectivity and ideological theater of our culture, no matter how unacceptable and repressed or neglected such experiences may be.

Design must articulate and inspire communication of real, often difficult lived-through experience, rather than operate as a substitute for it (i.e., the kitsch of Sharper Image design). The experience and its history are the often invisible and seemingly unimaginable complexes of problems, internal and external, that have been quickly covered up by the naive facades of all design "solutions" to these problems, and more recently by melancholic "deconstruction" of the design heritage of such cover-ups.

Design must put in doubt its search for all such often well-intended design solutions or self-deconstructions, to open the way to explore, discover, uncover, and expose the hidden dimensions of lived experience. Doing so, design as a practice must acknowledge this experience as a history of resistance to the conditions of life and a history of one's destabilized identity in the process of often enforced reconfiguration.

A history, being a critical structure of experience, is a recollection of the lived events of the past infused with the criticism of the present.

Interrogative design must create the points and spaces of convergence for a multitude of internal and external enquiries to such experience and its history.

Design of any object, space, place, network, or system must become a technology and a technique of constructing an artifice that would function as an opening through which a complexity of the lived experience can be recalled, memorized, translated, transmitted, perceived, and exchanged in a discursive and performative manner. Design must not hesitate to respond to the needs that should not, but unfortunately do, exist.

Designers must work *in* the world rather than "about" or "upon" it. In an unacceptable and contradictory world, responsive and responsible design must appear as an unacceptable and contradictory "solution." It must critically explore and reveal often painful life experience rather than camouflage such experience by administering the painkillers of optimistic design fantasies. The appearance of interrogative design may "attract while scandalizing"—it must attract attention in order to scandalize the conditions of which it is born. Implicit in this design's temporary character is a demand and hope that its function will become obsolete.

The oldest and most common reference to this kind of design is the bandage. A bandage covers and treats a wound while at the same time exposing its presence, signifying both the experience of pain and the hope of recovery. Is it possible to further develop such a bandage as equipment that will communicate, interrogate, and articulate the circumstances and the experience of the injury, provoking so as to prevent its recurrence?

The proposed design should not be conceived as a symbolic representation but as a performative articulation. It should not "represent" (frame iconically) the survivor or the vanquished, nor should it "stand in" or "speak for" them. It should be developed *with* them and it should be based on a critical inquiry into the conditions that produced the crisis. Interrogative design can also function as a critical mirror questioning the user's preconceptions and assumptions about others and about the self. The equipment can reinterpret various existing materials and components, like protective clothing, portable tools, electronic gear, defensive armor or weaponry, prosthetic components, wearable digital equipment, alert devices, shields, or a combination of these. One of the objectives of the design is to extend the use of the media of communication to those who have no access to them but who need them the most, and to those who have full access to them but who fail to take critical advantage of them.

Originally published in a slightly different version as "Projektowanie i doświadczenie," in *Krzysztof Wodiczko, Sztuka Publiczna* (Warsaw: Centrum Sztuki Wspoczesnej, 1995), p. 29.

Beyond the Hybrid State?

with Warren
Niesłuchowski
(1992)

Where Are You From?

Instead of a simple answer, a prolonged silence meets the question. The silence says, "You are asking me the wrong question. Ask me, 'Which "where" am I from?'"

There are millions on this planet today whose silence, too, is an answer. We are among them.

The following text is an attempt at recording, in the act, an unfinished dialogue over the Paris-New York line, an attempt to grasp a fragile moment in the history of democracy and its forms as a political, social, psychological, cultural, and ideological enterprise, and to situate the place of art in such a moment.

We found ourselves, entangled, in a labyrinth of fragmented ideas, metaphors imposed on us by the context of events spanning more than two continents and crossing existing categories. The moment calls for a xenology (*xenos*, "stranger"), a new, nomadic, and yet undeveloped form of understanding and expression.

As empires extend and recede, the boundaries and territories they incarnate shift, as do the particular and internal ones of the subjects they comprise. Drawn by the collision of their histories into identities they may not have freely chosen, these subjects remain in an ongoing struggle over the hold of imperial powers, engines of war. The forces deployed in these wars are not always ones from without. Taking advantage of differences, empires have often succeeded, by enclosing and excluding (Deleuze), in fashioning their world along the lines of this force-field until they, too, fall victim to the crush of competing imperial formations.

This is true whether the empires in question are capitalist democracies or absolutisms. Although the premises—or the physics—of the forces may be different, the goals remain the same, the preservation and extension of a super-identity against the multiple and individual identities subordinated, assimilated, or integrated into the great whole. Although in the age of "Capitalism Militant" this was achieved almost exclusively by (external) warfare, in the age of "Capitalism Triumphant" it is precisely on the ruins of these wars (and in the maimed souls of its exhausted, wandering veterans) that future theaters of war will be staged.

19 (Re)mobilization

"America" is a state of war. Paradoxically, the social relations in the great standing army in the desert were more peaceful and more democratic and egalitarian—like those in the Napoleonic Grande Armée—than at home. In that self-contained civil society of soldiers, each *citoyen* has human rights, including rights to social space, public and private, and one must enjoy these rights, whether one desires them or not. Facing this great mobilization in the unpopulated desert is another civil society, composed not of soldiers but of warriors, fighting not a war against some enemy of freedom, but each other. These warriors constantly defend themselves against each other in an unsuccessful struggle, not for freedom in the abstract, but for their ration of rights.

The army in the desert represents an oasis of civilization compared to the society of permanently embattled individual warriors fighting in the urban jungle, a social desert. This is an army of deserters from the battlefield of the United States who have consolidated themselves as a new society in the desert, neither *polis* nor *rus* ("countryside"), abandoning the (e)utopian ("good place") but difficult project of America for the (o)utopian ("no place") and featureless *terrain vague* of desert and ocean, a new social project of staging a theater of operations in a space with no social problems—a Theater of War.

We propose as the obvious conclusion to that war the repatriation of this army back to the "American" *polis* and a general remobilization of society from its present mission as an outpost of (o)utopian society on the flawless surfaces of the desert for a social mission—*redeployed as a welfare rather than warfare warrior state*. No longer a state as Grande Armée, but as a homeless army, based on the social realities of our society, important parts of which are composed of ex-slaves, returning veterans from imperial, social, and civil wars, refugees, and immigrants—an Operation Social Desert. As new recruits continue to be drawn in large part from these strata, the ideological sets and decors of the theater of war will be converted to a broader theater of ideology. This new army will thus broaden its operational terrain and fill out its complement through a full and voluntary self-conscription. It will have to transform the egalitarian structure of the army into one of multi-ideology and multi-identity—each "welfare warrior" exercising his or her right to a multiplicity of particular identities and ideologies. The communications system of this army would have as its function the dissemination of the multiplicities of its individual and collective units, and its mission would be, after a transitional phase, its own "disarm(y)ing" and a passage to a state of *unwar*.

This new dis-army will require a new category of citizen, a member of nomadkind, defined not in opposition to state power, but rather as a returnee from the wars seeking a new status and means of conceiving a society *beyond the fatal dualism* of social jungle and utopian desert, a social fata morgana. The newly demobilized will at last be given a chance to see this unwar for what it is, not a question of individual struggle for some coherent identity based on notions of right to difference (usually a flat one like some advertising image and often quickly raised to the level of a new multicultural nationalism or other hegemonic mirage), but a struggle for the right not to be continuously embattled, *the right to be multicultural inside* and *to live one's multiple identities.* This, too, is a utopia, but a nomad's and nomadic utopia, that of the new veterans of homelessness looking for a new home away from wars, soldiers, and warriors.

(Dis)integration

This dis-army calls into question any notion of a state only for survivors and winners (racially, economically, politically), implying the elimination of the possibility of recognizing differences, in all their complexity and antagonism. The capitalist army, for example, has converted its memory of victorious battles (often crimes against humanity committed in common, to which our monuments are both memorials and cover-ups) (Freud, Bataille) into an ethos of social will or moral "necessity," that of constantly fighting designated enemies at home and abroad. The myth of this necessity—to fight and win—then becomes the primary social and political bond holding society together, a State fusion of differences into a hybrid, which comes at the price of the alienation (*Entäusserung,* "estrangement, externalization, driving out") of "passive" or "weak" elements that cannot be assimilated or integrated into the agonistic culture (Simmel).

As was pointed out in a proposal for the *Poliscar* and the Homeless Communication Network, these alienated elements, like those who live in the city but outside, the urban homeless, are treated, or at best tolerated, as aliens on their own planet. This "alienation"—making into legal aliens legitimate operators within today's city—has a vicious effect, not so much of excluding "them," those alien, nomad "homeless," as "us," "the community," from the masses of "strangers" from whom we are then estranged and with whom we presume to have no common language. In fact it is the strangeness of the situation that we project onto the other rather than confronting it together. This contradiction—to us they may seem strange in the city, but they are not strangers to the city—results in a contradictory and complex identity: savage alien nomads (the "homeless") in a noble state and society (the city), or noble alien nomads homeless in a savage state and society (the city). Squeezed between this play of images the nomads themselves, in their complexity in a complex city, remain out of the picture, which has no room for the real life of people who happen merely to lack a home or dwelling.

The State Hybrid

First proposed by the Enlightenment, the democratic project of social and cultural "integration" (in the strong sense of the word) as a political engineering of the liberation of the individual through assimilation and total incorporation into a modern state machine is still being extended today (for example, by the pyramidal Socialist apparatus in Mitterand's France through its official State policy of integration). It is endorsed by many social activists (S.O.S. Racisme) but opposed by some concerned intellectuals (Kristeva), and provides an inspiration for reactionary "criticism" from politicians of the radical right (Le Pen). It also reemerges in everyday language through attacks of utopianism in the form of Orwellian nostalgias for engineered hybrids superior to their base parts.

At least since the Bronze Age people have mixed metals together to obtain properties like hardness or ductility that are not present in the base materials themselves. Now scientists are improving on the alloying process by combining materials in many fine layers only a few atoms thick. This atomic engineering holds the promise of designer materials, ones whose properties are built in by blending elements that could not be combined in other ways. Scientists say the new materials represent a new state of matter that was previously unavailable. . . . Some of the multi-layer materials are deceptive in appearance. A thin piece of shiny reddish-brown metal looks like copper. But is does not bend easily the way a thin sheet of copper would. Instead it is resilient, snapping back in place after a bending force is removed.[1]

There are many ways of assimilating, deploying and fusing difference, as this appeal to the victories of Machine Age engineering in such an ambiguously Durkheimian quote (whose applicability to social engineering is obvious) shows. The State hybrid, too, is a transracial and transcultural war machine, one which fuses sexual, racial, or cultural differences and erects another, (abstract) economic one. This new difference rapidly transforms itself into the very engine of the machine, like the core of a nuclear reactor, which functions, so to speak, solely on the difference of energy levels in the states of various isotopes of radioactive elements.

Those who are too slow for this machine are down(ed) and out. Those who cannot transform into power and energy are eliminated, like nuclear waste, no longer of any conceivable use, even dangerous. This is such a fundamental trait of the ethos that it becomes difficult to appreciate and criticize from within the categories of the social system itself. America, which has thus freed itself of any other restraints on its activity, is in this sense ahead of the rest of the world. In one sense, of course it had no choice—"alienation" or "estrangement" in this sense has characterized its struggle from the very beginning, from the first wars against nature, "Indians," religious intolerance, etc. Even when physical liquidation is not involved, elimination, casting beyond the *limen,* the threshold, is a basic feature of this alienation. As Foucault indicated, we have passed from the repression of sexual (and cultural and racial) difference to its deployment. Technically this has been achieved by an impressive feat of social engineering. For reasons of ideological coherence, equality must still remain the basic tenet of this new state. Ignoring the consequences of the deployment of difference, political demagogy of the right, center, and left can all be useful as a tool for maintaining the machine.

From the Hybrid State to the Labyrinth

To counter such a pseudo-democratic egalitarianizing repression into the un-conscious of these differences and scrape away the veneer of sameness and unity, we strongly agree with Kristeva that a society must be founded on a dialectical recognition of the complexity within each "human being." Her hu-manism, however, is a somewhat confused notion (since it posits but one hu-man identity), as is the dialectical but dualist confrontation between "I" and "other," something close to the biblical conception of "neighbor." This in turn is different from a "multiculturalism" which proposes the coexistence of many societies in one larger state, without a real recognition of what the differences are. (The multicultural project is a more advanced one technically, in the same sense that Seurat's chromato-divisionism of complementary colors and forms was advanced for its time—and perhaps reflected Seurat's own anarchist-utopian but totalist positions.) What is required is a recognition of the multitude of identities and cultures coexisting and often embattled within everyone.

It is also possible to self-alienate this society of identities-within out into society at large (multiculturalism) without confronting differences, and in one superficial sense a "hybrid state" already exists as a State hybrid. Here, just as in its biological substrate, hybridizing always requires dealing with dominance and duality, and the danger of an integration, submersion, or simple disappearance into a "superior" strain, a hegemonic whole, with no inscription of one's own history, is always present. The more alien element risks being forced to function as an alter ego, a kind of complement to the citizen, the less alien. (One may, of course, hopelessly hope that one day soon dominant white culture will assimilate into weak minority ones.) The State will argue that assimilationism is an important step forward, perhaps even a prerequisite for its affirmative-action program for aliens, but in fact this may be simply impossible for those who remain outside with no access to power. This constitutes a remoralizing of the problem in the same way that the "Protestant Ethic," the "New Socialist Man," or "liberation" have all moralized and psychologized the various stages of the historical forced march of the modern capitalist individual (Weber).

Far from being a wilderness, the vast and featureless wastes of Desert Storm are the perfect background for the new multicultural army—women, blacks, citizen-soldiers from the reserve army of the otherwise morally unemployed. We insist once again that this tremendous force must be turned inward—*crossing the barriers we erect within* and destroying the hold that our categories have over us.

Paraphrasing Brecht's point about cities, the following paradox arises: "America" is allowed (or forced) to change, but the individual may not. Something more than this technical and contradictory liberation must come into being as rights are extended to ever greater sectors of society, as was done in the case of slaves after the Civil War. If we cannot necessarily rid ourselves of the repertory of masks that social categories generate, we must at least understand what lies beneath them. Societies exist only in social forms, the most complex of which, democracy, is still in the process of development, and this is the battleground. Seeing this form not as a fixed essence but as a constant circulation is already an important victory. Yet, if multiculturalism is to be more than a liberal('s) liberation, it too must learn to deploy its forces, inward as well as outward, psychologically as well as socially.

Strategy must be developed for the passage from monocultural society (the "repression" or "expulsion" of difference) through multicultural society (the "deployment" and organization of difference) past the transcultural State "hybrid" (the "integration" of difference, its "crossing," in this vitalist and biological metaphor—a kind of superstate)—*the passage from the fort* through the panopticon and the pyramid of difference toward a labyrinth (Bataille) where one is lost only when one tries to find a "way out" (the illusion or utopia of exit) instead of finding oneself or another in it, a "way in," an entry.

Alien Art

For art today, as one entry (in)to this labyrinth, the task lies in finding its relevance in the midst of the political, demographic, and psycho-social transformations—relative to the shifting and crossing of collective and individual boundaries. Shifts in *external* boundaries (ethnic and state borders, for example, North-South, East-West) are closely bound up with migrations and the crossing of these boundaries. The face of Europe and North America in particular is being transformed in this way. These in turn impose themselves on shifts in *internal* boundaries—ideas, beliefs, ideologies, languages, metaphors, slogans—psychological traces, lines, both shortcuts and roadblocks, running across the individual territories of human minds. The migratory movements within each of us necessarily include crossing one important internal boundary, the line drawn between the person one has been but no longer is and the person one will become, thus establishing, by transgression, an *extraterritorial demilitarized zone,* which is where the alien feels most at home. Coming to terms with the varying directions of these internal shifts and crossings (and their corresponding demilitarized zones) is a complicated process, but the mapping of these zones constitutes one of the most important social movements taking place today.

For the alien, living is a series of entries, "crossings," not in the biotechnical sense usually implied by the term "hybrid" (although the latter does have the attractive force of transformation on its side), but rather the often painful and problematic crossing of spaces and borders, with concomitant changes in mental and moral position, which, as in the labyrinth, are as much (or more) internal as external. Here "alien" means both a political and metaphysical (nomadic and migrant) state of being and "becoming," perhaps even a psychological encampment in space and time in today's displaced and estranged world. In this new work, borders, internal and external, shift and cross in perpetual movement and transformation, and so do the identities they determine. "Who am I?" can only be answered in terms of "Who, where, why, (in the name of) what, have I been?" (Just as it is for the proton in quantum physics, which constantly and instantaneously "becomes" a sequence of eleven elementary particles, then a neutron and a pion, and then an individual proton "again," this observed unending transformative process is the "definition" of a proton, and its only "identity.")

The artist who would dare make a contribution to this present, understood as a home where past and future dwell together (Benjamin), as well as to the history of this present and future (Nietzsche, Foucault), would need to learn how to operate much like a nomadic Sophist in a migrant *polis,* providing new tools of language for it (in the performative sense of metaphoric speech-acts) for aliens alienated from themselves for lack of language. Like the Sophist in ancient Greece, the new Sophist, as a practitioner of democracy in that politically guaranteed but practically nonexistent empty space called "public," must practically recreate an agora or forum each time she or he wishes to speak or listen. Even in a democracy, the liberal state or corporate estate fills this space with its own "publicity" (Habermas), instead of leaving it for the "free communication of thoughts and opinions" (Declaration of the Rights of Man, 1791), becoming in effect a "tyrant of opinion" (Tocqueville). The Sophist must be prepared for an adversarial role in going beyond corrupted forms of communication. In a democracy the most important right is the right to representation. Neither a pedagogue nor a demagogue, the Sophist is an *interrupteur,* a "switch" always ready to open rather than close the communications circuit. There must always be room for this empty space, open to a multiplicity of expression and interpretation (Lefort). Alien art is this empty space, existing only between the lines.

Among all the more-and-less alien in this world lives one even more alien half. These are the double-aliens, women aliens, many of whom, often enveiled, have learned to operate as double agents, skillfully crossing borders between antagonistic alien compounds and the embattled zones within them (Carrie Mae Weems). Crossing by force of commerce or marriage a multiplicity of boundaries and identities, women become aliens not only to aliens, but aliens *of* and *from* aliens—the most nomadic of aliens, *cross-aliens.* In this depth of the depths of alienation, women's memory, thousands of years long, conceals and discloses sources of knowledge and philosophy for creating social space as de-alienating space, another private and public agora. One might even look to women as the first Sophists. Based on the special alchemy in the metaphors and expressions within this knowledge (devised under the most

26

alienating chains of circumstances), these traditions constitute an important artistic education for the contemporary alien artist.

The most difficult and critical challenge is the changing and nomadic status of the *metaphor* and the directions of *its* shifts and crossings. How one disarms or deactivates dangerous metaphors, deciding which of them to preserve (disarmed but not destroyed) as critical monuments, specimens of the dark past, and which to publicly unmask or destroy, and creating space for new metaphors to serve as elements of new aesthetic modes of communication among today's (alienated) aliens, are important practical questions facing the Sophist. The artist who would undertake such a project should be aware of the dangers of repeating or "repatriating" old and habitual preconceptions, in particular preconceived notions of (alien) "identity" as a uniform category, and of turning a blind eye to the internal and external antagonisms within and between it and aliens.

In this labyrinth, art must be not only psycho-demographic, but also democratic, and it must contribute to the transformation of this democracy through new nomadic forms and modes—art as *xenology,* a new form of inquiry (*historia*). Its critical, historical, and prospective voice is necessary equipment for aliens in transit, for whom an outdated history book, as much as any fading blueprint for the future, is a suspect, even useless, *pièce d'identité.*

Paris–New York, January 16, 1992
(On the first anniversary of the Gulf War)

Note

1. John Holusha, *New York Times,* December 1, 1991, p. F9.

Originally published in *The Hybrid State,* exh. cat. (New York: Exit Art/The First World, 1992), pp. 92–98.

Avant-Garde as Public Art: The Future of a Tradition (1984)

Before I attempt to characterize briefly the strategies of public art today in light of public practices of the avant-garde of the past, I must express my critical detachment from what is generally called "art in public places." This bureaucratic-aesthetic form of public legitimation may allude to the idea of public art as a social practice but in fact has very little to do with it. Such a "movement" wants first to protect the autonomy of art (bureaucratic aestheticism), isolating artistic practice from critical public issues, and then to impose this purified practice on the public domain (bureaucratic exhibitionism) as proof of its accountability. Such work functions at best as liberal urban decoration.

To believe that the city can be affected by open-air public art galleries or enriched by outdoor curatorial adventures (through state and corporate purchases, lendings, and display) is to commit an ultimate philosophical and political error. For, since the eighteenth century at least, the city has operated as a grand aesthetic curatorial project, a monstrous public art gallery for massive exhibitions, permanent and temporary, of environmental architectural "installations"; monumental "sculpture gardens"; official and unofficial murals and graffiti; gigantic "media shows"; street, underground, and interior "performances"; spectacular social and political "happenings"; state and real-estate "land art projects"; economic events, actions, and evictions (the newest form of exhibited art); etc., etc. To attempt to "enrich" this powerful, dynamic art gallery (the city public domain) with "artistic art" collections or commissions—all in the name of the public—is to decorate the city with a pseudo-creativity that is irrelevant to urban space and experience alike; it is also to contaminate this space and experience with the most pretentious and patronizing bureaucratic-aesthetic environmental pollution. Such beautification is uglification; such humanization provokes alienation; and the noble idea of public access is likely to be received as private excess.

The aim of critical public art is neither a happy self-exhibition nor a passive collaboration with the grand gallery of the city, its ideological theater and architectural-social system. Rather, it is an engagement in strategic challenges to the city structures and mediums that mediate our everyday perception of the world; an engagement through aesthetic-critical interruptions, infiltrations, and appropriations that question the symbolic, psycho-political, and economic operations of the city.

To further clarify my position on public art, I must also express my critical detachment from the apocalyptic visions of urban design and environment suggested by Jean Baudrillard in terms of "cyberblitz" and "hyperreality": however brilliant his metaphorical-critical constructs may be, they cannot account for the complexity of symbolic, social, and economic life in the contemporary public domain.

For Baudrillard the Bauhaus proposed "the dissociation of every complex subject-object relation into simple, analytic, rational elements that can be recombined in functional ensembles and which then take on status as the environment." Today, however, we are beyond even this: "When the still almost artisanal functionalism of the Bauhaus is surpassed in the cybernetic and mathematical design of the environment . . . we are beyond the object and its function. . . . Nothing retains the place of the critical, regressive-transgressive discourse of Dada and of Surrealism."[1] And yet this total vision omits the powerful symbolic articulation of two economically related but distinct zones in the contemporary city: state architecture and real-estate architecture. The two work in tandem: state architecture appears solid, symbolically full, rooted in sacred historic ground, while real-estate architecture develops freely, appropriating, destroying, redeveloping, etc. A monstrous evicting agency, this architecture imposes the bodies of the homeless onto the "bodies"—the structures and sculptures—of state architecture, especially in those ideological graveyards of heroic "history" usually located in downtown areas.

Now in the current attempts to revitalize—to gentrify—the downtowns, cities legally protect these graveyards as meaningful ideological theater, not as places of "cyberblitz" where "the end of signification" has been reached. In this regard Marc Guillaume is only partially correct when he states that the contemporary downtown is just a "signal system" for touristic consumption:

The obsession with patrimony, the conservation of a few scattered centers, some monuments and museographic remains, are just such attempts [to compensate for the loss of social representation in urban architecture]. Nonetheless, they are all in vain. These efforts do not make a memory; in fact they have nothing to do with the subtle art of memory. What remains are merely the stereotypical signs of the city, a global signal system consumed by tourists.[2]

And yet it is still possible to establish a critical dialogue with state and real-estate architecture or even, as described by Guillaume, with monuments to pseudo-memory. Not only is it still possible, it is urgently needed—that is, if we are to continue the unfinished business of the situationist urban project:

People will still be obliged for a long time to accept the era of reified cities. But the attitude with which they accept it can be changed immediately. We must spread skepticism toward those bleak, brightly colored kindergartens, the new dormitory cities of both East and West. Only a mass awakening will pose the question of a conscious construction of the urban milieu. . . .

The basic practice of the theory of unitary urbanism will be the transcription of the whole theoretical lie of urbanism, detourned [diverted, appropriated] for the purpose of de-alienation: we constantly have to defend ourselves from the poetry of the bards of conditioning—to jam their messages, to turn their songs inside out.[3]

Of course, the situationist project of intervention now requires critical evaluation; some of its methods and aims seem too utopian, totalitarian, naive, or full of avant-garde aestheticism to be accepted today. In this respect we can learn much from past and present avant-garde practices, which I will schematize below in terms of their relationships to: the cultural system of art and its institutions; the larger system of culture and its institutions; the system of "everyday life"; and mass or public spectacle and the city.

Historic Avant-Garde (1910–40s)
Futurism, dada, suprematism, constructivism, surrealism. Artistic interventions against art and its institutions; critical and self-critical manifestations of the rejection of its cultural system. Discovery of direct public address: e.g., futurist synthetic theater, evenings, actions, and manifestos. Discovery of media art; discovery of critical public art as contestation. Roots of situationist aestheticism (rejected by new avant-garde as well as by engaged and neo-avant-garde).

Socially Engaged Avant-Garde (1920–30s)
Bertolt Brecht, George Grosz, Vladimir Tatlin, El Lissitzky, Dziga Vertov, Aleksandr Bogdanov, Varvara Stepanova, Lyubov Popova, Galina and Olga Chichagova, John Heartfield, etc. Critical-affirmative action of culture and its institutions; critical transformation of the institutions of the cultural system of art. Engagement in mass publications, design, education systems, film (Kino-Pravda, Kino-Oko), opera, radio, theater ("epic" form, "estrangement" technique), agit-prop, proletcult, spectacles, Novyi Lef (Sergei Tretiakov's "organic" intervention). Roots of present affirmative interest in media cultural programs and public domain; also roots of situationist interruption and *détournement*.

Critical Neo-Avant-Garde (1960–70s)

Daniel Buren, support-surface artists, Hans Haacke, etc. (Missing reference: British pop art.) Critical-affirmative action on art and its institutions; critical and self-critical manipulations of its cultural system. Artistic attack on art as myth of bourgeois culture; critical exposure of structural ideological links between institutions of bourgeois art and culture-politics, ethics, philosophy, etc. Critical infiltration of museums as official public spectacle, but no significant attempts to enter mass spectacle, popular culture, public design.

Situationist Cultural Avant-Garde as Revolutionary Force (1960–70s)

Henri Lefebvre, Situationist international, Guy Debord, etc. (Missing references: Fluxus, punk rock.) Cultural revolutionary intervention in everyday life and its institutions (environment, popular media, etc.); critical and self-critical abandonment of art as cultural system and of avant-garde as specialized procedure. Public intervention against spectacle; tendency toward alternative spectacle. Creation of situations "concretely and deliberately constructed by the collective organization of a unitary ambience and game of events"; manipulation of popular culture against mass culture. Organization of *dérive* (drift), urban wanderings to contest modern structures, dominant architecture, city planning (surrealist tactics). Influence of postmarxist cultural studies and sociology; city as "rediscovered and magnified" festival to overcome conflict between everyday life and festivity. Attack on passive reception of the city: "Our first task is to enable people to stop identifying with their surroundings and with model patterns of behavior."

Present Critical Public Art: New Avant-Garde as "Intelligence"

Dennis Adams, Dara Birnbaum, Dan Graham, Alfredo Jarr; Barbara Kruger, Antonio Muntadas, etc.; also Public Art Fund (New York), Public Access (Toronto), Artangel Trust (London), etc. Critical-affirmative action on everyday life and its institutions (education, design, environment, spectacle, and mass media, etc.); critical transformation of culture from within. Critical collaboration with institutions of mass and public media, design, and education in order to raise consciousness (or critical unconscious) regarding urban experience: to win time and space in information, advertising, billboards, lightboards, subways, public monuments and buildings, television cable and public channels, etc. Address to public viewer, alienated city-dweller. Continuous influence of cultural studies enhanced by feminist critique of representation.

31 **Notes**

1. Jean Baudrillard, "Design and Environment or How Political Economy Escalates into Cyberblitz," in *For a Critique of the Political Economy of the Sign* (St. Louis: Telos Press, 1981), pp. 185, 203.

2. Marc Guillaume, [statement], *Zone,* nos. 1–2 (1986), p. 439.

3. See Ken Knabb, ed., *Situationist International Anthology* (Berkeley: Bureau of Public Secrets, 1981).

Originally presented as part of the panel discussion "Strategies of Public Address: Which Media, Which Publics?," which also included statements by critic Douglas Crimp and artist Barbara Kruger, at the Dia Art Foundation in New York on February 17, 1987. Published in *Discussions in Contemporary Culture,* ed. Hal Foster (New York: Dia Art Foundation, 1987), pp. 41–53.

For the De-Incapacitation of the Avant-Garde in Canada (1983)

The Canadian cultural state bureaucracy, with its "parallel" tentacles, appears today more charming and unchallenged than ever. Its appealing premise is that every "left" or "libertarian" idea can be incorporated with no delay into the centralized state bureaucratic system, starting, of course, with appropriating any idea of the decentralization of "culture" and the need for alternative organizations. This is especially effective when, in exchange, the art community itself, conveniently reviving the most questionable side of its avant-gardist unconscious, a glorious modernist myth of a "liberating" technology, suggests blindly to the central administration its own bureaucratic, technocratic, totalitarianlike projects.[1] Or when the artistic "left" attempts to "use" or to "take over" (but in fact assimilates itself to) the existing Canada Council "supporting" economic programs and the "parallel" bureaucratic artistic institutions.[2] In writing this I am aware of my advantage of freedom from the right to apply for Canada Council grants, a freedom which helped to save me from the danger of integration with the very subject of my critical focus: the present central bureaucratic process of political, social, or cultural incapacitation and moral capitulation of the entire artistic culture.[3]

Feedback

My own and my friends' lives in my native Poland of the sixties and seventies consisted to a large extent of conducting, as a daily routine, a continuous critique of the cultural policy of the central bureaucracy. The main place of the exercise of our opposition was, of course, the coffee shop, an important cultural site of intellectual and artistic discourse in Poland. Remaining continuously in the state of being-against-"them" (against the "oppressor"), but not able to imagine any concrete action (practice), we were, in a *negative sense*, unknowingly becoming more and more vulnerable to an osmotic assimilation to bureaucratic "reason." The more liberal and flexible in their strategies the "state ideological apparatuses" were (the coffee shop is one of them), the more difficult it was for us to see to what degree our sharp, restless, and detailed critique was adopting the enemy's linguistics and subjecting us deeper and deeper to its seductive site, to its mastery at indoctrinating our souls, and awakening our unconscious drive for collaboration, and desire for bureaucratic habits, style, language, aesthetics, philosophy, and power.

Through the same coffee shop, with its microphones in the walls and informers (real or imaginary), the bureaucracy could learn which sections of our

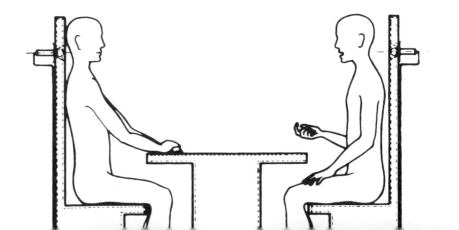

statements, complaints, and naive fantasies (we called it critique) could be appropriated by the state as an illusion of its liberalizing processes, to reinforce their operational capabilities and, in the end, to serve the mechanisms of bureaucratic *legitimation*.

Hot Beer

The intoxicated, stuffy, and feverish-by-hot-and-strong-espresso atmosphere of a decorated and illuminated Warsaw coffee shop is in great contrast to the cooled down, air-conditioned, and tranquilized-by-the cold-if-not-freezing climate of the dark Toronto bar. This contrast could be explained by the "cool" character of an authoritarian one-party system and the "hot" (warm) character of a "liberal" stoic democratic organization.

But the situation is not so simple in the case of the artist bar in Toronto; it is becoming increasingly warmer here—warmer than in any other bar. New improvements are ideological stratification of the tables, heavy air, ambitious design, and slightly better lighting (one can see the faces and dresses). All of this was remodeled not long ago. This might all appear confusing to the foreign visitor or the immigrant artist. After years of being far from a native cultural life, the life dissolved in cigarette smoke and coffee-table debates, now far from that avant-garde-like style (of a Baudelairean state-socialist *flâneur*), here one again finds oneself resubmerged (to one's immigrant dismay) into a quite familiar "artistic" atmosphere and "cultural climate." One learns that within the capitalist-liberal state of Canada, this bar belongs to another state (a state within the state), that is, to the aristocratic "state" of the Canada Council. The Toronto site of the romantic dialectics of capitalist madness! This is a Canada Council Toronto bar, in which the trapped spirit of a middle-class artist is tossing between a desire for democratic egalitarian capitalism and that of a postcolonial bureaucratic aristocratism. Surprised (and there will be more surprises), the expatriate-artist, through his discovery, recognizes a serious similarity, not between Poland and Canada, but *between Poland and the Canada Council*. Brrrrr!

The present state of high-cultural affairs in Canada is taking more and more complex institutional forms. The Canada Council "state" is trying to keep its naturally shaking authoritarian balance by employing typical (and, I believe, naturally hopeless—I am still a Polish optimist) "feedback" critical mechanisms.

The one party totalitarian regime is an unstable form—it defuses the political scene, it no longer assures the feed-back of public opinion, the minimal flux in the integrated circuit which constitutes the transistorized political machine.[4]

The Canada Council, as in Poland and in every authoritarian machine, must neurotically produce its own "coffee shops," alternative publications, and spaces, in order to control its own position and direction and to serve *itself* as a medium of critical discourse on its own future. The beer is getting hot (warm).

In this permanently unstable survival process, the Canada Council is acting permanently against itself (in a controlling self-controlled sense), and superficially fragmenting and camouflaging its main cultural effect: a total bureaucratic pacification of the intellectual creative power of the artistic intelligentsia and artistic culture.

The only remaining difference between Toronto and Warsaw (if one can see it through the smoke of the battle of artistic bars on Queen Street—or the coffee shops on Foksal Street in Warsaw) is that the distinction between the language and gestures of a bureaucrat and those of an artist is much less recognizable in Toronto (as a matter of fact, it is so blurred that it is almost invisible). Looking closer, one will be able to disclose a horrifying phenomenon: what was for Warsaw a nightmare or an imminent danger (not yet reality) received its total three-dimensional realization in Toronto. Finally *everyone appears to be both the artist and the bureaucrat.* In the happy and comfortable atmosphere of life in this state-hi-cultural-bureaucratic musak, in the climate of final reunion of old enemies, artistic (antibourgeois) and modern state (bourgeois) avant-gardes, in the aura of communion of the bureaucratized artist and the aestheticized bureaucrat, the Toronto artistic intelligentsia elevates itself to a much higher level of collaboration than artists in Poland. It approaches the conscious level, the level which I shall call *cultural corruption!*

Militant Melodrama

Every reversal, being essentially similar to its original, appears to us as an opposite. Such a reversal deludes us (as a revelation on the original image) and pretends to reveal the reality behind it, the typical dilemma of every avant-garde critique.

To claim an objective position necessary for the fulfillment of one's own destiny (to reverse the world image), the avant-garde must start first with itself, turning its own image upside-down, and presenting itself as either non-art-

35 in-life and antibourgeois antiart (dada, futurism, constructivism), or as a non-philosophy-for-world-revolution or antiphilosophy (Marxism), or finally, as an anti-avant-garde-art-as-cultural-work (present-day leftist art). In reversing itself (its own pre-avant-garde image), the avant-garde never actually recognizes, admits, or presents itself publicly or discloses itself as the reversed second-degree image (meta-image). It is a dangerously blind denial by the political avant-garde or artistic left (anti-avant-garde avant-garde) to recognize *itself as ideology,* its own perception and production as being dependent on ideology (anti-ideology = ideology), or finally, as producing ideology itself.

The artistic left suffers from a great confusion. The political ideology is confused with artistic utopia.[5] The distrust of the artistic left toward artistic avant-gardism (toward its own roots) expresses itself in a desire to reject the experimentalism of artistic work "in studio" or "in gallery," and in a tendency to hunt for "formalist witches."[6]

Artistic avant-gardism leads historically to the total and immediate degradation of art (as bourgeois art, official art, etc.). Political avant-gardism, being artistically conservative and *nostalgic* for forms which it believes appeal to the working class (often forms of bourgeois romantic art), cannot allow for such a degradation of art. Not calling for the "death of politics" and for the liberation from the ideological language, the political avant-garde could not accept and join the artistic avant-garde's radical critique of art ("death of art") nor could it support artists' utopian work toward the new social theory of form, leading to the liberation of artistic (and any) language from falseness.[7]

The utopian aesthetic-linguistic project of the artistic avant-garde failed as much as the ideological strategic project of the political avant-garde. Yet the artistic project was politically, aesthetically, philosophically, and ethically more ambitious. Its failure was, and still is, intellectually challenging to those whose work deals with art, language, and representation in relation to ideology, culture, revolution, and political theory. The political avant-garde's strategic (as opposed to utopian) program was unsuccessful because, among other reasons, it never considered the questions raised by the artistic avant-garde.

By refusing to analyze the structures and the mode of ideological production inherent in its own logic, Marxism is condemned (behind the facade of "dialectical" discourse in terms of class struggle) to expanding the reproduction of ideology, and thus of the capitalist system itself.[8]

Through the false notion of a strategic revolutionary necessity (even if there is no revolutionary situation, or no revolution as such), and specifically in the name of not giving ammunition to the enemy, the embattled artistic left does not allow for any *public* critical discourse within its own ranks, even if the only clear critical challenge to the left can arrive almost exclusively (due to the critical weakness and apathy of the enemy) from the left itself.

In the absence of a revolutionary situation this ideological trap of the left might lead to its total degeneration and its reduction to the point of an absurd revolutionary ornament in the state's liberal bureaucratic cultural firmament. The absence of self-critical discourse within the left leads to its dangerous appearance of seriousness about itself and its "mission," and consequently about everything else, which functions often as a mask of ignorance itself. Wearing the militant mask, it is important to remember that its owner is masked *both* from outside and from inside. In a challenging intellectual discourse, the unmasking of the enemy should mean the unmasking of yourself. In other words, in the process of an intellectual concretization and formulation (such as art, critical writing, etc.) the public discourse leading to the cultural deideologization must realize itself through the process of unmasking its own ideological, critical, linguistic, and theoretical limitations and cultural mystifications. (It would be better to conduct this discourse artistically through work on aesthetic practice and theory, and not only through popularizing didactic art, magazines, editorials, and "culturalizing" popular writings.)

This unmasking process cannot be arrested by any institutional self-governing desires or decisions. There is no end to mystification (signification) and ideologization processes. Even "deideologization" can assume an institutional and ideological form. If part of our own ideological limitation is a self-mystification process, the battle against ourselves as myth (and our masks) is perhaps more urgently needed than the battle against the "enemy," which may often only appear as an illusive result of the limited visibility produced by our own ideological outfit, our camouflaged armor, our militant mask.[9] The cultural performance of the artistic left avant-garde is not only dependent in a negative sense on its enemy (such as dominant culture and official art) but also unfortunately is dependent in a positive sense on its main allies: the artistically conservative, if not artistically reactionary; the political and the independent cultural left.

And so, hypnotised by his enemy—of whom he makes an infinitely cunning and terrifying monster—the avant-gardist often ends up forgetting about the future. The future, he seems to imply, can take care of itself when the demons of the past are exorcised.[10]

In this militant but dependent ideological left atmosphere of struggle, the intellectual, artistic, and cultural program of the positive and critical left is unlikely to be built. Before anything else, the left would have to liberate itself from its dependence on the right. Such a program would, with no paradox, lead to the final phase, the ultimate liberation of the left from the left itself, after which there won't be any room for a reactionary shift to the right or toward the center, but a need for the beginning of a constructive intellectual artistic *work-in-depth* in the direction of the new movement of the artistic intelligentsia, which I shall preliminarily refer to, not as the new avant-garde, but as an INTELLIGENCE.

Spirit

The process of neutralization—the transformation of culture into something independent and external, removed from possible relation to praxis—makes it possible to integrate it into the organization from which it untiringly cleanses itself. Furthermore, this is accomplished neither with contradiction nor with danger.

Today manifestations of extreme artistry can be fostered, produced, and pretested by official institutions; indeed art is dependent upon such support if it is to be produced at all and to find its way to an audience. Yet, at the same time, art denounces everything institutional and official.[11]

Canada has become a promised land, if not a paradise, for the modern cultural administrator—a realization of the oldest high-ranking bureaucratic dream, a reintegration with the detached "spirit." The initial separation from the spirit was, for the modern bureaucrat, a primary step and ethical condition to the formulation of an administration, whose objective mission was to protect the "spirit" outside of the walls of the governmental office in the new democratic society. The "spirit" then achieved for bureaucracy as status of desire, used with religious intonation, the sacred word-spirit, before the words "excellence" and "beauty," became a key term in the highest-ranking official speeches:

I can't help but hear an echo of the philosopher Henri Bergson of my youth, invoking a "spiritual supplement for democracy, in these times of enormous technological achievement . . .".

. . . I have a respectable accomplice in the philosopher Jean Lacroix. In effect, he says that democracy can only exist in a *climate of spirituality.* Democracy is not in opposition to the notion of aristocracy but rather in favor of applying the notion to all men. One cannot define democracy in terms of institutions, Lacroix says, no matter what their importance. To say that democracy is government "of the people by the people" does not have any concrete meaning: *there are only oligarchic, or rather, aristocratic, governments.* Democracy makes use of oligarchies, whereas oligarchies make use of people. The problem is to find a way to bring the best people to power and, once there, to require them to maintain their excellence and integrity.[12]

The cultural, or artistic, bureaucracy is becoming a modern aristocracy and (similar to the caste of art historians) functions as a high priest which not only protects the spirit, but coordinates it, steers it, governs it, and understands it for everyone.

The Canada Council is serving its national duty well and contributing effectively to the general politics of bureaucracy, the politics of saying and doing politically nothing (or as little as possible). By "not-doing," bureaucracy is supporting the existing political balance.

A mature political system needs to be partly non-political so as to possess adequate managerial capacity. By helping to provide such capacity, the bureaucracy has had a hand in the making of the contemporary state.

If this be action, the bureaucracy has mostly acted by seeming not to act, by being neither heard nor seen.[13]

As such, zero-degree bureaucracy is developing politically zero-degree language. Such public duty requires permanent linguistic coverage of every political moment, applying to each official speech terminology which camouflages any clear meaning. The bureaucratic zero-degree rational discourse is encumbered with the concepts of the individual human "destiny" and "catharsis" in the application of such terms as "spirit," "beauty," "climate of spirituality," "quality," "creation," "excellence," "integrity," etc.

By not saying anything, on the one hand, the Canada Council reinforces the modern liberal state, and on the other hand, by overstating the romantic notion of "creativity," it degenerates art to cathartic kitsch and separates it from any political, social, or philosophical sense.

Not only does the Canada Council have to produce the feedback mechanisms within the art community, but also within the Canadian democratic corporate/capitalist system which cannot continue forever to be host to its feudal, aristocratic parasite. The Canada Council might then be transformed from the existing centrally appointed "oligarchic" subsystem into a democratically formed (i.e., proportional political-cultural representation) parliamentary apparatus—a total appropriation of the political differences of the art communities in Canada.

Alternation . . . is the end of the end of representation. . . . Democracy realizes the law of equivalence in the political order. This law is accomplished in the back and forth movement of the two terms which reactivates their equivalence but allows, by the minute difference, a public consensus to be formed and the cycle of representation to be dosed.[14]

"Democratic" transformations might challenge all feudal subsystems within the bureaucratic machine. It is possible that we are witnessing a long-term strategy, or better and integral to the apparatuses, an irreversible process of gradual absorption, assimilation, and incorporation of the left avant-garde into the democratic system. Applying Baudrillard's terminology, we will see in this completely balanced system a "back-and-forth movement of two terms" ("artistocrats" versus "cultural workers"), a permanent spectacle which will not be the spectacle for us—*we will be the spectacle*.

The political debate (reflected on the screens in video bars) between the left avant-garde (artistic left) and the liberal aristocracy will constitute a hot (warm) medium, cooling down our bars to their normal freezing darkness: from the idiotic to the worse; to the final movement of official culture: the glorious progression to "the end of the end of representation."

Once again (as if nothing ever happened in the '60s), we are living the time of a corporate/commercial and bureaucratic incapacitation of art. This time it manifests itself culturally in various forms of dissolution or capitulation of the artistic intelligentsia and takes the form of a decadent revival of a pseudo-critical, anti-intellectual "expression" in art and the ornamental, skating irresponsibly on the surfaces of history—"postmodern" design manipulation.

Only the formulation of self-governing artists' economic organizations and agencies, the gradual detachment of the artistic cultural community from the

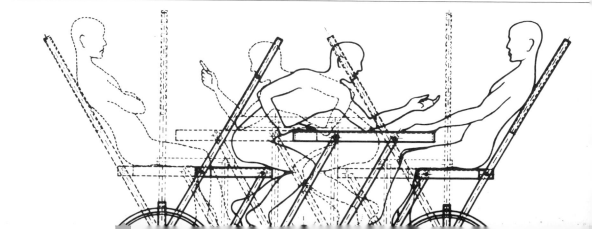

centralized state bureaucracy, and the organization of nonbureaucratic, small and flexible "Intelligence"-like working institutes and other, yet to be defined, artistic-educational institutions (always ready to dissolve themselves) will help to educate and recondition; to decaptivate our bureaucratized minds; to rescue and revive our stolen souls from bureaucratic protection, annexation, assimilation, and appropriation; to return to collective or individual constructive critical knowledge, independent and systematic artistic research, and a sense of social place.

This would be precisely the practical (not moralistic or ideological) *cultural action* which is needed more than anything else at this time. This would be an effective challenge to the monstrous system which, as we have learned in and from Eastern Europe, has to be challenged first; the system of the "national liberal culture" as a totally administrated and planned bureaucratic operation.

Notes

This essay is based on the lecture, "The Bureaucratization of the Avant-Garde," given at the Rivoli Café in Toronto on June 14, 1983. The author would like to thank Philip Monk, Leslie Sharpe, Karl Beveridge, and Christina Ritchie for their moral support and critical encouragement in addressing this sensitive and controversial subject.

1. Here, as in the case of the "Living Museum," a monstrous "Orwellian" proposal (see *Parallelogramme*, Retrospective 3), the myth of technology is cynically revived by the present pseudo-avant-garde as it is a common old sentiment of *both* the artistic avant-garde and the modern (stoic or capitalist/corporate) administration.

2. As the best example, the 1983 victory of the artistic-cultural left in the election of the Toronto A Space Board of Directors, or the process of (more or less successful) use of Canada Council grants for financing radical-cultural magazines, film, video distribution centers, etc.

3. Under the "independent" Canada Council "Law," *after* they obtain formal permanent resident status, immigrant artists must wait *five years* before they have a right to participate in the "democratic competition" for the artists' awards (apply for grants). In some cases immigrant artists work and live in Canada for many years while waiting for their formal permanent resident status.

4. Jean Baudrillard, "The Orders of Simulacra," in *Simulations* (New York: Semiotext(e), 1983), p. 131.

5. I am applying here the concepts of "ideology" and "utopian thinking" in the light of the discussion on their interrelationship by Karl Mannheim in *Ideology and Utopia: An*

41   *Introduction to the Sociology of Knowledge* (San Diego: Harcourt Brace Jovanovich, 1985), p. 40.

6. Attacking the shallow Greenbergian concept of artistic modernism, with its orthodox "disciplinism," it is easy to forget that art is and always was a specific method of questioning and reinventing itself through the practice of analyzing older concepts and forging new concepts from reality. In this practice, the formal method is the only one art has at its disposition.

7. In the '20s the Soviet and Eastern European avant-gardes called for the rejection of art and demanded the immediate construction of a new and "better" (that is, freed from the social chains of capitalism and the bourgeois heritage) socialist language and theory of form. The programs of Opoyaz, Novyi Lef, Vkhutemas, and the work of Rodchenko in the Soviet Union; Blok, Praesens, and the work of Strzemiński and Kobro in Poland; and the program of Disk in Czechoslovakia, can serve as examples of different choices. These avant-garde artistic/decorative/aesthetic (utopian) proposals were too advanced and too theoretical for the ideologists of the left-wing political avant-garde, who (like most of the members of today's artistic left) still do not understand the politics of social and formal revolution proposed by the artists of the '20s.

8. Jean Baudrillard, *For a Critique of the Political Economy of the Sign* (St. Louis: Telos Press, 1981), p. 89.

9. Of course, this applies not only to the artistic left, but also to all the factions and professional groups fighting each other inside and outside the art community.

10. Matei Calinescu, *Faces of Modernity: Avant-Garde, Decadence, Kitsch* (Bloomington: Indiana University Press, 1977).

11. Theodore Adorno, "Culture and Administration," *Telos,* Fall 1977.

12. Charles Lussier, "The Canada Council: The Principle of Excellence and Its Implications in a Democratic Society," Speech No. 7702, July 5, 1977. General Wojciech Jaruzelski would certainly be in agreement with the idea of democracy put forth by Charles Lussier, director of the Canada Council. Oligarchy: "a form of government in which power is reserved for a small number; also, a state so governed." *Funk and Wagnalls' Standard Dictionary* (New York: Signet, 1980).

13. F. Marx, "Bureaucracy as a Political Action Group," in Joseph LaPalombara, ed., *Bureaucracy and Political Development,* Studies in Social Development, no. 2 (Princeton: Princeton University Press, 1963).

14. Jean Baudrillard, "The Orders of Simulacra," op. cit., pp. 131–32.

First published in *Parallelogramme,* 1984.

two **Projections**

**Public
Projection** (1983)

Motto
It's not a matter of emancipating truth from every system of power (which would be a chimera, for truth is already power) but of detaching the power of truth from the forms of hegemony, social, economic and cultural, within which it operates at the present time.
—Michel Foucault, "Truth and Power" (1977)

The Body

We are looking at the multiple sites of its body, and at the shapes of its external organs: the colonnades, porticos, domes, helmets, arches, columns, pilasters, pediments, stairs, doors, windows. . . . Attracted by its appearance, we begin to gravitate around its body. Gazing, viewing, observing, and staring, we are trying to fathom its mysterious grammar. Standing face to face with the front, pacing along the facade, touring all of the elevations of its vast structure, we are being transformed into the mediums of a gigantic cultural seance. We are being drawn into the magnetic field of its architectural appeal and symbolic influence.

The Aura

Crossing the monstrous shade of its elevation, we are halted by the blow of a cool wind which is cruising around the corners of its lofty massif. As we approach its body, we are confronted by an intimate protective warmth radiating through the walls, wings, and open doors, confused with the heavy breath of the air-conditioning ventilators.

We feel desire to identify with or to become part of the building. We recognize the familiarity of the building, like that of our own body. We feel a drive to "complete" the building and we desire to be "completed" by it. We sense that there is something about us which is incomplete, and which can only be completed by a full integration with the building.

Superficially, we resent the authority of its massive monumental structure. We rebel against a tyranny of its deaf, motionless, immortal walls; yet, in our heart of hearts, we not only allow ourselves to be outwitted by an academic methodicalness of the hierarchical order, by its charm, the loftiness of its parts, and the harmony of its proportional body, but, more dangerously, we allow ourselves to become intoxicated and seduced by its structural ability to embody and to grasp artistically our intimate, unspoken drive for a disciplined collaboration with its power.

Social Body

Its body is both individual and social; its harmony is based upon the same discipline, governing a totality of relationships of the whole structure to the parts and of each part to the other. This embodies and physically represents the concept of the organization of a utopian society in the form of a disciplined-disciplining body, allowing for both the multidirectional flow of power and the controlled circulation of the individual bodies.

The Father

In the process of our socialization the very first contact with a public building is no less important than the moment of social confrontation with the father, through which our sexual role and place in society are constructed. Early socialization through patriarchal sexual discipline is extended by the later socialization through the institutional architecturalization of our bodies.

Thus the spirit of the father never dies, continuously living as it does in the building which was, is, and will be embodying, structuring, mastering, representing, and reproducing his "eternal" and "universal" presence as a patriarchal wisdom-body of power.

The Medium

The building is not only an institutional "site of the discourse of power," but, more importantly, it is a metainstitutional, spatial medium for the continuous and simultaneous symbolic reproduction of both the general myth of power and the individual desire for power.

For these purposes, the building is "sculptured" to operate as an aesthetic structure, thus assisting in the process of inspiring and symbolically concretizing (reflecting) our mental projections of power.

Social Effect

The prime occupation of the building is to remain still, to be rooted permanently to the ground, abstaining from any visible movement.

This static occupation—annexation of time and territory—creates both a dynamic and a somnambulistic social effect. The "aura" of the unmoving building hypnotically animates and sustains our ritualistic movement around its body.

Circulating around and between the buildings, we cannot stop moving. We are unable to concentrate and focus on their bodies. This establishes an absent-minded relation to the building, an unconscious contact, a passive gaze.

47

By imposing our permanent circulation, our absent-minded perception, by ordering our gaze, by structuring our unconscious, by embodying our desire, masking and mythifying the relations of power, by operating under the discreet camouflage of a cultural and aesthetic "background," the building constitutes an effective medium and ideological instrument of power.

The Method of Projection

We must stop this ideological "ritual," interrupt this journey-in-fiction, arrest the somnambulistic movement, restore public focus, a concentration of the building and its architecture. What is implicit about the building must be exposed as explicit; the myth must be visually concretized and unmasked. The absent-minded, hypnotic relation with architecture must be challenged by a conscious and critical public discourse taking place in front of the building.

Public visualization of this myth can unmask the myth, recognize it "physically," force it to the surface, and hold it visible, so that the people on the street can observe and celebrate its final formal capitulation.

This must happen at the very place of myth, on the site of its production, on its body—the building.

Only physical, public projection of the myth on the physical body of myth (projection of myth on myth) can successfully demythify the myth.

The look, the appearance, the costume, the mask of the buildings is the most valuable and expensive investment. In the power discourse of the "public" domain, the architectural form is the most secret and protected property.

Public projection involves questioning both the function and the ownership of this property.

In defending the public as the communal against the public as the private, the projection reveals and is effected by the political contradiction of the culture of capitalism.

As a private property, the architectural appearance is well protected by the police, the guards, and the city bylaws.

The attack must be unexpected, frontal, and must come with the night, when the building, undisturbed by its daily functions, is asleep and when its body dreams of itself, when the architecture has its nightmares.

This will be a symbol-attack, a public psychoanalytical seance, unmasking and revealing the unconscious of the building, its body, the "medium" of power.

By introducing the technique of an outdoor slide montage and the immediately recognizable language of popular imagery, the public projection can become a communal, aesthetic counterritual. It can become an urban night festival, an architectural "epic theater," inviting both reflection and relaxation, where the street public follows the narrative forms with an emotional engagement and a critical detachment.

Warning

Slide projectors must be switched off before the image loses its impact and becomes vulnerable to appropriation by the building as a decoration.

Post Scriptum

It may be noted, by the way, that there is no better start for thinking than laughter. And, in particular, the convulsion of the diaphragm usually provides better opportunities for thought than convulsion of the soul.
—Walter Benjamin, "The Author as Producer" (1934)

Originally published in *Canadian Journal of Political and Social Theory/ Revue canadienne de théorie politique et sociale* (Winnipeg) 7, nos. 1–2 (Winter-Spring 1983), pp. 185–87.

Memorial Projection (1986)

Demonstrations! Clashes! Rallies! Voluntary and involuntary assemblies! Battles! Events pregnant with far-reaching consequences!

Surprisingly seized by these social and political outbreaks, the old memorial has no choice but to accept its new role and meaning as a revolutionary site. To legitimize its historical indispensability during crowded, dramatic, and risky moments, the crafty monument must welcome and accommodate the optimistic and full-blooded events cankering into its skeptical, pale, and wrinkled facade.

If the memorial were to allow itself any resentment or disrespect toward these events, they would forcefully and mercilessly impose themselves upon it. Such meaning-forcing acts would be carried out either by physical destruction of the memorial or, in a worse and more pathetic case, by cultural abandonment, exposing the now-absurd-in-remaining-there poor structure to its shameful and prolonged death from de-signification.

State celebrations ... tourism ... free entertainment ... health and recreation.

The newly erected memorial was an ideological creation of the posteventful state, which did not camouflage but, quite the reverse, exhibited outright throughout its entire site its joyless, deadly, and heavy duty: the duty of the emotional consolidation of the myth of the event as embodying official public value. The previously respectful distance ("historical perspective") of the memorial from everyday life is now being broken. Cold, tombstone benches, regimenting, mountainous stairways, brainwashing fountains, architortured bushes, and windswept floors were intended to banish unofficial life from the memorial's territory.

Today, the authorities want to add life and "social function" to the memorial site, to turn it into a "humanized" place for cultural relaxation, a zone of free festivity, tourism, permanent recreation, and so-called art in public places. Misattracted by refurbishing and by trivial cultural "events," the confused public must now learn how to live closer to the obscene necro-ideology of memorial icons, the naked, cold bodies of the monumentally frozen goddesses, gods, and heroes of our glorious massacres of humanity.

In extreme cases of life-with-memorial, the public will enter into very close, intimate, psycho-political relations with memorial architecture, which can then lead to disastrous neuro-patriotic reactions.

Thus administered by the department of "parks" and "recreation," submerged in newly planted vegetation and tranquilized by bureaucratically

guaranteed positive social reception, the relaxed memorial continues more effectively than ever its unchallenged ideological life.

Father

The son's unsuccessful rebellion was not aimed against the legal rules and moral, republican guidelines. The rebellion was against the father's absolute sexual, political, and social control. David's fathers, Brutus and the Horatii, serve as the monumental lesson on the system of the patrio-patriarchate as well as the ultimate social definition of the form of the father's body: the imperturbable, unshaken, inflexible, sober-minded, sexless and lifeless, silent, cold, odorous with death, ghastly pale (all blood transfused to the state's disposal), tired but powerful and self-disciplined, disciplining structure. The body of an unmoving father, barricading vast social territory, creates heavy traffic, the traffic which the father will then regulate himself. His lifelessness will regulate life; his sexlessness wants to castrate.

The spirit of David's model body continues to live its imaginary existence in the bodies of fathers and in all structures built by them. At the cost of their own aliveness, their repressed particular bodies must continuously supply life-power to their monumental bodies as memorials to themselves-as-patriarchs. Thus the body of the memorial, erected in the name of a particular father and a particular war, carries out the eternal ideological mission to secure symbolically and legitimize "historically" the *perpetuation* of the ghastly double myth, the myth of a patriarch as a great, heroic father and that of the war as a sacred, noble *sacrifice*.

Picture

Where else can one take one's own camera and one's own son for a walk?

Only in the atmosphere of "nature" and the environment of "history" can the enjoyment of a walk be sanctioned: a meaningful family pastime, the amusement instructive, the chat memorable, the picture-taking purposeful. While I mimic the memorial's grand gestures, the loud click of my father's camera freezes my body. This sound serves as a signal of formal encouragement of, if not applause for, bravado.

His busy movements are similar to the merciless procedures of land triangulation. Following photographic strategy for a full-scale survey, he repeatedly runs across the memorial grounds, moves from one shooting position to another, changes the vast battery of camera lenses suspended from his body,

compensates for the difference of their focal lengths by short runs back and forth. Following his sniper desperation for perfecting a shooting position (as if it were a real combat operation), he will suddenly fall flat on the flagstone or gravel, go down on his knees, squat, hop or jump over branches, flowerbeds, and fountains. But the real reward is yet to come: the shiny color pictures and bright slides. It is, of course, too early to imagine which particular pose of my body, juxtaposed with which parts of the memorial body, will please my father the most. Only the picture itself will tell. If Mother approves it, the family-memorial-picture will be selected and find its place on a prominent page of the official family album.

Memorial

Frolicking, making faces and excessive gestures, running, and climbing, every height is somehow less restricted here than bodily conduct there, on the street, at school, at home, in church, shopping center, cemetery, zoo, post office.

To straddle its knees, to ride its imperial lions bareback, to slide down along their bronze, monstrously long, thick hair, to climb the shining tangles of their tense muscles. Suddenly, and again, a familiar click of Father's camera interrupts my journey . . . yet I continue traversing the edge of the bases of all four grand bas-reliefs as if nothing at all has happened. With my stomach and chest adhering to the sharp shapes of their belts, holsters, buttons, and insignias, I continue clothing myself in their uniforms, arming and equipping myself with their rifles, bayonets, grenades, and packs. I learn through my fingers and cheek, letter by letter, sign by sign, emblem by emblem, all the lessons there are to learn. I sculpt myself through the recesses, nooks, and corners of the halfway liberated form, halfway rooted into its flesh, its permanently thrown-out chests, heroic bodies, and corpses.

Assuming their poses and gestures, my body grasps their heroic style. Synchronizing the focus and direction of my gaze with the position of their blank stare, I see . . .

Projection

The aim of the memorial projection is not to "bring life to" or "enliven" the memorial nor to support the happy, uncritical, bureaucratic "socialization" of its site, but to reveal and expose to the public the contemporary deadly life of the memorial. The strategy of the memorial projection is to attack the memorial by surprise, using slide warfare, or to take part in and infiltrate the official cultural programs taking place on its site.

In the latter instance, the memorial projection will become a double intervention: against the imaginary life of the memorial itself, and against the idea of social-life-with-memorial as uncritical relaxation. In this case, where the monumental character of the projection is bureaucratically desired, the aim of the memorial projection is to *pervert this desire* monumentally.

Originally published as "Memorial Projection," *October* (New York), no. 38 (Winter 1986), pp. 4–10.

The Venice Projections (1986)

The new world empire of tourism (travel, entertainment, art, and leisure) has turned the ruins of the old world financial-military empire of Venice into an art-Disneyland and shopping-for-the-past plaza. In alliance with the international "Save Venice" movement, this new empire has converted (renovated) the once lavish and decadent capital of capital, that glorious, floating pioneer of the multinational corporate World Trade Center, into a tourist playground, an imaginary "refuge" from the politically and economically troubled world of today. Such a refuge cannot, however, really succeed in Venice. The escape it offers must function as a semiconscious return to the golden roots of today's global reality.

The gilded architecture of Venice, thin as its own image, has been copied, perfected, magnified, and mass-produced throughout the cities, suburbs, and entertainment centers of Europe and North America. Thus the imaginary escapes and semiconscious returns of Venice are easily furnished by the "gondolas" of the Chicago World's Fair, the "Piazza San Marco" of Disneyworld in Florida, the "Grand Canal palaces" of apartment towers, the "campanili" of city halls, factories, churches, banks, fire and train stations, and by the "Condottieri Colleoni" of all colonial and postcolonial urban monuments.

The tourist, familiar with contemporary commercial, religious, and militaristic slogans, draws upon this "knowledge" in order to discover Venice. Armed with the popular literature of art history, travel guides, and Italian dictionaries, the tourist begins a consumer love affair with the Venetian past, shopping for its difference, its richness, and its seductive historical atmosphere.

Today, mercenary pirates of political terrorism are threatening to cut off the commercial routes of tourism's global empire, of which Venice is the strategic center. To secure this empire's operations, in particular its overseas summer crusades, the imperial jumbo-jet fleet demands military protection. Thus the contemporary fear of terrorism joins with the fear of the entire empire of tourism, finding its center today in Venice, whose embattled history and architectural memory are haunted by it already.

—To recognize the imaginary Venice as the true Venice of today! As the site of the merciless cultural and economic "terrorism" of the world empire of tourism, and the site of fear of the merciless "tourism" of world terrorism, ancient and contemporary!

—To infiltrate the Venetian tourist entertainments with counterfeit spectacles aimed at the uncritical consumption of historical Venice and her present-day myth!

—To interrupt this Venetian tourist romance, this shopping for the imaginary past and present!

—To call off this consumer marriage to the sea!

—To take Venetian architecture as a historical "screen" for the critical projections of the present!

—To turn the projectors upon Venice as a historical fetish of a contemporary reality!

—To project the symbols of the present onto those of the past!

—To confront publicly their illusive difference and embarrassing similarity!

Originally published as a flyer distributed during public projection in Venice, published by the Canadian Pavilion at the 12th Venice Biennale (1986); reprinted as "The Venice Projections," *October* (New York), no. 38 (Winter 1986), pp. 17–20.

The Homeless Projection: A Proposal for the City of New York (1986)

Architecture

What has been called architecture is no longer merely a collection of buildings with "stable forms" and "permanent structures." Architecture must be recognized today as a social system: a new economic condition and a psycho-political experience. The new meanings ascribed to architecture through their interplay with changing circumstances and events are not new meanings but exist only as concepts in semiotic texts (Umberto Eco) and slogans in real-estate advertisements for the gentry (Zeckendorf Towers). If architecture does on occasion preserve its traditional and sentimental appearance in an attempt to "interplay" with new events, this serves only to create, impose, and ultimately reject or appropriate these new social circumstances. In this way, "architecture" demolishes, relocates, rebuilds, renovates, rezones, gentrifies, and develops itself continuously. Mimicking and embodying a corporate moral detachment, today's "architecture" reveals its inherent cynicism through its ruthless expansionism. What has been defined as architecture is really, then, a merciless real-estate system, embodied in a continuous and frightening mass-scale *event,* the most disturbingly public and central operations of which are economic terror, physical eviction, and the exodus of the poorest groups of city inhabitants from the buildings' interiors to the outdoors.

The New Monument

Such forced exteriorization of their estranged bodies transforms the homeless into permanently displayed outdoor "structures," symbolic architectural forms, new types of city monuments: *the homeless.*

The surfaces of *the homeless*—over-or underdressed, unwashed, cracked from permanent outdoor exposure, and posing in their frozen, "classic" gestures—weather and resemble the official monuments of the city. *The homeless* appear more dramatic than even the most colossal and expressive urban sculptures, memorials, or public buildings, however, for there is nothing more disruptive and astonishing in a monument than a sign of life. To the observer the slightest sign of life in *the homeless* is a living sign of the possibility of the death of the homeless from homelessness.

The homeless must display themselves in symbolically strategic and popular city "accents." To secure their starvation wages (donations), the homeless must appear as the "real homeless" (their "performance" must conform to the popular *myth of the homeless*): the homeless must become *the homeless.*

Adorned with the "refuse" of city "architecture" and with the physical fragments of the cycles of change, the homeless become the nomadic "buildings," the mobile "monuments" of the city. However, fixed in the absolute lowest economic and social positions and bound to their physical environment, *the homeless* achieve a symbolic stability, while the official city buildings and monuments lose their stable character as they continuously undergo their real-estate change.

Unable to live without the dramatic presence of *the homeless* (since their contrast helps produce "value"—social, economic, cultural) and denying the homeless as its own social consequence, "architecture" must continuously repress the monumental condition of the homeless deeper into its (political) unconscious.

Projection

If the homeless must "wear" the building (become a new, mobile building) and are forced to live through the monumental problem of Architecture, the aim of the *Homeless Projection* is to impose this condition back upon the Architecture and to force its surfaces to reveal what they deny.

—To magnify the scale of the homeless to the scale of the building!

—To astonish the street public with the familiarity of the image and to make the homeless laugh!

—To employ the slide psychodrama method to teach the *building* to play the role of *the homeless!*

—To liberate the problem of the homeless from the unconscious of the "architecture"!

—To juxtapose the fake architectural real-estate theater with the real survival theater of the homeless!

Originally published in *Jana Sterbak and Krzysztof Wodiczko,* brochure (New York: 49th Parallel, Centre for Contemporary Canadian Art, 1986); reprinted in *October* (New York), no. 38 (Winter 1986), pp. 11–16.

Projection on the Monument to Friedrich II, Kassel (1987)

On the monument to Landgrave Friedrich II of Hesse-Kassel, I confront his glorious but also egomaniacal heroic acts—the spreading of ideas of the Enlightenment and the popularizing of aristocratic culture, the promotion of art and science—with his dubious economic and political acts, which served as the monetary source for all of his cultural and artistic projects. His politics, incidentally, were a source of criticism even in his lifetime. Gazing proudly at one of these projects, the Museum Fridericianum, his obscene white body too bloated from gluttony to fit its heroic Roman armor, the Landgrave cannot conceal his ravenous hunger for conquest, his imperial appetite for plundering foreign territories (look at Austria). He is interested in political and cultural power over the world. (One thinks about the Polish crown.) He also knows that the *Soldatenhandel,* a trade in soldiers in the eighteenth century (22,000 peasants were sold to Great Britain for 21,276,778 talers in order to support that country's war against American independence), is hardly different from Daimler-Benz's use of slave labor today by exploiting "guest workers" to make military equipment such as the Unimog S (a four-wheel-drive military truck, parts of which are produced in Kassel) and deliver it to South Africa, where it is used to subjugate blacks; or from accepting donations from Mercedes and the Deutsche Bank, though knowing of their South African dealings, in order to organize *Documenta 8* in the Fridericianum and the Orangerie Gardens—places Friedrich II built with money from the trade in soldiers.

To expose the relation between Daimler-Benz and *Documenta 8* as a clear example of the way the shameless "history of the victors" perpetuates itself today, I had decided to recall the Landgrave's monument in order to critically actualize it.[1]

This slide projection superimposed onto the large base of the monument an image of a crate containing axles to Unimog S military trucks produced by the Daimler-Benz plant in Kassel. The content, the manufacturer, the origin, and the South African, Salvadoran, and Chilean destinations of this shipment were clearly marked on each side of the crate. The statue itself was subjected to similar superimposition. Projected over his Roman armor, a white shirt, tie, and Daimler-Benz identity badge had transformed the Landgrave into both warrior and company executive. The face of Friedrich II, which according to many spectators resembled that of the *Documenta 8* director, as well as tubes held by the statue containing architectural and cultural designs, were both strongly illuminated.

Note

1. For an elaboration of the operation of the "history of the victors," see "Designing for the City of Strangers" in this volume. The phrase is Walter Benjamin's.

Originally published as artist's statement in *Documenta 8,* exh. cat. (Kassel: Fridericianum, 1987), vol. 2, pp. 278–79.

City Hall Tower Illumination, Philadelphia

(1987)

In the name of "progress" our official culture is striving to force the new media to do the work of the old.
—Marshall McLuhan

For the city of today does speak to us, but it is also at certain points and in certain orders remarkably silent. There are things that it speaks of and others that it does not speak of at all, there are places where it speaks and others where it does not speak, or quite often has ceased to speak.
—Raymond Ledrut, "Speech and the Silence of the City"

Illumination of any public institution, in particular one located in the crowded center of the city, is an act of speech that should both assist and encourage a vast majority of people (crossing all strata of society) in their participation in the social discourse of the city. Ideally, such illuminating public acts would help the city-dwellers to speak to each other and to keep their fingers on the pulse of the city. Such acts should also help parents to teach their children to "think the city" and to measure critically the city's pulse.

In some ways, the architectural body of City Hall is already busy in helping us to unite and speak to each other, as well as to speak to the government officials working inside. It provides an ideological framework through its allegories of law, labor, trade, civilization, culture, nature, moral values, history, and the contributions of citizens to progress in every field. Day and night, the clock tower is synchronizing the rhythm of the city: work, vast constructions, real-estate developments, revitalizations, gentrifications, and rezonings that are progressively fragmenting and dispersing blocks, neighborhoods, communities, and, on occasion, entire districts of the city. Increasing alienation of city-dwellers from each other and from the city as meaningful environment is occurring in the context of an invasion of architectural (yuppie) pseudo-historicism and sentimental, uncritical, superficial attachment to heroic monuments of the past.

The moral and political machine of the body of City Hall is focused on the past and on a history to which the residents of Philadelphia may not have a clear relation; there is no room for any evidence of problems, tensions, or desires experienced by contemporary Philadelphians. In light of the presence of thousands of people who use the area of City Hall both day and night, the responsibility to secure contemporary meaning to such a dominating structure is particularly important. The new task for City Hall will be to transform the sense of the entire public institution and its architectural body into something sensitive, responding, and responsible, to acknowledge the daily rhythm or daily life of the city. Our task is to reattach the public domain's hold on contemporary life and to challenge its alienating, elusive effect.

My proposal attempts to expand the symbolic function of City Hall, to its moral authority adding pulses synchronizing the city's rhythms of employment, housing for low-income inhabitants, education for everyone—the most critical issues in urban life and politics. The highest level of public consciousness and alertness about these issues is crucial for the survival of the city as a whole and for its unity and solidarity.

The City Hall Tower Night Illumination Key should be posted on signs surrounding City Hall, in locations where City Hall is visible, in subways and buses and their stations, in schools, churches, and shopping malls, in restaurants and bars, in local media (newspapers, television and radio announcements), with utility bills mailed to customers, and in public and private institutions and services for housing, labor and unemployment, and education.

The City Hall Tower will be illuminated by a series of strokes and flashes of light according to the following program:

Night Illumination Key

SHORT BLUE LIGHT (one short stroke)	A homeless person has signed a lease agreement today with private or public landlord (for one or more years)
LONG BLUE LIGHT (one longer flash)	A homeless family has found a home today and signed an apartment lease agreement with private or public landlord for one or more years
SHORT RED LIGHT (one short stroke)	An unemployed person has found employment today with private or public employer
LONG RED LIGHT (one longer flash)	An unemployed single parent has found employment today with private or public employer
SHORT YELLOW LIGHT (one short stroke)	A school dropout has returned to school today (has been readmitted today to elementary school, high school, or college)

SHORT ABSENCE OF LIGHT (one short blackout)

A person has today become homeless, unemployed, or a school or college dropout

LONG ABSENCE OF LIGHT (one longer blackout)

A family has become homeless or a single parent has become unemployed today

The Timing of Flashes and Strokes of Light

Short stroke	1 second
Longer flash	3 seconds
Between each stroke or longer flash	1-second interval of white light
After each color light cycle	10-second interval of white light
Short "blackout"	1 second
Longer "blackout"	3 seconds
Between each "blackout"	1-second interval of white light
After each "blackout" cycle	10-second interval of white light

Each image of the City Hall Tower (or visible absence of such image) "lasts" 1 second

Night Illumination Hotline

Anyone who has found employment, secured a place to live, or returned to school or college is requested to call before 4 p. m. that same day the Night Illumination Hotline number:

1-800-111-1111

Anyone who has lost employment, lost a secure place to live, or dropped out of school or college is requested to call before 4 p. m. that same day the Night Illumination Hotline number:

1-800-111-1111

The City Hall Tower Night Illumination Key must be publicly discussed and altered (in terms of its issues and system) each year, particularly through public debate on television.

Originally published as "City Hall Tower Illumination: A Proposal by Krzysztof Wodiczko for the Fairmount Park Art Association of Philadelphia," in *Light Up Philadelphia: Presentations and Discussion* (Philadelphia: Fairmount Park Art Association, 1988).

Speaking through Monuments
(1988)

Among observers of the economic, social, political, and semantic transformations of urban space, there is growing concern that the city, with all its old and newly built architectural structures as well as their spatial configurations, is losing the ability to operate as a communicative environment.

In today's contemporary real-estate city, the mercilessly dynamic space of uneven economic development makes it extremely difficult for city-dwellers and nomads to communicate through and in front of the city's symbolic forms.

The unstable and uneven situation around and between the monuments is complemented by the transformation of the monuments themselves, which become victims of the same social and aesthetic manipulation as the entire city. Aesthetic simulation and trivialization turn historic sites into decoration representing the past. Our historic harbors are being turned into seafood restaurants.

The meaning of city monuments—whether intentional or unintentional, historic or contemporary—must be secured today, as in the past, through the ability of the inhabitants to project and superimpose their critical thoughts and reflections on the monument forms.

We are witnessing the return of themes of nationalism and militarism in politics in the context of gentrification and the gradual destruction of social programs that affect urban life. In front of our memorials and monuments, which were built to commemorate heroes of liberation, the flight to freedom, civil liberties, and the right of the individual pursuit of happiness, are facts such as homelessness, segregation, the isolation of individuals, and the destruction of community ties—all processes that project themselves already on these monuments. My projection is a clarification or specific articulation of those projections.

Not to speak through city monuments is to abandon them and to abandon ourselves, losing both a sense of history and the present.

Today, more than ever before, the meaning of our monuments depends on our active role in turning them into sites of memory and critical evaluation of history as well as places of public discourse and action. This agenda is not only social or political or activist, it is also an aesthetic mission.

Originally published as a statement in the brochure *Krzysztof Wodiczko: Works* (Washington, D.C.: Hirshhorn Museum and Sculpture Garden, 1989).

City Hall Tower Projection, Kraków (1996)

In this work, I managed to combine my experience in earlier monumental public projections with the social, performative, and ethical agenda of my more recent *Alien Staff* and *Mouthpiece* projects. As with those two communication instruments, the Kraków projection was open to people who were marginalized and voiceless, those whom no one wanted to hear. For the first time in my projectionist practice, I used video projectors rather than slide projectors. And, also for the first time, I used loudspeakers to introduce sound. This created a completely new possibility: transmitting through a public monument a narration of a particular person's actual experience, "completing" this landmark structure by projecting "into" it bodily movement, gesture, and human voice. This afforded the participants/performers the opportunity to magnify and articulate architecturally a voice and gestural expression and to make their experience public. The process of video recording, editing, testing, and revising the images and voice recordings became an important experience for the participant/performers, who learned how to use the tower as a psychological artifice, to develop their confidence and powers of self-expression.

Public architecture was appropriated here as a transitional object (Winnicott) and as a communicative artifice (Kristeva).[1] Imagine oneself as a tower! For those whose voices were heard through the tower, addressing the mass of people gathered in the square below provided a bizarre and comical opportunity to reveal painful secrets either to a particular person or simply to anyone. Such truths may sometimes be unveiled more safely and more freely speaking in an open agora or forum, protected by the aura of democratic public space, than in private, speaking to a friend, or even silently to oneself. And for those looking and listening in the square below the projection, it may have been easier to empathize with the person-as-tower than with the actual speaker.

The video and sound images transformed into a human being the most prominent architectural structure in Kraków, the fourteenth-century City Hall Tower, which stands in the middle of the Central Marketplace (Rynek Głowny). This brought the people speaking through the tower to the center of public attention and turned them into strangely prominent public figures. Everybody in Kraków identifies with this tower. Everyone has a special relation with it. Even people who live far away, on the outskirts of Kraków, see this tower as a special partner—a lonely, if not heroically alienated, but authoritative, stable, protective, and trustworthy civic structure. Even the most critical and ironic minds of Kraków share with the rest of the city's population this secret psycho-architectural addiction and sustain a lifelong affair with the tower. Having al-

ready mentally projected themselves onto this tower, viewers were now faced with somebody else being projected onto their projections. The tower that they already inhabited (or that inhabits them) was now inhabited (or cohabited) by someone else—someone who was different from them, marginalized, relegated to the realm of "otherness," yet now strangely familiar. The animated tower communicated the loneliness and alienation of someone suffering a nightmare, for example the experience of domestic violence—an occurrence that is not uncommon in Kraków but which is rarely communicated in public.

In this way, the tower became a very unsettling junction between me (the viewer) and the Other, overseen by a "third party," the crowd witnessing the dialogue. The third party—the real person standing next to me in the crowd, who could be my boyfriend, girlfriend, husband, wife—could speak through this tower on another night, or I could speak to them through this tower, in front of everybody. What a frightening, liberating possibility. It is easier to be honest with someone who abuses and neglects you when you are fifty times taller than that person, when you can speak with your face masked by a huge city clock and your head protected by a gigantic Baroque helmet, clad in the fourteenth-century masonry of the City Hall Tower. Suddenly the secrets of the city and all its nightmares—powerful personal experiences that lie hidden inside homes or workplaces in the darkness of night—came to light and were publicly shared through our tower, everybody's tower.

The tower acts as the stranger's double, as an artifice and memorial, as something that is in between him or her and me, something that can represent and help the Other to come to terms with his or her personal experience. It is what enables viewers gathered in the square below to confront what is being conveyed—the Other's experience—as well as to accept the painful similarity between their own experience and that of the Other. Like an *Alien Staff* or *Porte-Parole,* the tower allowed the speaker/performer to play creatively or to be playfully creative in storytelling and using gestural expression to the point of virtuosity. At the same time it created a possibility for the spectators to respond to such a performance in a critical and discursive way while safely sharing the responses. All of those processes were made possible because the event was partially artistic and partially lifelike, partially real and partially virtual; both science fiction and nightmare, personal tale and crime story. It is easier to accept reality as fiction or as a mixture of reality and fiction than as reality itself. In this way, the uncanny feeling can be accepted rather than expelled through the

rejection of the Stranger. It takes a complicated work of art to transmit (and to make one accept) what looks and sounds strangely familiar.

The projection on City Hall Tower used high-power video projectors placed on the ground of the plaza, 65 meters from City Hall Tower at a 35-degree angle. A powerful loudspeaker was installed at the top of the tower below the clock. Several months before the event, contacts were made with the homosexual community, the disabled, the Kraków Women's Center, and with organizations and individuals dealing with the problems of drug users and people living with HIV. The eight actual participants emerged directly and indirectly from those contacts. They shared their troubling accounts in recordings of their voices and hand gestures on video. For the hand gestures, they selected everyday objects appropriate to their story, performing such simple domestic tasks as peeling potatoes, wringing a washcloth, grinding coffee, mixing *kogel-mogel* (a frothy mixture of egg yoke and sugar used in Poland to cure laryngitis), and other symbolic gestures such as pulling petals from a flower or holding a lit candle while protecting it from the wind. The loudness of the soundtrack awoke the city, revealing these nightmarish experiences that are normally kept hidden.

All the recorded accounts described personal events that took place at night. Three women spoke of their experiences as victims of domestic abuse (suffered by them and their children) at the hands of their husbands. One, for example, spoke of her many years of "imprisonment" in her own home, not knowing why she allowed herself to become such a prisoner. Her husband, who was well respected, had been imprisoned in the past, and was now acting as a prison guard of his wife. One woman told of trying to calm her screaming infant one night to protect it from her drunk husband who had earlier beaten the child. Because she could not quiet the child, she too was beaten by the wakened husband. Their stories addressed two of the most serious problems in Poland today, that of domestic violence and alcoholism. A young homosexual described his painful experience of being discovered by his brother in bed with a man, and irreversibly losing his brother's love. A drug-addicted man who was being treated as someone who had committed a moral crime, not as a sick person, described his experiences, especially with city agencies and at the illegal drug market in the train station nearby. At this train station, addicts were treated superficially and allowed to die by police and emergency medical technicians. An older blind man talked about his tragic experiences of trying to walk

67 at night in the city (including the area around the tower), announcing publicly the unbearable secret he held: that his son had always been ashamed to walk with him in the streets of Kraków.

The City Hall Tower Projection was very well advertised in various media as part of the Andrzei Wajda Festival, sponsored by the city of Kraków as part of the "Kraków 2000" celebration. There were many Polish and foreign tourists. Transcripts of the tower's narratives were widely distributed in English and Polish. During the first forty-five minutes of the projection, organizers counted 4,000 spectators. The projections lasted from 10:30 p. m. to 12:30 a.m. for three nights from August 2 to 4. Large numbers of people also witnessed seven evenings of tests conducted in the plaza beforehand. Media including radio, television, and newspapers, national, regional, and city, reported on the projections, taping events with audio and video recordings and conducting interviews with spectators. The Women's Center organized a special public event on the occasion of the projections. One spectator was heard remarking to another, "How is it possible that one does not believe a person, while one believes the Tower?"

Note

1. For an elaboration of these ideas, see "Designing for the City of Strangers" in this volume.

This text is published here for the first time.

The public projection on the City Hall Tower, Central Marketplace (Rynek Głowny), Kraków, was produced in summer 1996 by Contemporary Art Center Bunkier Sztuki, the Andrzej Wajda Festival, and the City of Kraków as part of the "Kraków 2000" celebration, with the cooperation of Centrum Kobiet (the women's center) and the technical sponsorship of the Barco company (video projectors). Coordinator of projection: Beata Nowacka. Photographs: Jagoda Przybylak, courtesy Galerie Lelong.

Voices of the Tower (1996)

Hands Holding a Candle

When a baby wakes up, it's going to cry. And when it cries, *he* gets even more upset. So he goes after the kid. He never hugs him—he rejects him. He rejects him because he's just something that cries. And then there are those days when Daddy doesn't drink, when Daddy picks him up in his arms, when Daddy fixes his little bike. It no longer matters that Daddy is the one who broke it in the first place—he broke it when he kicked it. For the child what's important is that his Daddy is a good Daddy, that this Daddy fixed the brakes on his bike. But when night comes, Daddy threatens to kill everybody in the house. Now the child doesn't know what happened to that other father. That other father is such a good person. This father is so . . . , so . . . And he starts to wonder, maybe I'm the one who's been bad; maybe it's all my fault. Maybe it's because of me that this father is so mad.

(Then begins the child's interior drama—that of the child who doesn't know how to please his father, even though he really loves him so much. He loves him because he's his father, and yet he's afraid. He's also afraid for his mother . . . and his mother's the only one who can help him.)

(Loud sound of the candle being blown out.)

Hands with a Cigarette

I dream about drugs at night. I once had a dream in which some unidentified persons—someone healthy, at any rate, I know that much—put me in a situation. . . . That is, I was supposed to get a box of paints, good artist's oil paints, which I very much wanted to have. Under one condition, the condition that along with this box of paints I also take another box. A box of amphetamines. Amphetamines—the drug I take, the one I'm also heavily addicted to.

. . .

In Kraków the drug market—the illegal drug market, since there's no legal one; the legal one doesn't exist—is located in the tunnel underneath the railroad station, over there, just behind you. One day, a friend of mine OD'ed on heroin. His heart stopped, and then he stopped breathing. I started to give him CPR. It was late evening. A friend went off to call an ambulance. They came and gave him a shot. After the shot, he came to for fifteen minutes. But they left right away. Fifteen minutes later he had collapsed again. His heart stopped beating, and he stopped breathing. I gave him more CPR, my friend called another ambulance, and they came a second time. They gave him another shot,

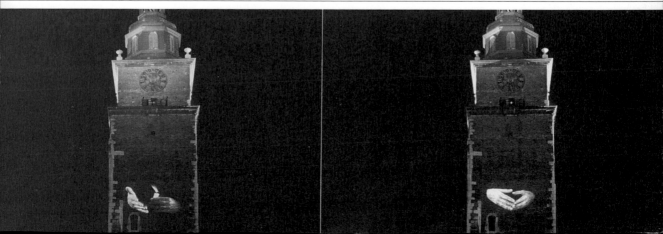

and then they left again. We spent the whole night trying to bring him around. He survived, but several months later he died.

   . . .

Hands Wringing a Rag

Everything was going real good for us until the baby was born. But he was there at the hospital. He came to pick me up with flowers. My mom was there. . . . Everything was going fine. Later it was all turned upside down. He was good until his grandmother started turning him against me.
(Sound of the rag being wrung out, water dripping into the sink.)

Hands Playing with a Wedding Ring

The nights were the hardest for me, the nights when I didn't sleep, when I just sat in the armchair, my feet up on the footrest, stayed up waiting. I stayed up and watched my baby sleep. I was afraid of his reaction, of my nightmarish drunken husband. I never knew what he would do. I didn't know what kind of situation would erupt during the night. I just waited and watched. I'd stay awake the whole night. I was really just watching over this drunk's sleep. When I left him, I could sleep at last. . . . The first and foremost thing for me, and to this day it is still the most important, is to be able to undress in peace. To be able to put my nightgown on in peace. This is very important to me. It is what has allowed me to rebuild my life, to recreate a family, with no more nightmares, without those nightmarish sleepless nights. Without fear, vodka, or cursing. And that's the most valuable thing I got out of leaving.

   I wish that all women everywhere be able to sleep in trust and peace, and that men respect their night with a woman, that it be their night together, and not some kind of public night.

Hands Pulling the Petals off a Flower

He liked to lock me up in tight places like the toilet. And then turn out the light. Later, when he found out I was terribly frightened of rats. . . . I'll never forget it. . . . He came home drunk and in a bad mood. I was asleep; it was late, after midnight. He ordered me to take some pickles down to the cellar. I was so upset I cried, and begged him, but when he started pushing me around and looking at me with that look of his. . . . The children used to say that Dad looks and smiles like some wild beast. . . . I went down to the cellar in silence with a bag full of pickle jars. I was in my nightgown. I didn't even have my slippers on, but

at that point I didn't even notice that I didn't have them. But that wasn't the worst thing. Each time he would come down with me, and while I was putting the jars on the shelves he would keep calling me horrible names and insulting me. I didn't want to provoke him, so I kept quiet. After I went down for the last time he locked me up in there and turned out the light. And then I found out why. Because I didn't wait up for him with his supper. So I got put in jail. He told me he'd often spent a week in jail. I only had to do time until morning. Every little rustle was the scuttling of rats coming to eat me. I could see them. I could see them climbing all over me. . . .

It was then encoded into me that no one was supposed to find out about any of this. To his friends my husband was a wonderful husband. I was supposed to pretend to be happy. But he treated me like a prisoner. He liked to watch me through the keyhole. He said I had to be kept under surveillance.

I spent fifteen years in jail and I still don't know why.

Hands Gesticulating

We were alone together, he and I. When it got to be evening, we just went to bed together. I didn't expect anybody to be coming home so early. We were together, and we fell asleep. I woke up and saw my brother standing over me. He flew into a rage. He grabbed me by the arm and pulled me out of the room. He told me that I had gone beyond the pale, and that what I was doing was just intolerable. How could I bring some guy to the house and do something like this? We started to quarrel. I explained that this was *my* guy, and it's not like I go with just anyone. Then he dealt with me . . . he dealt with me physically, damn it, very physically. He had no idea that I might be feeling something, too, that I'm his brother, and the fact that I'm gay doesn't change that, does it? We started shoving each other, and then he hit me hard, and that's how I ended up on the floor. I wanted to say something more, to explain, in spite of what he had done to me. Because it isn't a disease; it's something natural. I can't get over the fact that my own brother could treat me like that. We've had no contact ever since. He's ashamed of me. I hope that it's not all over between us, that if you're here somewhere, it's not too late, and that you'll call me.

Hands Mixing *Kogel-mogel* in a Mug

I was angry at my situation. I was angry that this had to happen to me, to me and my children. I was crying and was very upset. Nobody knew how to help me. The neighbors were afraid of my husband, and so were the police. When

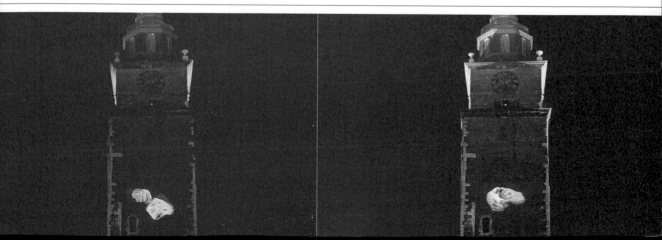

I reported him, they said it was nothing. Finally they came with the juvenile authorities, but so what? They said that if I paid the court costs, they would take my husband away. If not, he would have to stay. He pulled out an ax from under the featherbed and came after us. I don't want to go on living like this. I want to change my life, and the children's, too.

Hands Holding Dark Glasses

My son is embarrassed even to walk down the street with me, for no other reason than the fact that I can't see. Of course, I don't let him see that I know what's going on, that I realize that he's ashamed of me, but it makes me feel alone, even bitter, in a way. I smother those feelings.

I'm in the middle of this very Market Square, and I don't even know which way the sidewalk is. More than once I've been in a situation where I stumbled into a bench where people were sitting. When that happens, it's just a bench, nothing more. I make my way around it, and after a while I finally get there. Eventually I find the sidewalk.

Hands Peeling a Potato with a Kitchen Knife

He used to come home drunk at 11, 12, even 2 in the morning. The first thing he would do is go to the refrigerator, into the freezer. He'd order me to pull out some frozen meat and cook it. By then the kids were already asleep. But if there wasn't any meat, then it would start. He'd smash the pots against the windows, or pour out what was in the pot. . . . Even if there wasn't any meat, he'd declare that he always had to have meat; he had to eat meat, especially when he was drunk. When he was sober he would eat some soup, or a poached egg with some potatoes, whatever there was. . . . But he would often start beating the kids, throwing me to the floor, kicking me in the stomach. Then he would leave the room. He'd go to sleep, or go drink some more. Several times I called for help. My mother-in-law came and tried to protect me. He cut her in the finger, too. He put a knife to her throat and told her not to come there when he's drunk—not to butt into our affairs, and not to try and protect me. Once he came home drunk carrying two puppies. I told him, "What did you bring the puppies for? You know very well we don't even have enough money for food." As for Wojtek—well, he never took any interest in little Wojtek. He'd hit him in the stomach so there wouldn't be any marks—hit him with his fists. Once he threw him against the wall. He beat him because he, our son, was finicky. Several times he threw him against the wall, just like that. . . . Little

73 Wojtek didn't lose consciousness, but . . . at night he would wake up in a fright, and leap out of bed screaming. The three of us used to sleep together. If the two of them were asleep and I wasn't there yet, he'd wake up in a fright and shout, "Mommy!" If he saw that I was there, or that there was someone next to him, he'd fall back to sleep. But after a bit, it would be the same story all over again.

This is a new English translation, by Warren Niesłuchowski, of the Polish sound-track accompanying the video projection and broadcast from the balcony below the City Hall Tower clock. Part of this text was distributed as a flyer during the public projection in Kraków, including a transcription of the "Voices of the City Hall Tower."

three **Vehicles**

Vehicle (1971–73)

The vehicle moves in a uniform motion in a straight line and in one direction only. The artist, walking up and down the tilting platform, causes a seesaw movement; the energy thus generated is transmitted by a system of cables and gears to the wheels which, as a consequence, move the vehicle forward.

The vehicle is for the exclusive use of the artist.

"On the road of progress," picking up speed on the "highway to a better future," the intelligentsia was to contribute to the rational progress. Progress was guaranteed, on condition that everyone, including artists and intellectuals, devote themselves to that machine and accept it as a given. Within the machine, it was they who would revive and inspire it. . . .

You couldn't just go around thinking too much or too critically; you, the artist, had to function like a poet "creatively" lost in the clouds, for whom there was also allotted a certain amount of room in the machine. . . . One could say that the subject who operated the vehicle was in fact an object, a part of this machine. And yet there was, in this vehicle, a certain illusion of freedom, moving back and forth and seeing the world independently, in peripatetic fashion. And for all that the independence was limited by the dimensions of the machine and the manner in which one moved upon it, there emerged a dubious dialectic based on this dual point of view. The thesis and antithesis were to influence the synthesis, but the synthesis had a direction determined in advance. It was not simple locomotion, just moving along the ground—dangerous terrain—but rather involved elevation above it, to the level of the platform of the vehicle, somewhat closer to the clouds.

First two paragraphs originally published in *Krzysztof Wodiczko: Pojazd/Vehicle* (Warsaw: Galeria Foksal, 1973), and *Krzysztof Wodiczko* (Urbana: Krannert Center for the Performing Arts, University of Illinois, 1975); with excerpts from a conversation with Jaromir Jedliński, 1997 (published in full in this volume).

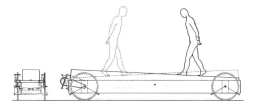

Vehicles (1977–79)

1. Vehicle-Café
- The voices of the conversants activate the engine of the vehicle.
- The liveliness of the conversation sustains the vehicle's continuous motion.
- The vehicle moves in a straight line and in one direction only.

2. Vehicle-Coffee Shop
- The movement of the bodies of the conversants causes a swinging motion of the table and seats of the vehicle.
- This motion is transmitted through a system of gears to the rotation of the wheels.
- The vehicle moves in a straight line and in one direction only.
- The speed of the vehicle is dependent upon the dynamism of the discussion.

3. Vehicle-Platform
- Movement of people operating on the surface of the large, square platform of a vehicle that is free and multidirectional.
- The movement generates energy which, through mechanical and pneumatic systems installed in the floor of the platform, is accumulated and transmitted to the rotation of the wheels.
- The vehicle moves slowly in a straight line and in one direction only.

4. Vehicle for the Worker
- The movement of a mass pushed cyclically forward and backward by a worker along a tilting platform causes its seesaw motion.
- The energy thus generated is transmitted through an adjustment of gears to the rotation of the wheels.
- The momentum of the vehicle and the dynamism of the labor sustains the vehicle's motion in a straight line and in one direction only.

5. Vehicle-Podium
- The strength of the orator's voice controls the speed of the vehicle.
- The vehicle is propelled by an electric engine and moves in one direction only.

———

Thanks to my experiences in Poland I wasn't completely useless [in Canada]. I leapt at the most Polish thing, something other people perhaps couldn't see: the similarity between the Canada Council in the seventies and Poland. [See also the essay "For the De-Incapacitation of the Avant-Garde in Canada," re-

1.

2.

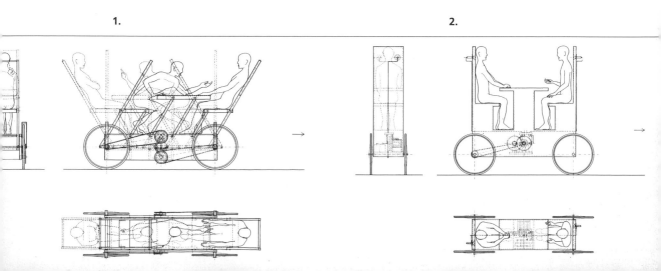

printed in this volume.] The Canada Council represented the bureaucratization of culture and there was nothing I could analyze better than this. It was a centrally controlled cultural machine. It resembled Poland not so much in its external mechanisms as in the internal mechanisms that incapacitated artists. Artists and critics in Canada did not immediately see the relevance of my projects to their situation, but I continued to design more versions of my metaphoric vehicles. I wanted to see to what degree they should change to become applicable to the Canadian context. One of the vehicles that was a kind of Canadian machine was The Platform. In a drawing, you see me sitting on the edge of this vehicle looking critically back at an increasingly distant point (Poland) while still being fascinated by a possibility of becoming part of this new "democratic" platform. . . . The "liberal" movement of people on the platform automatically propelled the vehicle forward.

Original description published in "Krzysztof Wodiczko: Vehicles," *Impulse* (Toronto) 8, no. 2 (1980), pp. 47–50; with an excerpt from Ine Gevers and Jeanne van Heeswijk, "Interview with Wodiczko," in Gevers and van Heeswijk, eds., *Beyond Ethics and Aesthetics* (Amsterdam: Sun, 1997), pp. 452–54.

3.   4.   5.

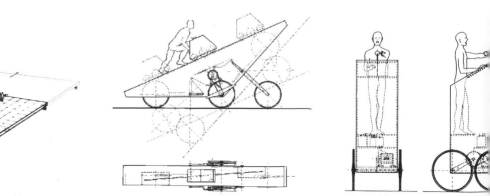

Homeless Vehicle Project
with David Lurie
(1988–89)

I was not insane when they picked me up, I was homeless.
—Joyce Brown, homeless person forcibly hospitalized by the New York City government[1]

During the winter of 1987–88, an estimated 70,000 people were homeless in New York City.[2] A large portion of this population is made up of homeless individuals. Unlike families with children, homeless individuals are not given priority for placement in the city's transitional housing facilities or in welfare hotel rooms. Instead, the city government offers space to the single homeless in its growing system of dormitory shelters.

Most city-run shelters—though they provide food and respite from the elements—are dangerous and unfriendly places that impose a dehumanizing, even prisonlike, regimentation on residents. Guards routinely treat clients as inmates, allegedly denying them food for the violation of rules. Some shelter residents are bused from place to place for food, showers, and sleep. Charges of violence by shelter security guards and clients are common.

According to the mayor of New York City, a homeless person who chooses to live on the street rather than accept placement in a shelter during the cold of winter is, by definition, to be suspected of mental illness. But given the city's official response to the problem of homeless individuals, it is not surprising that many have made a rational choice to live on the streets.

Though a significant proportion of homeless individuals are the deinstitutionalized mentally ill, a growing majority of them are not. Furthermore, both the sane and insane homeless share the same immediate, life-threatening condition: they have no permanent shelter and no safe place to go.

Their alternative has been to develop a means of survival on the streets of New York City. The nomadic homeless people we all observe and encounter on the streets have been compelled to develop a series of strategies for self-sufficiency under constantly changing—and always threatening—circumstances. Problems of garnering food, keeping warm, remaining safe from personal harm and relatively undisturbed during sleep all present challenges that are never perfectly resolved.

The fact that people are compelled to live on the streets is unacceptable. But failing to recognize the reality of these people's situation or holding up the fact of their living on the streets as proof of their universal insanity is a morally and factually untenable position. Advocacy for permanent, safe, and dignified shelter for all people is essential—and is being pursued. But a recognition that all individuals need and deserve permanent housing must also lead to an

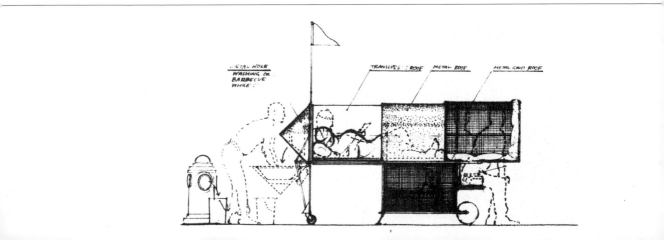

examination of the immediate needs of homeless people. Given the failure of the city's shelter system, what can we do for individuals struggling for self-sufficiency on the streets today?

Our proposed vehicle is designed to play a role in filling a dangerous gap in shelter needs. It seeks to be of use to the significant number of individuals who will, for the foreseeable future, continue to be compelled to live a nomadic life in the urban environment. Rather than an ideal shelter, the vehicle is designed with attention to the specific limitations and compromises imposed by urban nomadic existence. Though it cannot appropriately be called a home, the vehicle is a potential means for ameliorating the conditions of life for people surviving under trying circumstances.

When I came to New York I was struck by the occasional form lying on the street, with people standing over it as if it wasn't there.
—John Bowers, *New York Times*[3]

Although in our daily encounters with homeless people we are aware of their status as refugees, we generally fail to recognize that they are refugees from the transformation of the city itself. The redesign of city parks to allow for better surveillance and easier removal of homeless people signifies an institutional ignorance of the fact that the destruction and renovation of entire neighborhoods has left no place for these people to go.[4] We are reluctant to discern the relationship between the physical transformation of the city—through real-estate development and economic displacement—and the creation of homelessness. An ABC official stated that his company is hesitant to construct a public plaza next to its midtown headquarters because it does not want to see a "tent city for the homeless here."[5] But with or without a plaza, the homeless will not disappear.

Homeless people's marginalization is directly tied to the refusal of other city residents to recognize them as fellow urban citizens. The dominant notion of the homeless as mere objects largely explains why we allow people to live and die on our streets without doing much to help them.

In a television forum, columnist George Will argued that the presence of ragged masses camped out in front of midtown New York office buildings was an infringement of the legitimate rights of executives working there. In Will's view, dodging the bodies of homeless people and enduring their incessant demands for small change is an unnecessary addition to the already stressful lives

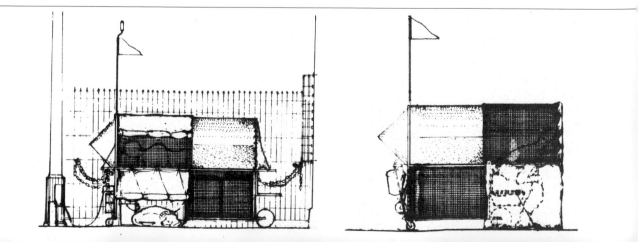

of businessmen.[6] In the activity of moving through the city, described by Walter Benjamin as a "series of shocks and collisions," the homeless are apprehended as immobile barriers to travel. This description, from a recent *New York Times* article, of seasoned commuters' strategies for dealing with their daily encounters with homeless people in the Port Authority bus terminal is typical: they block out recognition by "locking their eyes forward" and "striding purposefully" toward the exits. The homeless are seen as identity-free objects that must be negotiated rather than recognized. The article describes acknowledgment of the presence of the homeless as a sign of inexperience, a trap that only temporary visitors to the city fall into: "They stop and stare, eyes wide open to the unfamiliar, raw suffering."[7]

Of course, the dramatic image of the homeless as faceless, rag-encased bundles signifies an elision of these peoples' actual modes of survival. Though we encounter the homeless as figures anchored to a grate or bench or asleep in the subway as we rush to work, surviving on the streets of New York is actually dominated by the constant necessity for movement, often in response to the actions of authorities. In recreation areas such as Tompkins Square and Riverside Park, uniformed police officers are routinely deployed to remove homeless people. All of Grand Central Station and portions of the Port Authority bus terminal are closed to homeless residents during the night. Survival, therefore, compels mobility. Especially for those who live entirely outside of the shelter system, the ability to travel from place to place with one's personal belongings in a swift and efficient manner is a key to functioning successfully in the city.

Through the use of adapted, appropriated vehicles, some homeless individuals have managed to develop a means of economic sustenance in the city. These people, known as "scavengers," spend their days collecting, sorting, and returning cans to supermarkets in return for the five-cent deposit. Shopping and postal carts and other wheeled vehicles are used for collecting and transporting cans and bottles during the day and for storage of collected materials during the night. Crowds of homeless redeemers outside of supermarkets have become commonplace since the Bottle Bill went into effect in 1983.

In their familiar position of supplication and helplessness, homeless individuals do not stake a claim to the territory that has been taken from them. They are reduced to mere observers of the remaking of their neighborhoods for others. Their homelessness appears as a natural condition, the cause is dissociated from its consequence, and the status of the homeless as legitimate members of the urban community is unrecognized.

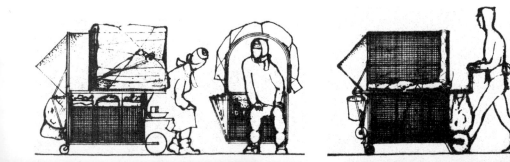

The activities of scavengers and the growing numbers of what one reporter described as their "gaily decorated" shopping carts have played a role in altering the public perception of homeless individuals. Their visibly purposive movement through the city gives them an identity as actors in the urban space. Since scavengers are mobile, they cannot be walked away from or easily dismissed as silent nonpersons. Where the immobile figure's status seems provisional and ambiguous, the scavenger stakes a claim to space in the city and indicates his or her membership in the urban community.

The shelter vehicle attempts to function usefully in the context of New York City street life. Therefore, its point of departure is the strategy of survival that urban nomads presently utilize. Through discussions with scavengers, we developed a proposal for a vehicle to be used both for personal shelter and can and bottle transportation and storage. An earlier design was shown to potential users and modified according to their criticisms and suggestions. Since the design developed through reference to the needs of a specific group of homeless people, all of whom are tall, male, and physically strong, it is possible that it may not be appropriate for other homeless people. As the project develops, the needs and interests of other groups of potential users must be addressed, particularly those of homeless women. We have yet to speak with any homeless women and learn of their particular strategies for survival. Though certain features of the vehicle as it is presently designed, such as a possible built-in toilet, might be of use to homeless women, discussions with them will be necessary to develop a design responsive to their needs.

An initial proposal, the project is not put forward as a finished product, ready for use on the streets. Rather, it is conceived as a starting point for further collaboration between skilled designers and potential users. Both parties will have to play roles in the design and production of future versions of the vehicle, with continued adaptations in the design made in response to the survival needs of users and additional strategies devised by designers. Though such a collaborative relationship may sound unlikely or even impossible, it is the key to the project's success. Only through such cooperation can the vehicle function usefully. Direct participation of users in the construction of the vehicle is the key to developing a vehicle that belongs to its users, rather than merely being appropriated by them.

A false notion of the homeless as individuals functioning in isolation from the urban community and from each other contributes to their current status as exiles in their own city. We hope the vehicle will aid in making visible and strengthening the modes of cooperation and interdependence that now exist in

the homeless population. The possibility of grouping, even linking, the vehicles together could be explored.

The signifying function of the vehicle is as important as its strictly utilitarian purpose. Building upon the existing image of the scavenger as an autonomous, active individual, the vehicle attempts to function as a visual analogue to every-day objects of consumption and merchandising (such as food vendor carts) and to create a bridge of empathy between homeless individuals and observers. The use of a vehicle fashioned specially for their collection activities makes visible the fact that scavengers, like other urban citizens, are working for their subsistence.

The goal of the vehicle project is, therefore, twofold: to fulfill the need of homeless people for a means of transportation and shelter, and to aid in creating a legitimized status for its users in the community of the city.

The prototype vehicle bears a resemblance to a weapon. In our view, the movements of carts through New York City are acts of resistance, opposing the continuing ruination of an urban community that excludes thousands of people from even the most meager means of life. Though the transformation of the city, which has compelled so many people to survive through collection of its detritus, is an outrage, we must all be forced to recognize the value and legitimacy of their daily work.

Since its first presentation at the Clocktower in January 1988, the Homeless Vehicle underwent preliminary tests on the streets of New York City. The working model was discussed with scavengers and passersby. Drawings and documentary material were shown to architects, artists, urban geographers, social workers, activists, and journalists. These tests and discussions resulted in many practical suggestions, critical comments, new concerns and ideas. New developments in urban politics, such as the Koch administration's construction of floating shelters for the homeless and the confiscation of homeless people's belongings and destruction of their habitat in City Hall Park, as well as resistance to the curfew and the related antigentrification riot in Tompkins Square, have intensified the gravity of the situation for which the vehicle was intended, requiring additions to and reinforcements of its functional and symbolic program. These include the following:

Mobility:
- A simple suspension system, larger wheels, and other adjustments to facilitate increased maneuverability over curbs, potholes, and steps.

Safety:
- A simple brake system both for slopes and for parking while resting or sleeping.
- An emergency escape system in case of fire or attack.
- A lock and alarm system to protect collected goods and personal property.
- Rearview mirrors and emergency signals to protect against traffic.

Variants:
- Versions of the vehicle responding to the needs of various users, in particular those of women scavengers.
- Transformation of the vehicle into a vendor's cart for selling found goods, such as clothing, magazines, etc.
- Assembling vehicles in groups as collective habitats or defensive encampments against police harassment.

Notes

1. Quoted by Josh Barbanel, *New York Times,* January 19, 1988.
2. Coalition for the Homeless estimate, reported in *New York Newsday,* January 4, 1988.
3. *New York Times,* April 4, 1987.
4. See Rosalyn Deutsche, "Krzysztof Wodiczko's Homeless Projection and the Site of 'Urban Revitalization,'" *October,* no. 38 (Fall 1986), pp. 63–99.
5. Quoted by Paul Goldberger, *New York Times,* January 17, 1988.
6. "David Brinkley Report," ABC-TV, ca. January 1986.
7. Jane Gross, *New York Times,* November 9, 1987.

Originally published by the authors as a photocopied brochure distributed during the exhibition *Public Image: Homeless Projects by Krzysztof Wodiczko and Denis Adams* (New York: The Clocktower, 1988); reprinted as "Homeless Vehicle Project," *October* (New York), no. 47 (Winter 1988), pp. 53–67.

In 1988 and 1989 four variants of the *Homeless Vehicle,* differing in the materials with which they were constructed and resulting in various technical improvements, were tested, used, and publicly presented in the following places: Variant 1 in City Hall Park and the parks across from the Criminal Court and the Municipal Building (Manhattan); Variant 2 in Tompkins Square Park and the surrounding area, Wall Street, and the area around Battery Park (Manhattan); Variant 3 in Central Park, Grand Army Plaza, Fifth Avenue, across from Trump Tower, and Battery Park City (all Manhattan), and in Greenpoint Park (Brooklyn); Variant 4 in Washington Square Park and the surrounding area and the area around Broadway-Lafayette (Manhattan), and in Dilworth Plaza, Rittenhouse Square, the area around the Liberty Bell, the area around City Hall, and the National Temple Recycling Center (all in Philadelphia). Those who tested and used them include Robert of "Dinkinsville," New York; Allan Benjamin, Oscar, Victor, and Daniel of Tompkins Square Park, New York; and Vanessa Brown, John Alston, and Vernon Wilson of Philadelphia.

Conversations about a Project for a Homeless Vehicle (1988)

Wodiczko: Now, don't laugh, because after what you told me last time . . . I feel that the basket part designed for collecting cans is not that good, but the rest. . . .

Oscar: It's all right, man.

Wodiczko: What you see here is the traveling position. That means that the inner shell, which you don't see, is inside of the external shell. You see, this is like a wedge of cheese, or a slice of pizza, and there is another one inside, so right now the space is half. . . .

Oscar: It's empty.

Wodiczko: No, you can use it as a locker, for personal belongings, when you travel. Also, for a mattress and maybe a sleeping bag. And . . . this is the part that should be redesigned, after what you told me.

Oscar: This would be the container where the bottles are kept?

Wodiczko: Yes, and other parts—external parts—can be designed to hold bags and attach other things to it. What you see here is a relatively large wheel, something you don't have on shopping carts. The wheels would have to be smaller if they are . . .

Oscar: . . . to be stable.

Wodiczko: Yes, and the front wheels would also have to twist. To make it cheaply, they would have to be smaller, just to keep that level.

Oscar: To keep the balance.

Wodiczko: Yes. I already rejected the additional door because it's too complicated. There would be enough space here, on this side, for a door, so you could actually enter from the side, and then it would be protected from rain and snow.

Oscar: Right. I could go for that.

Wodiczko: This is a little shorter and narrower than a standard bed, because we don't want to make it too large.

Oscar: Right, you've got to be able to keep it consumption size. If you make it too bulky, the person operating it will have a lot of problems behind it.

Wodiczko: Meaning its weight?

Oscar: Not the weight, but police, traffic, people in general.

Wodiczko: But folded, this shape is the minimum size, because the length of the bed, that is, the length of the vehicle unfolded, determines its height, but that's also a good height for sitting up.

Oscar: Right. So why did you say I would laugh at this? I think you have a very good idea. The size will be appropriate, a cabinet with a shell of itself that can hold a person's belongings, his personal items, his money, so I don't see anything so ill-informed about that. This doesn't have to be a complicated matter, because it can be cheaply made. Traffic won't be a pain in the neck, the police won't hassle you about having such a long vehicle. You can crawl inside, you can sit up, you can lie down, you can keep your personal belongings. The only complication that you might run into is that you have to make it big enough for collection. The minimum weight that people take is ten cases. You have to be able to hold, say, a least 500 bottles and cans . . .

Wodiczko: 500?

Oscar: 240 is ten cases, so you double 240, you get 480, so 500 bottles and cans. Your weight comes from the bottles, not from cans or plastics. A good time to collect is summertime, a very beautiful time, when you have festivals, parades, and so much activity. The weather's nice, there's lots of outdoor drinking—restaurants, clubs, what have you.

Wodiczko: So do you think that this will be enough space? When I look at your vehicle, I . . . Would it be necessary to design separate areas for bottles?

Oscar: That's what I do. I keep the glass away from the cans. The reason that separate compartments are good is that when I go to the grocery store, or to the distributor, whoever's going to take my bottles and cans, it's easier and faster. You want the simplest way to unload your cart, get your money, get everything processed, get out, because as soon as you turn that first corner, there's another can. I could circle this park three times and come up with shit every time. I only work specific little areas. I don't have to work too far. I can fill up one cart in one block.

Wodiczko: Where do you take the cans once you've filled up the cart? What's the nearest place from here, for instance?

Oscar: Oh, wow, it's a long way.

Wodiczko: That's why you've got to do 500 cans?

Oscar: Right, then it's worth it. You've got to take a walk, take the stuff out, box it up, then possibly stand in line. Somewhere along the line, we can talk about an idea I have. I'd like to open up a redemption center. There's a few ideas I have to make life easier for the bottle/can man.

Wodiczko: If you were to imagine yourself having this vehicle, how would you use it?

Oscar: All right, this is the front of the vehicle. This right here is the opening of the front, right? This is where I'd put my bottles; you get more bottles than anything else.

Wodiczko: And plastic bags on top of it?

Oscar: No. If possible, cans and plastics, but, you see, you have beer cans, tall and small, tall cans, little cans, soda cans, so you want to keep your soda cans with other soda cans, tall cans with tall cans, little cans with little cans, glass with glass, beer bottles with beer bottles.

Wodiczko: So plastic bags are good?

Oscar: Plastic bags are beautiful. Unless you have to travel a long way, like I've got to do tonight.

Wodiczko: What about the other part of the vehicle, about using it as a home? As a place to sleep?

Oscar: It's a good idea. It's a bad idea. My product's on top, I'm underneath. Now I've got to think about thieves.

Wodiczko: But won't you have sold those cans?

Oscar: No, man, there's no way in hell you can have an empty cart. Once you start collecting, there's a can lying on every street that you walk down. I can empty the whole cart right now, and as soon as I empty it, there'll be a can right there. So you gonna dump it? Of course, you're gonna take it.

Wodiczko: So you want to have all this above you? or below you?

Oscar: Victor had a good idea. If you could possibly come up with an idea for a sealtight.

Wodiczko: You could use a tarp.

Oscar: No, you need something to seal it.

Wodiczko: But you don't need to waterproof cans.

Oscar: Yes you do, because when you take them to the store, if they're all wet—you've got to think about the weather, too—you put them in a box, and the box will fall apart, and you can lose everything right there.

Wodiczko: Look at this drawing over here. It will give you a sense of proportion. You can sit up inside, because this is the whole length of the body when you sit up.

Victor: Why do you want to sit over here?

Wodiczko: Sit over here? No, sit inside.

Victor: And lie down?

Wodiczko: Yes, but if you're lying down, you might want to sit up, too.

Victor: Make another drawing. Like I told you before, the cart a little higher than this, two feet longer than this, have a top over here that you can open and close, and still have this space for somebody to lie down and stay out of the wind and cold. If people lie down here with this closed, ain't nobody going to steal anything or come around bothering anybody.

Wodiczko: So you think all those bottles and cans could be stored above you?

Victor: Let's say you make it high like this and this longer and this a little wider—a lot of cans will go in there. You can be out in the park and sleep in the park, and that will have a top to close it.

Wodiczko: But, you see, it won't be able to be as long as this one, because you cannot make this the length of the body or the vehicle will be too long. I already made some drawings similar to what you are saying, but I rejected them because it appeared to be too long to be maneuverable in the city, and, as Oscar said, it looked to be unacceptable for the police and the traffic.

Victor: That's nothing. I mean, we're not talking about building a car.

Wodiczko: But for him—you see, now there are two different approaches. He is interested in the collecting part, and you are interested in the sleeping part. Now we have the option of combining the part for bottles and cans with the sleeping part below. What he is saying is that it doesn't have to be the entire length of the body because you can sleep with legs bent. So that means it could be shorter, and then all the storage area could be above and closed with a plastic seal.

Oscar: Right, not only is there protection from the wind, but it's theft-proof. The most important thing is that you've got to think about when you're underneath, and somebody attacks you.

Wodiczko: I'll show you a drawing. Remember, you mentioned a vehicle . . .

Daniel: Yeah, the U.S. Postal vehicle.

Wodiczko: Do you think this is a good amount of space for collecting cans and bottles?

Daniel: Sure, but instead of carrying those bags to the supermarket, the supermarket should have a place where you could go with the postal cart, because the bottles are too heavy for the bags, so you could put them in the postal cart.

Wodiczko: I was thinking about combining the function of collecting bottles with an emergency place to sleep.

Daniel: Yeah, but that's too small for a human being to fit in, and it's also good if you sleep in there without the bottles, because its more protected from the wind.

Wodiczko: I'm designing it in order to produce it, and to establish a workshop with interested people, like maybe you and Oscar. We could start making these vehicles in the fall or the spring, or anytime.

Daniel: Oh, whenever you're ready, man, you let me know. I'll make you all the best I can, as long as you've got the wheels.

Wodiczko: What about the temperature? What is the best material to use?

Daniel: Insulation, like cotton and wood and aluminum, insulation.

Wodiczko: All of those panels folded around the cart could form some kind of little building on top. Oscar told me that there is no need to have the full length of the body, because you can bend your legs a little bit when you sleep.

Daniel: Some people don't feel comfortable like that, so you've got to build it the full size of a person.

Wodiczko: That means that I will have to unfold it a little more to create a longer . . . So you would suggest a special insulation, using two aluminum sheets and maybe something in between?

Daniel: They call that expanded insulation, and it's very good, because it'll take the wind.

Wodiczko: So you think with this you will survive most of the winter?

Daniel: You'll survive, but you're going to have to attach yourself, you're going to have to have two empty screws here for the key chain. That way, if the wind is too strong, it won't take you away.

Wodiczko: So you attach it to a fence or something?

Daniel: Yeah, the fence or pole or something, you know, because otherwise you'll go bump bump bump, and it's no good.

Wodiczko: So I'll have to design this part to make it a little longer. I can't have this cart as long as a human body. It would be too long.

Daniel: That's what I'm trying to tell you. If you have it this size, it's okay, a person can fit in there, but, you know, it's gonna have to be on top, so they have room to stretch out.

Wodiczko: But, still, a person is longer than that, but you could bend the legs a little bit.

Daniel: Right, and fit inside, I've done it, too. But I'm saying that other people don't sleep the same way.

Wodiczko: So you have to have other parts that unfold to compensate for the difference.

Daniel: You could expand this part just a little more.

Wodiczko: I'll do that, I like the idea. What would be the best material for the bottom part?

Daniel: Plywood, because when you put in the boxes of bottles, they won't slide back and forth.

Wodiczko: But when you replace this canvas here with plywood, you'll be much heavier.

Daniel: The problem is you can't make it heavier than what it is, because if you're going to build a cart that's too heavy to push, who the hell is going to push it?

Wodiczko: You mentioned fiberglass for the top?

Daniel: You know why? Because the roof you want to see.

Wodiczko: But a small hole is good to see out of.

Daniel: That's okay for some people. How would *you* do it?

Wodiczko: But I don't live outside.

Daniel: But I *do*. I know. You ever seen those snowcone carts? They have a big thing, all glass. That way, people can see what they're buying, like chocolate or vanilla.

Wodiczko: But you're not chocolate to be purchased, you are a person. Maybe you need some privacy.

Daniel: But I'm saying that what they use on top is glass. And for *you,* for your *safety,* for you to sleep.

Wodiczko: You're saying that it's better to be visible, to show that you're there, rather than to be hidden?

Daniel: Yes, that you're there, because what if someone comes along and turns you over? At least you could see that somebody's there. You gotta think of that, too, 'cause there's a lot of crazy motherfuckers around on the street, too.

Wodiczko: What about at night, an emergency light, to show you're there, because of garbage trucks?

Daniel: Yeah, 'cause they might take you and just put you in . . .

Wodiczko: Right, okay, this is very helpful.

Daniel: See, I gave you a lot of good ideas.

Originally recorded in Tompkins Square Park, New York City, and published as "Conversations on a Homeless Vehicle Project," *October* (New York), no. 47 (Winter 1988), pp. 68–75; reprinted in *File* (Toronto), no. 29 (1989). The conversants asked that their last names not be used.

Poliscar (1991)

The name of the vehicle, "Poliscar," comes from the same root as "police," "policy," and "politics," namely from the Greek word for city-state, *polis*. In ancient Greece the word referred more to a state of society characterized by a sense of community and participation of the citizen (*polites*) than to an institution or a place. To be a citizen is by definition to be a legitimate and protected member or inhabitant of the community and, as such, entitled to the rights and privileges of a "freeman." The *Poliscar* is meant both to underscore the exclusion of the homeless from the city community and to provide them with some means of participating in it.

The homeless population is the true public of the city in that they literally live on the street, spending their days and nights moving through the city, working and resting in public parks and squares. The contradiction of their existence, however, is that while they are physically confined to public spaces, they are politically excluded from public space constitutionally guaranteed as a space for communication. They have been expelled from society into public space but they are confined to living within it as silent, voiceless actors. They are in the world but at the same time they are outside of it, literally and metaphorically. The homeless are both externalized and infantilized, and as externalities and infants they have neither a vote nor a voice. As long as the voiceless occupy public space, rendering them their voice is the only way to make it truly public.

The *Poliscar* is designed for a particular group of homeless persons, those who have communications skills and the motivation to work with the homeless population in organizing and operating the Homeless Communication Network, an important part of which will be the fleet of mobile communications and living units—the *Poliscars*. The vehicle will respond to some of the most urgent communication needs of the different groups within the homeless population. It will be serving mostly those who live on the streets and in empty lots, helping them learn and expand communicative strategies and technologies, some of which are already well developed by the homeless who inhabit abandoned buildings—the squatters. It will establish links between various encampments, forming new social ties and leading to greater intercommunity and urban organization for this emerging constituency.

Through the Homeless Communication Network and its equipment, the *Poliscar* will:

A. Increase the sense of security among those who live outside by transmitting emergency information, such as early warning of planned evictions and other dangers facing both the homeless and nonhomeless in troubled areas. Its

use can help them organize quick and massive social action in the face of impending actions against these populations. In this way the position of the homeless living in empty lots will be closer to that of squatters who are already developing telecommunications systems for the same purpose.

B. Help develop forms of communication necessary for the participation of homeless populations in municipal, state, and federal elections. The Homeless Communication Network and *Poliscars* will provide a medium for articulation, exchange, and confrontation of ideas, opinions, experiences, visions, and expressions among different groups in the homeless population. Concurrently, it can take advantage of material and information transmitted from other networks.

C. Develop a sense of social and cultural bonds among the members of the groups. This implies an increased understanding of antagonisms and differences, resulting in a decrease of tensions and alienations of one homeless group or individual from another. At the same time, the preconceived, fixed, and a priori image of the homeless population and its identity produced and reproduced by existing official networks of communication will be challenged by this experimental speech-act machine for homeless self-representation and expression.

D. Help create and record not only images but also individual histories of the homeless. History in this context means the relationship between the present situation and the changing city, and the changing life of that person within it. Democracy, liberty, and identity are all forms of continuing practice that cannot be separated from the instances of their expression, communication, and, by implication, reception by the larger population.

E. Produce both image and sound programs that could aid different groups and individuals to considerably extend and expand existing action groups' constituencies and constantly update the information in professional areas such as:

1. legal aid—listings and interactive forums for issues within the realm of the law,

2. medical aid—health and drug advice,

3. social crisis aid—helping people to communicate with one another in critical situations, taking into account the specificity of their life on the streets, encampments, and squats through counseling by homeless and nonhomeless psychologists, sociologists, etc.,

4. expression and individual histories,

5. formulation of political, educational, and aesthetic strategies.

F. Help the economic system of the homeless population enter the larger economic system of the city. There is a possibility of advertising skills and commodities and using the communication system for job listings within certain labor markets. Employers who wish to employ homeless people could use the network as a data base as well as advertising for their own needs. Events (fairs, theatrical, and musical performances, etc.) could be listed as either public or private listings.

Equipment: Portable Microwave Link

Key *Poliscars* within the Homeless Communication Network will be outfitted with Ikegami PP-70 Portable Microwave Links. This is a line-of-sight video transmission signal requiring a low-power transmission license from the Federal Communications Commission (FCC). A parabolic antenna with split RF units mounted on the top of the *Poliscar* will be equipped with Transmitter and Receiver Control Units capable of two-way transmission on a single-frequency band.

A 13-GHz unit with a 0.5-foot parabola antenna can operate at a distance of three to seven miles from its field pick-up site on the eighty-second floor of the Empire State Building. *Poliscar* locations not capable of direct line-of-sight transmission will require an IF Through-Relay System positioned on a nearby rooftop to provide the necessary link from the ground to the Empire State Building.

Video signals from a *Poliscar* in one community can be directed to the repeaters on the Empire State Building and transmitted as scheduled communications to *Poliscars* across the city, providing a political and cultural information link between communities within the Homeless Communication Network. Manhattan Cable receiver antennas also positioned on the Empire State Building can provide access to the larger community of the city through public-access cable systems.

CB Radio

The Homeless Communication Network is a mobile land-radio service. The FCC allows the existence of such networks for private and special-interest public communications. The CB-radio component of the network is comprised of mobile units (*Poliscars*) and one or more base stations. A "mobile station," such as the *Poliscar,* according to FCC definition, is used while in motion or during halts at unspecified points. Usually, a mobile station means a radio-equipped

car, truck, motorcycle, or other single-operator vehicle. A base station is installed at a fixed location to communicate with the mobile units and other base stations. CB-radio systems operate independently from other communication systems.

CB land-radio services use half-duplex and full-duplex audio operations. A half-duplex system allows communications in two directions but not simultaneously. First one communication takes place, then the other. A CB system's half-duplex modes require only one frequency. The range between mobile units is shorter than between mobile units and the base station. Vehicle-to-vehicle range is from three to ten miles, vehicle-to-base from five to fifteen miles, and base-to-base from ten to fifty miles. FCC regulations limit station antenna height to twenty feet above natural formations and existing architectural structures.

Electronic Communication and Other Equipment

Each community equipped with a *Poliscar* will generate information and communications with video recorders and surveillance cameras. A Star Tech Video Sender can transmit a high-frequency video signal for short distances between an active camera and its *Poliscar*. This allows mobility of a camera unconstricted by cables.

Beside the motor is a locker for the various materials that the urban nomad must carry with him or her at all times: water and other beverages; food supplies (e.g., special-diet food); baby food; dog food; cooking tools; equipment for washing; emergency medical kit (including emergency shots for infections, medication for asthma, diabetes, and for malnutrition, poisoning, and drug or alcohol overdose, sleeping aid, vitamins, birth control, pregnancy tests, AIDS tests, etc., along with a medical history); gas mask; umbrella; suntan lotion and sunglasses; alarm clock; stationery; books; toys and games; audio and video tapes; disposable bags; spare parts; tools (e.g., flashlight, binoculars, tools for emergency repairs and for attaching the vehicle to other *Poliscars*); and valuables (money, personal and official documents, food stamps, drug and alcohol reserves, etc.).

The homeless are treated, at best tolerated, as aliens on their own planet. This "alienation"—making into legal aliens legitimate operators within today's city—has the vicious effect of excluding not only the homeless, but us, the "community," from those real masses of "strangers" from whom we are estranged and with whom we presume to have no common language. In fact it

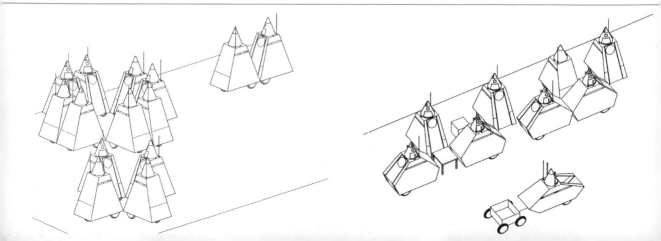

99   is the strangeness of the situation that we project onto the other rather than confronting it together.

This contradiction—to us they may seem strange in the city, but are not strangers to the city—results in a contradictory and complex identity: the savage homeless in a noble city, or the noble homeless in a savage city. Squeezed between this play of images, the homeless themselves, in their complexity in a complex city, remain out of the picture, which has no room for the real life of people who happen to lack a dwelling.

Originally published as a brochure titled *Poliscar* (New York: Josh Baer Gallery, 1991).

four **Instruments**

The Personal Instrument (1969)

The instrument transforms the sounds of the environment.
The instrument functions in response to hand movements.
The instrument reacts to sunlight.
The instrument is portable.
The instrument can be used any place and any time.
The instrument is for the exclusive use of the artist who created it.
The instrument permits him to attain virtuosity.

A microphone placed on the forehead receives the sounds from the environment and transmits them to the electroacoustic filters located in two sound-proof shell-earphones. Filters are controlled by two photocells fastened to each hand. The moving of hands regulates the amount of light reaching the photoreceivers and thus the intensity of filtering. When both hands are closed in fists (photoreceivers dark), the filtering device works at the top of its performance and no sound is heard. Turning the hands directly toward the light switches off the filters and all sounds from the environment are heard. The right hand's photoreceivers control the low-pitch filter (higher-pitched sounds are heard). The left hand's photoreceivers control the high-pitch filter. The waving of hands creates the glissando sound effect.

———————

It was difficult [in Poland] to find an artistic voice which could interrogate ethical and political voicelessness. On the other hand, life became the art of attempting to do exactly this, to speak indirectly about having no voice. One was forced to listen directly but not speak directly. This sparked the formation of a peculiar culture of indirect listening, sharing it through veiled speech. At that time I tried to see industrial design as somehow related to the design of the state—on the one hand, relating the operator of designed equipment to the "citizen," and, on the other hand, relating the state ideologist to the designer or artist. I was in a strange position: a designer employed by the state industrial corporation while trying to establish a critical and ironic dialogue with a real and monstrous designer—the communist state itself—who was in total control of the entire society and treated it as a single work of art or design. . . . In the Personal Instrument, I somehow represented myself, my colleagues, and possibly many others, swimming "freely" in a world of sounds and speech, yet remaining silent. I represented the individual within the state, trying to listen selectively. Or I presented a person who made an art work out of the art of

listening, switching on one part of a frequency and switching off another; rein-terpreting what was happening without speaking.

Original description published as "Instrument Osobisty / Personal Instrument," in *Autoportret / Self-Portrait,* exh. cat. (Warsaw: Galeria Foksal, 1973); with an excerpt from Ine Gevers and Jeanne van Heeswijk, "Interview with Wodiczko," in Gevers and van Heeswijk, eds., *Beyond Ethics and Aesthetics* (Amsterdam: Sun, 1997), pp. 450–52.

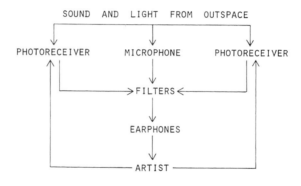

Alien Staff
(Xenobàcul)
(1992)

No aliens, residents, nonresidents, legal or illegal immigrants have voting rights, nor any sufficient voice or image of their own in official "public" space. When given a chance by the media (mainstream or ethnic) to communicate their experience or to state their opinions, demands, and needs, immigrants find themselves already framed and silenced. Feeling set up by preconceived categories of strangeness and difference, they have no chance to convey the often unbearable complexity of their lives, the world of differences between them and the confusing and antagonistic voices within each immigrant group, family, or individual. These are the strangers in the process of becoming nonstrangers, double aliens in dealienation.

The *Alien Staff* is a piece of storytelling equipment and a legal and ethical communications instrument and network for immigrants. It is an instrument that gives the singular operator-immigrant a chance to "address" directly anyone in the city who may be attracted by the symbolic form of the equipment, by the character of the "broadcast" program, or by the life presence and performance of the operator. The *Alien Staff* resembles the biblical shepherd's rod. It is equipped with a mini video monitor and a small loudspeaker. A video player and the batteries are located in a specially designed shoulder bag. The small size of the monitor, its eye-level location, and its closeness to the operator's face are important aspects of the design. As the small image on the screen may attract attention and provoke observers to come very close to the monitor and therefore to the operator's face, the usual distance between the stranger and the observer will decrease. Upon closer examination, it will become clear that the image on the face of the screen and the actual face of the person holding it are the same. The double presence in "media" and "life" invites a new perception of a stranger as "imagined" (a character on the screen) or as "experienced" (an actor offstage, a real-life person). Since both the imagination and the experience of the viewer are increasing with the decreasing distance, while the program itself reveals unexpected aspects of the actor's experience, the presence of the immigrant becomes both legitimate and real. This change in distance and perception might provide the ground for greater respect and self-respect, and become an inspiration for crossing the boundary between a stranger and a nonstranger.

The first model of the *Alien Staff,* called *Xenobàcul* in Catalan, was built and tested in Barcelona in June 1993 with the assistance of Fundació Antoni Tàpies and SOS Racisme of Barcelona. The first user was an immigrant from Burkina Faso. A second model was built and its design further transformed in New York during the fall and winter of 1992–93. This new variant of the *Alien Staff* differs from the first model in the ways it was developed with the input of a singular

person—a storyteller/video-performer, who was willing to present her own experience and function as a legal and ethical advisor for other immigrants. This version, with a vertically oriented screen of the "xenoscope" (the top or crook section of the *Alien Staff*) for a closer view of the owner's face, is made of stainless steel to look more powerful and respectable in the New York context. The new "xenolog section" (the central part of the rod of the *Alien Staff*) is made up of interchangeable cylindrical containers for the preservation and display of precious relics related to various phases of the owner's immigration history. This version has become something of a reliquary, with containers for such relics as rejected visa applications, immigration and legal documents, apartment keys, old photographs, and the various identity cards acquired by the owner. Through prerecorded video broadcast and live narration, these accounts of the immigrant past are recalled in the face of the immigrant present and become an art of critical history and a critical vision of the future.

The first operator of this version of the *Alien Staff* was Jagoda Przybylak, a prominent Polish artist-photographer, who moved to New York in 1981. Forced by immigrant circumstances, she took various jobs of Polish women: "plejsy" (cleaning private apartments), "ofisy" (cleaning corporate offices), and "kompaniony" (accompanying elderly American women). Since 1986 she has worked as an assistant professor at the New York Institute of Technology, where she presented herself with her *Alien Staff* to give the students, professors, staff, and maintenance personnel an opportunity to hear and see the stories of her "plejsy," "ofisy," and "kompaniony." The process of telling these stories required recording and much editing. She has found recounting and revealing her often hellish past emotionally difficult, but morally constructive in terms of self-respect from others. Details forgotten or suppressed return, providing the possibility of the discovery through language, both Polish and English, of identities old and new that go far beyond what is usually taken for granted.

Parts of this text were originally published as "The Alien Staff (Bâton d'immigré)," in *Espaces de transit* (Paris: Ecole nationale supérieure des Beaux-Arts, 1992); reprinted in *Krzysztof Wodiczko: Instruments, Projeccions Vehicles* (Barcelona: Fundació Antoni Tàpies, 1992), pp. 303–6. Between 1993 and 1997, more than twenty persons used various variants of the *Alien Staff* in Barcelona, Paris, Marseilles, New York, Houston, Stockholm, Helsinki, Warsaw, Rotterdam, and Boston. These were refugees, immigrants, and in some cases citizens who are perceived as foreigners in their own countries.

Alien Staff, Variant 2
with Joshua Smith
(1992–93)

The new interactive and digital version of *Alien Staff* invites an improvisation and virtuosity in replaying the prerecorded content. The electric field sensors respond to the operator's and interlocutor's gestures, modulating both sound and image.[1] Unlike in the previous versions, the monitor does not expose the entire face but only the eyes of the operator. The quality and strength of the speaker has been improved. Additional covers give the operator the choice of exposing or concealing the relics. If necessary, the containers can be easily detached during the performance for closer examination of their content. In the near future, a new design will allow for two-way radio transmission between the operators and the xenological base.

The new *Alien Staff* is capable of sensing and responding to hand and body gestures of the operator or interlocutors. This *Staff* was developed with the research assistance of Joshua Smith of the MIT Media Lab, and with the participation of Noni, an immigrant from Peru living in Boston. As a hand approaches the top relic container, the eyes that appear on the small screen open and blink. A quick up-and-down motion of the hand when it is in the vicinity of the top relic container "triggers" several story fragments prerecorded by Noni, whose eyes appear on the *Alien Staff* screen. The fragments of the story repeat themselves as long as a hand or body remains near the central portion of the *Alien Staff*. This instrument allows the operator to replay the audiovisual content, using gestures to navigate through the prerecorded stories, for example recalling a particular episode or moment in response to a question from an interlocutor. Pointing at a particular container recalls an experience associated with the relic inside. In addition to the main audiovisual program, the operator is able to compose a "counterpoint" of several short, repeating audio lines played against the main narrative. These audio programs are associated with the relics and may emphasize, contradict, or provide other viewpoints on the main narrative. Because these repeating "audio relics" may differ in length from one another, the juxtapositions will shift over time.

A pair of translucent, Plexiglas doors can be closed, partially obscuring the relics and sensors from view. The sensors function unimpeded by the closed doors, but a small receiver wire mounted on the bottom edge of one of the doors allows the computer to detect the configuration of the doors: open, closed, or anywhere in between. The position of the door in turn affects the audiovisual program with the meaning assigned to the operator's gestures. We are still experimenting with various programs for opening and closing the doors. The closed doors "muffle" the soundtrack of the stories associated with the specific relics; when the doors are open, the soundtrack plays at a volume comparable to that of the main program. When the doors are closed, the gestures no longer refer to particular relics but to the entire body of the *Alien Staff*

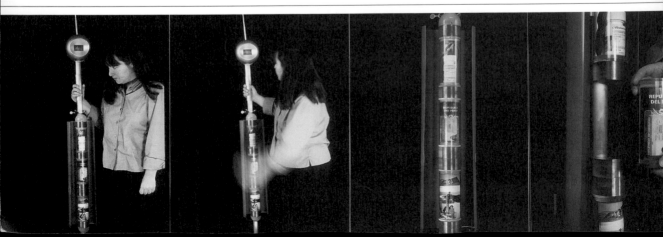

and may only play with the main audio narrative. The doors will conceal the relics from sight while revealing them through sound. When the doors are closed, only sound fragments associated with the relics will be heard, as if the immigrant relics were "asking" to be viewed and explored. This new capacity to play (or to replay creatively) the prerecorded stories will create a humorous distance from the immigrant's experience and will help the user to master his or her virtuosity in storytelling.

In the future, new illuminated relic containers will replace the present doors. The relics will be displayed in dark Plexiglas containers that will reflect outside light and conceal the contents within, but when illuminated from the inside will reveal the objects. The brightness of the illumination may be controlled by the sensors. The antenna atop the *Staff* and a microphone installed in the back of its "head" open a possibility that singular units could communicate with each other across the city and worldwide, allowing for an ongoing transmission of information and a dialogue between the operators and the "xenological" base or bases run by *xenologists*—legal, psychological, and ethical experts in displacement.

Note

1. In a future variant of the *Alien Staff,* we hope to move to a better sensor design based on new field sensing circuitry known as the "school of fish." The design of the school of fish circuitry is in part a response to the challenges posed by the *Alien Staff* project. Each school of fish board contains all the circuitry needed to drive an electrode as either a transmitter or a receiver, and to switch between these two modes in response to software commands. The school of fish is designed to allow the sensing electronics to be located with the electrode. This would eliminate the present need for shielded coaxial cables carrying very small (mA), sensitive signals from the electrodes in the *Staff* to the sensing circuitry in the operator's bag. Eliminating these cables would also eliminate the fragile connector through which these sensitive signals leave the staff. Instead, only power (+12V), ground, and the two RS-485 digital serial bus lines would need to travel between the electrodes and out of the staff. Because the school of fish units are transceivers, we would also be able to eliminate the "extra" fifth electrode in the present *Staff.*

This text was previously unpublished. The electric field sensing technology utilized in this prototype staff is a descendant of that found in the Theremin, an early electronic musical instrument. Electric field sensing was invented by members of the MIT media Lab's Physics and Media Group, Neil Gershenfeld and Joshua Smith, who collaborated on the design of this staff, which was built by John Kuntzsch of Brooklyn Model Works.

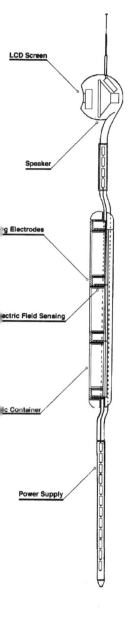

LCD Screen

Speaker

g Electrodes

ectric Field Sensing

ic Container

Power Supply

Voices of the Alien Staff

(1992–96)

Jagoda Przybylak, Greenpoint, Brooklyn, N.Y.

Ofisy is a difficult job to get. You have to have special connections and a large bottle of alcohol for Miss Stella, who does the hiring and overlooks the lack of a green card. On our floor there are women from South America, from Haiti, and from the most remote parts of Poland. Everyone has a particular job to do and then at dinner break we come together and laugh and joke and get to know one another. It's a good job. . . .

And suddenly—panic—immigration raid! The doors of the elevator open and Stella chokes out, "*Immigration! Hide!*" Hide where? The only place was the fire escape. It was dark and in the back. We stood there, shaking with fear. Actually, I wasn't as scared as they were because they wanted so much to be here and work here and live here. I could go back to Poland anytime and go on with my work as an artist. They were terrified of being deported. One girl from Colombia tore off her blue cleaner's uniform and stood there in black underwear, trembling from the cold. "If they catch me, I won't admit I work here. In a few weeks I'm getting married. I have to stay in this country. I'm not going to let them throw me out." Every one of us had problems trying to stay in America.

We stood there in that cold, dark, dirty place for a long time, still shaking, whispering together. We didn't know if they were still out there looking for us but we were afraid to open the door to find out. Finally, as the least vulnerable of us, I sneaked to the toilet and there I was completely astonished when I saw my face in the mirror. It was white as a sheet, almost green—huge, round, frightened eyes. I looked terrified. I *was* terrified. Just like they were.

Anonymous, Brooklyn, N.Y.

Our employer was a distinguished lady, charming and friendly. I loved her. We were singing songs on the way to her residence, and I could have hugged and kissed her if I had not had to keep my feelings back. She was our redemption at that moment. But never trust the appearance. Our paradise was lost the next day when we were given a long list of duties and rules. Our precision was of the essence, even if it did not make any sense. I had to clean and polish the silverware with special care everyday. Setting a table, I was told to put the plates with their pattern vertically to the edge of the table, and I still have this habit serving dinner for my husband. I was not allowed to do the dishes in the dishwasher. I still ask, what was there a dishwasher for? We started our working day at seven o'clock in the morning and never finished before midnight. There

were always several people in for dinner, and I was always in the kitchen preparing extraordinary dishes which I had to learn how to prepare the night before. When Lady Ellen went out for dinners instead of cooking, I had to sew and mend dresses for her. My husband had not only to vacuum the carpets but to comb them in one direction as well. When we were hired, we were told there would only be cooking for two.

We did not have any minutes resting, and when I asked for a one-hour nap one day, she said with exclamation, "After what?"

The list of our duties was growing and our hard work was never appreciated. We felt like slaves not only because of our work but the situation, which put us in a position of mentally abused people. My husband couldn't stand it anymore and decided to leave this place. He wanted me to do the same, but at that moment I was not able to quit, in order to be loyal to my employer. I knew I had to save some money and to have my family together, and at the same moment I was so afraid of my future.

After he had left for New York, Lady Ellen tried to convince me that my husband was irresponsible and that I should leave him and stay with her. But at the same time, she treated me even worse than before.

I had to work daytime, but nighttime did not bring any relief. Even when I was together with my husband, there was always the same nightmare with a woman opening the door and coming to kill me. I was screaming with horrible fear of being touched by her. My husband tried to protect me, but I was still scared that he would not be able to shield me from that woman.

I really don't know why I am telling this story. Maybe I want to get rid of these memories and to become again a human being with self-esteem. I want this for my little son.

Honza, Warsaw

I had an offer of a job. But it was quite hopeless since, hearing that someone is a Gypsy, every Pole gets the wrong impression. My situation in Poland is now very difficult. I have no place to live or any work. If I were to return home, I would first have to give my decision a lot of thought.

As a deserter I face a penalty of 8 to 15 years' imprisonment. Here in Poland I am free, but miss working very much and cannot think about the future. I am upset by the fact that I cannot simply stay here just like anyone else, but only as a "Gypsy" or a "darkie." People immediately think I steal and cheat. I find this amazing. In Yugoslavia the situation is completely different. A Gypsy is a

Gypsy. What you do is your own business. If you have difficulties with the police, then that's your problem. In Yugoslavia, no one would say in the street, "Look, a Gypsy!" I would like to stay in Poland, because I like it here. I like the Poles as much as I do Poland itself, and believe that those who say "Gypsy," etc. are uncouth. If I were to introduce myself as a Gypsy when looking for work, I would have only a five percent chance of getting the job. Saying that you are a Yugoslav changes the way people think. They talk to you differently. I would like to be able to introduce myself as a Gypsy; I am not ashamed of being one.

Noni, Cambridge, Mass.

My state right now, at this moment, is like hanging from a thread. The word "limbo" describes my state well—of being in the middle of nothing, of not having control over anything. But a job is just out of reach. A decision between Dave and me is out of reach. It's like I'm in somebody else's hands but I don't know who that is. On top of everything is the immigration people, the INS. Even if I get hired, even if Dave commits to our relationship, it is finally they who decide my fate, whether I can stay or not. They are like a god in my life.

I am in a very vulnerable state. There is this feeling of not being capable of planning anything. It's an awful feeling. I can't protect myself for more than four months. I can't say, "This summer, I plan to go to Martha's Vineyard." I really don't have control of my life. For all practical purposes, I shouldn't even get a subscription for a magazine. Why go through the effort to do anything? I may never see the results.

I don't think that Dave realizes that all we have is four months. If I've waited for him this long, it's because I want things to happen in their own time. But I have exactly four months. That is when my student visa expires. This means that we'll see each other fourteen more times, once a week, four hours each time. We have fifty-six hours, which means we have two and a half days left. So, whatever we should talk about, that is our limit. It's like *Leaving Las Vegas:* we are in a terminal movie. I would like love to be like that. To be totally selfless, and with no expectations. To be only for love.

Abdelkader N'Dali, Paris

Two-thirds of the Moroccans found in France came under contract. At Simca, at Peugeot, in the mines, in the building trades, the cleaning trades, craftsmen.

Me, I don't understand why they turn against us now, because before, before in 1969, '72, '73, they were walking into foyers and cafes looking for workers. The French needed workmen from 1968 to '80. We were robots, we took the place of robots on assembly lines. The line went at forty an hour and a fellow put on the wheel, the door. Each put on a piece, each put a piece on the car. The car was complete . . . and, in fact, we were 26,000 and doing 2,000 cars per day . . . 2,000. They have installed robots now, there are a third as many who work. They have sacked all, sacked the foreigners, all. They are turning against foreigners, hiring a young man . . . they are sacking foreigners, hiring . . . every time, every time it is like that and it is shit . . . it is shit.

My father was a sharpshooter from 1939 to '49, with the Senegalese at the front, while the noncommissioned officers were traveling in England. General De Gaulle was traveling and foreigners were defending the French flag. And all that . . . they forgot that . . . that is serious . . . that counts. They forgot that, and when you bring it up, you say, my father is French, he says to you: it's not you . . . it's not you who went through the war, it is not you who was a soldier! But I tell him, it is my father! Here are his papers! They throw them aside, every time they throw them aside. An Arab before them remains an Arab, a Maghrebin remains a Maghrebin. An outsider, he is deported. After all, it is one Arab less.

Ambroise Wolking, Paris

Gobineau was a writer, the French intellectual who theorized racism. First he said that blacks are endowed with true aesthetic faculties. They have great sensibility, they have much drive, but because they do not have the power of reason, they have no understanding, and they cannot express this sensibility. For the black is almost an animal . . . almost an animal. Lots of sensuality, lots of emotion, but very little reason. That was the discourse of Gobineau. But on the other hand, he said that whites had very little sensibility, not much emotion, but that they had great minds, a great deal of reason. Senghor, a poet who was an apostle, a pope of negritude, was later to say that reason is Hellenic, that is to say, Greek, and that emotion is black. That's what Senghor would say, but I refuse both the position of Senghor and the position of Gobineau. I think all men are endowed with almost the same sensibility, the same reason, and it is up to man to externalize either his sensibility and reason. . . . And as far as racist theories are concerned, I should mention that even before Gobineau,

there were philosophers like Kant. Let's not forget that Kant was a contemporary of the French Revolution. We often have a tendency to consider Kant a thoroughly modern philosopher, a contemporary of Nietzsche, but Kant was a contemporary of the French Revolution. He read a lot of Rousseau, for example. In a text entitled *Considerations on the Beautiful and the Sublime*—the title is something like that—he said that since blacks don't have enough understanding, don't have enough power of reason, they cannot even master a Western language. That's what Kant said: they cannot even master a Western language, and that's why they have to be disciplined with the rod, or something like that. But I'm quite certain Kant said it. In South Africa, when they want to legitimize racism, they tell the students, both black and white, "The white is superior to the black; if you want proof, look at what Kant said. Kant was a great luminary. If he said it, it must be true. Therefore, blacks are imbeciles, and whites are intelligent."

Patrica Pirreda, Paris

If someone had told me that, I'd never have believed it. Why not? Because you don't display bits and pieces of old cups as your roots. I am very, very attached to these cups, because they're from the end of the 1800s. They were handmade, gilded by hand, and I know that's important now. [Laughter.] And they are completely—but completely—broken. But there, what's strange is that they are broken not because they were smashed, but because they were used for a really, really long time by many, many people. They were coffee cups. You can see where the break was caused by the coffee, because of the contrast of the heat. . . . In Italy, they make espresso. It's very thick coffee, very, very hot. It's served very hot, and the contrast of the heat with the cup is what caused it over the years, many, many years, to penetrate. And that's what I love about them. Why these roots? Because I adore dreaming about the people in my family.

All this is to say that if I find fertile ground, well adapted, if I find it, the seed could grow. Unfortunately, I haven't found that bit of ground yet. For the moment, Paris isn't the right place. It's a terrain where all the fractures in my life came to light for me, all the broken bits of myself. For the moment, there is no question of building anything; we're still in the demolition phase.

In this country, I have the impression that I don't exist. At best I do exist, but thanks to my child, my husband, my friends, but not for myself, not thanks to my own capacities, my own dreams. . . . With broken pieces like that, it's easy to make a cup like that, but not easy to make anything else. It's not easy, because when things are designed, they already have a form. That can't be changed. You can modify it, but it will always remain, and that's life.

Thanks to the birth of my child, I was able to get a residence card. The card was issued September 20, 1988, and my son was born on June 10, 1988. Thanks to the fact that I had a child, the powers that be granted me a residence card good for ten years. In ten years—that is, in five, now—we'll see what I do. I don't know what will happen.

A Few Reactions to the Alien Staff
Reaction: I don't understand.

Patrica: You can listen to my story a bit. I'm a foreigner.

R.: Ah, I see! You introduce yourself with it.

P.: Totally!

R.: But to what end? Professional?

P.: No. It's called the *Alien Staff.*

Comment: . . . Which retraces the life of an immigrant in France. It tells the story through . . .

R.: But what's the point? Is it originality, or that when you introduce yourself with it, you want people to get to know you?

P.: No, it's for people to ask questions. And they do ask questions. . . . My own goal is to be able to express this. My goal is to participate in a voyage, a voyage beyond borders. I have crossed borders. There have been plenty of fractures within myself. And this is another voyage I am making. I am trying to see if I can cross borders. . . .

R.: I thought you could buy one.

C.: Oh! You thought you could buy it.

P.: No, we are in a consumer society here, but you can't buy everything. [Laughter.] I'm not selling it. I'm a part of the *Staff;* we're together. We travel together. It's a kind of purification on my part. It's a concretization of suffering and tears, a way of embodying them differently.

C.: It's an analytic undertaking.

P.: It's my therapy. I would like it to also be the therapy of lots of other people.

C.: It's funny, because it's a slightly bizarre endeavor—not really bizarre—but surprising that we should need it to communicate with others.

R.: Does the cup have meaning for you?

P.: Yes, it represents my roots. It's a symbol, a metaphor. It's completely broken, and at the same time completely impregnated. I relate the bits and pieces of my story with respect to the change of country.

R.: And what is this?

P.: It's a part of my past. I have a master's degree in computer science. I'm a computer scientist, and that creates a circuit. When I lived in Italy, I had just finished my computer degree. I came to Paris on a trip, and in Paris I fell in love with a Parisian artist and I stayed. But it was very hard to fit in, extremely hard. It was only after the birth of my child five years ago that I was granted a residency permit. I've been here for eleven years, and my permit is good for ten years. That is, I'm dependent on my child and husband for my existence here.

R.: I really admire this thing.

P.: I'm not the one who made it.

C.: It's a totem pole.

Excerpts from video programs broadcast by the *Alien Staff* when used by various immigrants in Paris, New York City, Warsaw, and Cambridge, Mass., 1992–96; Noni and Honza asked that their last names not be used. The interview with Patrica Pirreda is from Jean-Louis Sonzogni, *Reactions to the Alien Staff* (color film, 30 minutes, produced by the French Ministry of Culture and Grand Canal Studios, Paris, 1993).

**Identity and
Community:
Alien Staff** (1994)

Strangers are treated as "those with no history." In crossing and trespassing new borders and territories, they must counter this perception and preconception by producing and disseminating, through the performative act, their experience and perception as their history, identity, and critical contribution. All this takes the form of storytelling. In this way they disrupt and insert their secret "tradition of the vanquished" into the "history of the victors." The performative act is a discontinuity interrupting the continuity of national pedagogy. The number of people who are in a migratory-symptomatic psychological state and who are in no position to exercise cross-cultural communication is extraordinary. It is a historical moment for designers and artists to respond to this in a constructive way (both a deconstructive and a constructive way).

The *Alien Staff* becomes a sacred object. It is an immigrant's companion and a historical (and "storical") double, displacing displacement and spreading communicative cure. It is an act of opening of a private case of strange experiences; opening up toward others who themselves might feel compelled and encouraged to share their experiences. In this way, the *Alien Staff* creates a performative space—a sacred space—around the alien and his or her staff. The object is sacred in the way it creates a sacred place.

To create a performance, dramatize, make a humorous comical story out of a painful tragic experience, find metaphoric ways to explain the unexplainable, find the words for unbelievable facts, construct, edit the story. Storytelling is a kind of creative manipulation of the facts, events, memories, reflections, conclusions. It is also a critical recollection of the past. As one of the rabbinical scholars said: "The one who believes the story is a fool, but the one who denies the story is a wicked nonbeliever." Storytelling is a manipulation, as is every work of art. It attempts to concretize metaphorically, not directly, the truth of human existence.

An important part of the encouragement for this performative situation is the fact that there is already a discourse developed between the staff and its owner, between the speaking monitor, the speaking owner, and the exposed narrative content preserved in the relic containers. This is the sacred place understood in the way Bataille described it, as "the place of unleashing of passion."

The task of the *Alien Staff* is to inspire, provoke, and assist in the processes of communication among and between immigrants and nonimmigrants.

The *Alien Staff* is an instrument designed for the exploration and expression of the complexity of the immigrant experience. Its task is to expose at the same time the limits of such experience, the moments of painful impossibility of representation and communication.

As a personal instrument, the *Alien Staff* focuses on and exposes the singularity and uniqueness of its operator's life experience. The owner is understood as a separate human being who happened to become an immigrant, rather than as one who conforms to any preconceived category of immigrant, population or community of immigrants, or any other kind or type.

The *Alien Staff* exposes the history of such a singular being in the process of becoming and being fabricated as an immigrant. Such a history, being recalled in the context of present moments of an immigrant's life, constitutes a particular constellation of experience of displacement.

The task of the *Alien Staff* is to concretize metaphorically, to translate this constellation into narrative, into an interactive performance, and into a public dialogue.

The *Alien Staff* is simultaneously an instrument, a performance, and a network. It is designed as public-speech-act equipment, which allows the singular immigrant to open up his or her own critical history of displacement to everyone whom it may (or even may not) concern, to open up to the Other and to the world the complexity of the often unstable and multiple configurations and reconfigurations of identities inhabiting the immigrant's mind.

As these identities are not only unstable but also often antagonistic to each other, the only common ground they share is their resistance against any imposed (even self-imposed) uniform or generalized notion of a so-called immigrant identity.

The resistance of these identities (which conflict with one another and transform themselves in the process) to the colonizing or multicultural categories imposed upon them (from outside and inside) is, in fact, the seed of new identity, not only for a particular immigrant but also for the surrounding society.

In the hand of an immigrant, the *Alien Staff* explores, exposes, and proposes this new discursive model of identity to the world as a possible model for a new community.

The new community, as much as the new singular identity, can be formed of the solidarity of those who are prevented from joining those who feel in-common and at home, of the pain of resistance to the imposed state of being-in-common, and of the desire to be invited to the state of being-in-common as a critical and transforming force.

117 More recently, the new community might be born of those aliens who are both objects and critics of multiculturalism, who resist functioning as Others in a new multicultural paradise organized by the Sames, who are still in charge.

Originally published as "Le Baton d'étranger: expérience, identité et communauté," in *Krzysztof Wodiczko: Art public, art critique,* edited by Marie-Anne Sichère (Paris: Ecole nationale supérieure des Beaux-Arts, 1995).

The Mouthpiece (Porte-Parole)

(1993)

The *Mouthpiece* is a piece of equipment for strangers. It covers the mouth of the wearer like a gag. A small video monitor and loudspeakers are installed at the center of the instrument and in front of the user's mouth. The monitor and the loudspeakers replace the real act of speech with an audiovisual broadcast of prerecorded, edited, electronically perfected and quickly searched statements, questions, answers, stories, etc.

The *Mouthpiece* "replaces" the immigrant's actual act of speech with the moving image of the immigrant's lips and the sound of the immigrant's voice. It is designed to be as attractive as contemporary virtual reality gadgets. The clear resolution of the liquid-crystal screen of the video monitor attracts viewers' attention. The small size of the screen (no larger than the actual size of human lips) forces viewers to come close to the user's face in order to see the image of speaking lips and to hear the voice clearly. Thus the distance between the immigrant wearing the *Mouthpiece* and the viewers, nonimmigrants and other immigrants, decreases physically and, hopefully, psychologically as well.

For a speechless stranger living in a culturally, politically, and ethically unnatural situation, wearing a piece of artificial and artistically conceived speech-act equipment is a natural thing to do. In today's migration era, the wearer of the *Porte-Parole* appears as a prophetic storyteller and a poetic interrupter of the continuity of established life in public space and the dominant culture. This stranger becomes an expert and a virtuoso in the technology and the artistry of speech, equipped to speak better than others who have yet to overcome speechlessness in their encounter with strangers.

The *Mouthpiece* is a further evolution of the *Alien Staff* as the next generation of speech equipment designed for immigrants. The previous instrument was meant to operate as an attribute, an artifice, a reliquary, a portable memorial to recall in public the "private history" of the immigrant experience. It functioned as a third party between immigrants and nonimmigrants and among immigrants themselves; it functioned as the immigrant's double, and as an inspiration for dialogue between the segregated worlds of the people who entered into conversation around it.

The new instrument is a more radical type of equipment. It is directly attached to the body (the face) of the immigrant, becoming an extension of the body. The user himself or herself is no longer delegating power to the instrument, but is integrated organically with it, transforming him or her into a kind of cyborg, a virtual subject.

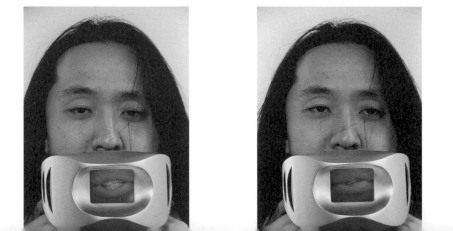

The *Mouthpiece* points to the absurdity of any attempt to deprive people of speech rights in a democratic society. It responds to the actual political process and experience of such deprivation, while at the same time it helps to translate this disadvantage into a new advantage. In other words, it is an instrument whose function is to empower those who are deprived of power. It is designed to assert the universal communicative rights introduced by the Declaration of the Rights of Man in France, assured by the First Amendment to the Constitution of the United States, and guaranteed by most national constitutions since. An implication of these declarations is that no artifice can be created to restrict communicative rights and, conversely, no artifice whose aim is to aid in the exercise of communicative rights can be legally banned. Its basic purpose is to provide a means of saying all the things that must be said and that no one wants to hear. In doing so it does not prevent anyone else from doing the same. The *Mouthpiece* is thus a democratic artifice.

The *Mouthpiece* allows its owner to compose and prerecord his or her act of speaking and to replay and reenact it later, in a particular chosen time and place, in private or public situations. This process reinforces a specific kind of power already acquired by immigrants, the artistic power of speech invention and storytelling. The storyteller has always been forced to develop an art of speech in order to tell what has usually been untold and for which there is no ready-made metaphor. The storyteller creates a situation in which repressed feelings, translated into stories, can be effectively expressed. The wearer of the *Mouthpiece* is a storyteller who is an expert in the technology of speech in the cyberspace era, an alien who has arrived in a xenophobic land and who looks strangely familiar to us who have yet to overcome our speechlessness in the face of our repressed fears.

This project, like the previous *Alien Staff,* creates an artifice that provokes or inspires communication or translation, a display of what is usually hidden. The instrument suggests an acknowledgment of the richness and complexity of people who combine both "natural" and "artificial" qualities in life. This means that feeling artificial (not at home, alienated from oneself or others) becomes a process that can open up new questions and introduce the possibility of different identities and communities beyond nationalisms and fixed notions of difference, crossing social and psychological boundaries, meeting on new common ground, however shaky and displaced such ground may be.

"Aliens" equipped with specially designed instruments might appear perfectly natural in the contemporary migratory environment of global strange-

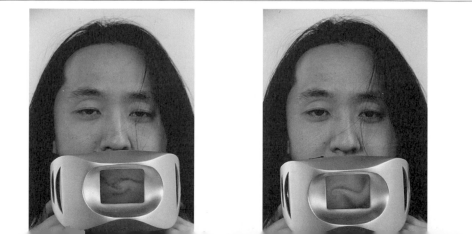

ness. Exposing their own disintegration and displaced identity, they provoke and inspire the larger process of the disintegration of identities among non-immigrants. They may spread the communicable (contagious) process of the exploration of one's own strangeness. They might help create new links and affinities between immigrants and nonimmigrants on the basis of the recognition of their common strangeness.

With the use of digital technology, the process of recording and editing the image and sound of a speaking mouth will become an artistic endeavor. The process of composing and prerecording each speech act in private is psychologically, politically, and artistically as important as public live performance and its social discourse. Advanced video editing, digital enhancement, and transformation of both the image and the sound of the speech (through the most recent Macintosh software) is critical to the project. The technology of video production will help to create a metaphoric synthesis of often overlapping and displaced memories, fragments of experiences, statements, stories, words, and sentences, all of which correspond to the unstable identity of the stranger who is living through the pain of displacement and becoming. Electronic montage will allow for changes in the speed of the lips on the screen and the change of frequency characteristics of the sound, for dubbing, correcting, playing with and multiplying accents and gender indicators. Fragments of films and other videos can be inserted and other people's lips can be juxtaposed with those of the immigrant, for example.

The careful choice of locations and situations for the performative use of the *Mouthpiece* is crucial. Official events and symbolic environments are the best, because they are the situations where immigrants are least expected. The presence of a group of *Mouthpiece* users is also essential. The image of a crowd of aliens appearing as if they have just landed from another planet (which happens to be our own) is most desirable.

In the next stage of development of the project, a portable computer and additional electronic devices will be added to allow for quick searching through a large repertoire of prerecorded speeches using the operator's voice as a command. In this way the immigrant will have a greater variety of speeches ready for all anticipated situations and will be able to choose the appropriate videotape to respond immediately to any question. As portable equipment improves technically, links to satellite communications and the Internet will allow an immediate dialogue among *Mouthpiece* users, enabling an exchange of experiences and coordination of their presence and their actions nationally and internationally.

Originally published in the catalogue of the exhibition *ARS 95 Helsinki* (Helsinki: Museum of Contemporary Art, 1995). Between 1994 and 1997 thirteen persons used various variants of the *Mouthpiece* in Paris, Malmö, Helsinki, Warsaw, Amsterdam, Trélazé, and Angers. These were refugees, immigrants, and other culturally displaced persons.

The Mouthpiece, Variants
with Joshua Smith
(1995–97)

A later variant of the *Mouthpiece* is equipped with a more powerful loud-speaker and a more stable and adjustable head attachment. The video-monitor section can function in two main positions: in front of (covering) the operator's lips, and next to (exposing) the lips. The second position allows for speaking simultaneously with two voices and "two lips": the real (natural) and the virtual (prerecorded and transformed electronically). The disclosure of the previously hidden mouth of the stranger helps to establish direct contact and dialogue during the public encounter between the operator and interlocutors on the street.

A prototype of this model was built by Brooklyn Model Works and was used in France in the summer of 1996 thanks to the support of the French Ministry of Culture.

The present proposal offers three further elaborations of an experimental, interactive *Mouthpiece*. The first two are technically straightforward. The equipment necessary for the third may be prohibitively expensive. The mechanical parts of the new *Mouthpiece* would be built by the Brooklyn Model Works, while the electronic part would be developed by the Physics and Media group at the Media Lab of MIT.

In the *first scenario,* the video and audio recorded speech would be interrupted by the operator's speech. The operator and the recording would take turns, creating a dialogue between prerecorded audio-video speech and direct, live, amplified speech. The gaps in the operator's speech would always be filled in by the recorded material, eliminating all silences. The acoustic sensitivity would be adjustable. Different sensitivity settings lead to different artistic effects. For example, the system might interrupt very fluidly, aggressively filling even the normal gaps between words. Or it might be set more sluggishly, hesitating several seconds after the operator had stopped speaking before "replying" to the operator.

In addition to the existing *Mouthpiece* unit, with its video display, speaker, and video tape player, the additional apparatus needed for this experiment includes a microphone to be added to the *Mouthpiece* unit, a simple custom speech detection circuit (to be built in the Physics Lab within the MIT Media Lab), and an improved amplifier-speaker system. The microphone would feed into both the amplifier-speaker and the speech detection circuit. When the operator begins speaking, the detection circuit suppresses the prerecorded material, and the operator's amplified voice is heard through the speaker. When the operator stops speaking, the detection circuit reconnects the prerecorded audio to the speaker and reenables the video display.

In the *second scenario,* the prerecorded audio-video speech would be activated by the operator's live speech. The prerecorded video speech would be superimposed over the direct, amplified acoustic speech of the operator, creating a sense of interruption and contradiction rather than dialogue. There would, however, be an alternating rhythm of speech and silence: when the operator stops speaking, the prerecorded speech stops as well, creating silence. When the operator resumes speaking, the silence is broken not by a single voice, but by the superimposition of the prerecorded audio-video speech and the operator's speech.

The equipment needed for this experiment is the same as for the first experiment, except that the custom circuit would be slightly different. In practice, we would make a single circuit with a switch to determine whether the system would operate in the first, "dialogue" mode, or the second, "contradiction" mode.

The *third scenario* would involve a more intelligent, though perhaps more unruly, *Mouthpiece* unit. The video tape player currently in use would be replaced by a small computer, and the video and audio would be stored, indexed, and retrieved digitally. Furthermore, the computer would continuously monitor the signal on a microphone inside the *Mouthpiece,* and would be hypersensitive and hyperresponsive to certain words and their configurations through the use of the voice recognition unit. When it detected one of a set of special words or phrases ("immigration," "home," or "where are you from," for example), it would trigger a related video segment on the display. The rhythm of the interaction between the operator and the prerecorded material would be "more chaotic" than in the first two scenarios: at certain times neither source of speech would be active, at others just one "speaker" would have the floor, and at still other moments both would be active. In variants of this scenario, the prerecorded video segments might be triggered by special words spoken by the interlocutors into an externally mounted microphone, or by either the operator or the interlocutors. This would lead to still more complex speech rhythms.

This digital video version of the *Mouthpiece* system might include a wearable computer, which would be responsible for both the voice recognition and digital video display. As an example, the Phoenix-2 computer is based on the Intel 486DX-33 processor, and comes with 680 megabytes of internal hard disk

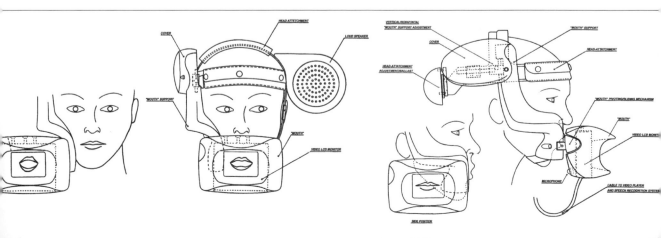

storage and built-in voice recognition capabilities. This amount of storage enables it to store substantial amounts of digitized audio-video footage.

To improve the sound quality of the *Mouthpiece,* a low-frequency speaker could be included as a part of the equipment worn by the operator, in addition to the medium- and high-frequency speakers already installed in the *Mouthpiece.* The low-frequency speaker would improve the perceived sound quality, making the operator's voice and the prerecorded material more understandable. But because the human ear uses only high frequencies to locate the sources of sounds in space, the presence of this additional low-frequency speaker would not change the apparent origin of the voice inside the *Mouthpiece.* This is a well-known and frequently used principle of sound design.

Previously unpublished proposal.

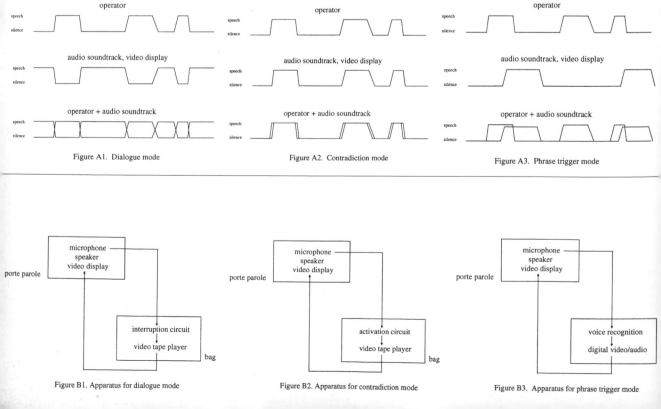

operator	operator	operator
audio soundtrack, video display	audio soundtrack, video display	audio soundtrack, video display
operator + audio soundtrack	operator + audio soundtrack	operator + audio soundtrack
Figure A1. Dialogue mode	Figure A2. Contradiction mode	Figure A3. Phrase trigger mode

Figure B1. Apparatus for dialogue mode

Figure B2. Apparatus for contradiction mode

Figure B3. Apparatus for phrase trigger mode

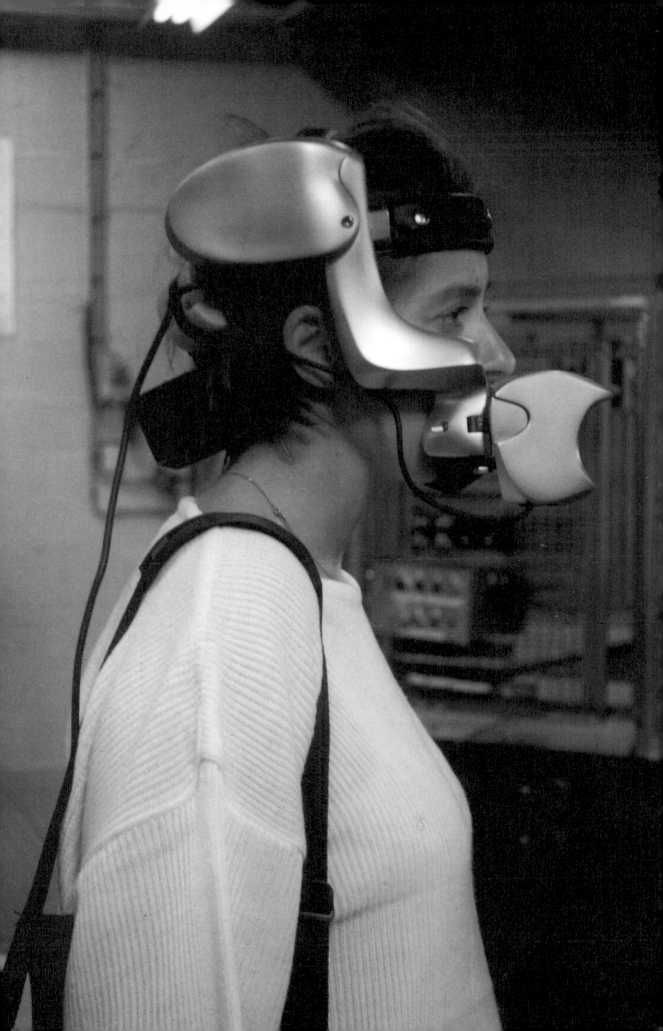

Voices of the Mouthpiece

(1994–96)

An Algerian, Warsaw

What I would like to tell you about bears the title "An Incomparable Tragedy." I address this message to the Polish nation so that it may understand the situation in my country from 1992 up to today. I appeal to all democratic countries like yours to assist my country in overcoming its problems.

By way of example, politics and religion cannot he combined. Religion is a question of faith and it never leads to violence and the destruction of the individual. Mankind, however, has something to fear. Once religious extremism mixes these concepts, it can produce dangerous consequences for a country which employs religion for political purposes.

I find the present a time of anxiety and sadness, of lengthy waiting for someone to make a decision about my fate. I fear that I may be ordered to return. I am left to myself.

Separation is insufferable. It is daily torture. I miss my children, my wife and my mother. They fear for me. I am afraid for them and for my uncertain destiny. A family torn apart by fear.

I ask myself, does man live in order to be afraid?

Awad Gabir Bashir, Warsaw

One day I was with my friends in a Russian restaurant in the Palace of Culture in Warsaw. A girl sitting at the next table looked at us and said something like, "I hate niggers." Finally she threw a salt cellar at us. The oldest of my friends tried to talk to her. She then threw a bottle. Silence fell. Everyone witnessed the incident, and the maître d' came over to us. We demanded that the girl leave. She replied, "What, you want me to leave for these niggers?" We were of the opinion that she should be asked to go. Her girlfriends and a man who was with them apologized to us. It became very unpleasant. At that moment I really wanted to return home to my country. But several tables away there sat an elderly married couple. They approached us with a bunch of flowers and apologized for the others, telling us not to think that all Poles are like that.

Now I find it difficult to describe the real nature of the Poles. I try not to judge them. I believe that such fringe groups exist in every society. We rarely go out to a disco or to concerts because my girlfriend just doesn't like them. But when we do go to parties with girls, we encounter reactions like, "Look, asphalt!" Once we went out in a group which included the Polish fiancée of a friend of mine. Two policemen appeared. "Hello. Documents, please." "What's going on?" she inquired. "Why are you asking? After all, you are the one asso-

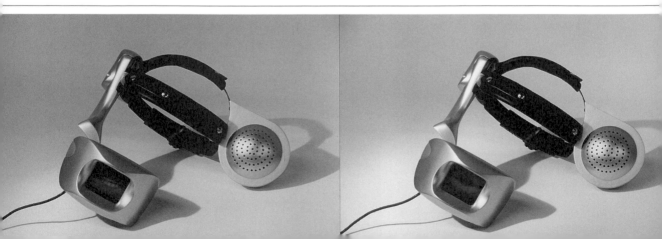

ciating with niggers," came the reply. We found this terrifying, because he was a representative of the law.

Whether the Poles like it or not, Poland has become a second home for foreign students, and after returning to our countries, each one of us would like to have pleasant memories, and not to associate Poland mainly with intolerance and aggression. At the same time, I believe that the solution to the problem depends both on the foreigners and on the Poles. The only way out is contact and dialogue about customs and the principles of how we treat each other. Only in this way can we live in a favorable atmosphere and environment. Mutual isolation will lead nowhere. Even if I were to be beaten or killed, this is my second homeland, because most of the time outside my own country has been spent here.

Nathalie, Trélazé, France

When my father died, my family wasn't there for me as moral support; my friends were, though. . . .

One day there was something strange about him. He had changed somehow: during the day he had been all smiles, but that evening he was in a terrible mood. He grabbed my mother by the hair and dragged her to the bedroom. He kept hitting her, and then slammed her against the wall. I tried to separate them, but he just slapped me in the face. It was horrible. . . . This had happened before, but this time I thought he was really going to kill her. . . . I never understood why my parents argued so much, or how he could change so much from one second to the next. . . .

Now my mother seems relieved. . . . But she keeps on heaping abuse on him, saying how bad he was. She is very, very hard on him. You get the feeling she is taking her revenge out on us. . . .

I keep having this nightmare. My father has been dead now for seven years. [Covers her face with her hand.] In my dream I go up to the attic of my house. There is a coffin there. I open the coffin, and there's my father, alive. . . . It still frightens me. [Wipes away her tears.] I never go up to the attic . . . maybe because my father's death affected me so deeply. Sometimes I wish he were here again, at my side. . . . My parents argued all the time, so I guess you could say I didn't have a very happy family life. I never had the pleasure of confiding in him, of telling him what was going on in my life. . . . Maybe I could have trusted him more. . . .

Now I tell myself, "That's life; have strength." But I'm not the only one. When I came here to Trélazé, there were lots of others with the same problem—a father who's gone—and they were able to get over it. I saw that in fact I was not the only one it had happened to. . . .

Interview with Nathalie

The fact of speaking to someone you don't know is like going to a psychologist. It has a completely different effect from talking to someone who is already familiar with your problems, like your family and friends. They know what's happening and take a position. The same is true when you exchange information with people who are having the same problems as you are; together you often get caught up in the details of your situation. . . . Speaking to someone foreign, a stranger who takes an interest in your problems, is really different. But there has to be the right atmosphere; you can't confide the heart of a matter just like that. . . .

Things are much better since I spoke to someone I didn't know, much clearer. I am no longer the same person. At first, while I was being filmed, the camera almost kept me from opening my mouth. I was very careful about what I said. Then I started to address the person behind the camera. I wondered whether I ought to divulge certain intimate details of my life, or whether I should remain silent and keep them to myself.

Krzysztof's presence was very important. He is a very humane person, one who gets very close to people. Someone who looks for solutions without quite looking for them. Like with the *Homeless Vehicle*—it's an object that could be used, but at the same time it's more useful in raising more complex issues. I felt both close to him and a little distant. We didn't communicate much. His French is elegant but somewhat stilted, a bit hard to understand. But he was mysterious and aroused my curiosity; I wanted to get to know him better. He has a greatness about him; that interested me and made me wonder what he thought, but he doesn't reveal himself much.

After I had bared myself, for five days I felt exhausted, tired and depleted. I wondered why I had told so much about my life. I felt guilty and wondered, "I said all that, but why?! No one could care less. . . ." Unconsciously, I wanted to talk about all of that, even though I had no wish to bring up my past. People have a need to talk, which is different from an intimate diary. That, too, allows for an exteriorization of oneself, but only for oneself. In the *Porte-Parole* the speaking is destined for others—for women, or others who think the same. We deal with an issue together. An intimate diary is of no use at all.

At first, I said to myself, "How does what I say fit into the project?" For me the point of the project was not to talk about oneself, but—and I only understood this later—to communicate a problem and to get people—including oneself—to understand it. Especially oneself! I realized that the *Porte-Parole* was intended for me, not for others.

Six months later, when I first listened to what was to be put on the *Porte-Parole,* it was quite strange. I wondered whether I still agreed with what I had said. During the recording, many things had been said, and I didn't think the cameraman would retain only certain points, like the battered women, for the tape. I was surprised and shocked; I didn't expect that at all. I thought the video would present the issues in a more general way, timely but more superficial. Fortunately I knew that only my mouth would be shown on the screen. If it were my face on the *Porte-Parole,* I wouldn't have worn it. There is nothing particularly singular about the mouth; for me the face is in the eyes. It's the eyes that convey feelings, not the mouth. We are recognized by our eyes or face. During the filming, when I touched on sensitive issues, I often cried as I spoke. But there are no tears on the tape.

Anyway, when you wear the object in the street, people can easily think that it is not your mouth that is on the screen. It's reassuring, and that feeling takes away some of the responsibility. You wear this object on your face, and it's something that is very, very close to you. Although the *Alien Staff* accompanies you, it does so at a distance. You wear the *Porte-Parole* on your person, and it's much harder. The hardest was the moments in public, and I hated them; I felt uncomfortable and anxious. First of all, the *Porte-Parole* doesn't make for a very aesthetic profile; physically it marks you and destroys the structure of your face. Yet at the same time, I noticed that some people were totally uninterested and did not even look over. You could wear just about anything on your face and they wouldn't react. It's too bad it takes something like that to communicate, that you have to wear something over your face to catch people's eye, for them to take an interest. It's a pity that this is what it takes to be heard, but if you have nothing and begin shouting in a supermarket, people will think you're crazy. . . . I think all those narrow people should be made to wear the *Porte-Parole.*

In any case, the issues I raised were intimate and personal ones, like that of battered women, and this was very hard to do in public places like train stations or supermarkets. People were not at all drawn to what I was saying; they don't

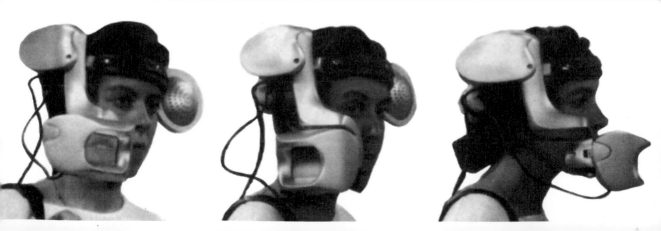

want their secrets revealed. . . . If I had been talking about something more general like racism or integrating foreigners into society, it would have been much easier to talk to them. But what I was saying was very personal, and my words went deep into people's hearts. I didn't feel comfortable, I felt like I was directly entering their private lives. I could feel the unease; I was cutting to the quick. I didn't want to approach people; I find that grotesque. Also, I was terribly emotional. It takes willpower and energy, and I didn't feel up to it. But I managed to continue, and I succeeded. I was amazed by how much willpower I was able to summon for the project. The morning they brought me the *Porte-Parole,* I felt like dropping the whole thing. But I said to myself, "I've got to go through with it," and I held up!

I did this project more for myself than for others. I didn't want people close to me to see the tape. I had told myself that I would never show the tape to my mother. . . . Finally I showed it to her. She watched it all the way through, but said nothing. I still don't know what she thinks of it. It was a big step just to show it to her. The next step would be to ask her what she thinks. But not now—the time isn't right yet. . . . But what she heard is what I really think. She heard my own voice; that's very different from a letter. A letter is you without being you.

During this project, we spoke a lot, but we never felt judged. No one ever said, "She said this or that. Why did she say that?" I think it's important not to judge people and to accept what they say. In fact, we self-analyzed ourselves! . . . Now I have another life. I analyze what I say, and it's the project that forced me to do that. . . . I live with my problems less, and that's the main thing. It is very hard, psychologically and physically, to wear the *Porte-Parole.* It's a burden, and it's crazy when you think we need something like that to communicate.

Excerpts from video programs broadcast by the *Mouthpiece* when used by various persons in Warsaw and in Trélazé, France, 1994–96; interview with Nathalie in Trélazé on November 20, 1997, one year after their performance, conducted by Emmanuelle Chérel; translated by Warren Niesłuchowski. Nathalie and and her fellow high-school student Peggy were the first nonimmigrants to use the *Mouthpiece.* They both asked that their last names not be used. For fear of being recognized in Warsaw by an Algerian fundamentalist network, the Algerian represented here asked another person to wear the *Mouthpiece* (while his voice and lips were speaking).

Xenology:
Immigrant
Instruments
(1996)

Xenology (from the Greek *xenos,* Latin *alienus*), the art and science of the stranger, is also the immigrant's art of survival. Historically the integrity of the community has often been measured by its openness to strangers. Today this openness to the stranger, whose contemporary form is the immigrant, has once again become a test for democracy. The representation of the stranger, the unfamiliar, interrupts the flow and continuity of the familiar. It seeks to convey its uniqueness, despite the fact that no one may be ready for such a presence. It proposes a vision of a better world, as an exceptional and difficult hope lived in the mode of the present.

This social and communicative utopia, as suggested by Walter Benjamin, emerges from a unique clarity discovered in the "revolutionary energy of the new," based on transporting personal experience into the historical. This new energy helps break the inertia that perpetuates past injustices provoked by fear of the stranger.

This is not only an ethical and philosophical program, but an aesthetic one. Based on an existing body of knowledge of the world—stories, histories, sacred and profane texts, literary and oral, lore and science, archives and correspondence, techniques of social and ethical know-how (with the Talmud as an example)—it constructs an aesthetics of self-creation and recognition. Being an immigrant is in some sense already being an artist, even a counterartist. It communicates the secret tradition of the vanquished (which never allows itself to forget) in opposition to the "history of the victors." It is an art of existential ethics, creating new communicative and performative forms for survival while employing ancient traditions of know-how in the design of tactically useful artifacts.

What occurs within each and every immigrant in our present world is far more interrogative, critical, and visionary than what occurs outside. A community for new Americans must be born of an unstable world of disagreements and antagonisms experienced within the newcomers themselves. One way to its realization is commitment to a community of artifice and play, a recognition that such an interior community is possible and can be developed. This requires the recognition of the presence of these strangers and newcomers in this community, which must continually question and delegitimize its own identity by asking strangers to play a central role as major actors in this vast ethical and aesthetic project on the stage of democracy. Xenology is the art of refusal to be fused, an art of delimitization, deidentification, and disintegration.

The life of an immigrant is an artistic process and requires special equipment. The *Alien Staff* and the *Mouthpiece,* immigrant instruments, are presented here as design contributions to xenology, inspired by it and intended to further its development. In one sense, the most important stage of the work is the psycho-aesthetic process that precedes the public appearance and operation of the *Alien Staff* or *Mouthpiece.* The immigrant operator's preparations: recollections, confrontations, and presentations of the self with the artifacts of his or her experience. Rather than proposing an art that refers to, interprets, or translates the experience of displacement, I propose the design of performative media equipment, albeit aesthetically conceived, to assist and inspire its migrant operators in the construction and exposition of their art as they take charge of their newly emerging identity.

Originally published as an exhibition statement distributed at the Galerie Lelong, New York, 1996.

Ægis: Equipment for a City of Strangers (1998)

The *Ægis* is the most recent instrument in my *Xenology* series, but, unlike previous instruments like *Alien Staff* and *Porte-Parole*, it may be freely used by anyone undergoing alienating experiences, not just immigrants. The *ægis* was the cloak of Athena, bearing a Gorgon's head, that she used to protect herself and others. The instrument is a piece of equipment designed to represent dual (and often dueling) truths, those living contradictions that both define, depict, and can sometimes destroy individual existence. Socrates, himself a stranger in Athens, appeared in three different roles: technician-teacher, prophet, and truth-teller. The truth (*a-lētheia:* that which is not to be forgotten; rescued from *Lēthē,* Oblivion) demands an ethics of "response-ability" that can withstand even the threat of being silenced. Revealing the complex truth of experience requires showing the contradictions—that between authenticity and assimilation, or between liberation of oneself and being bound to or for another. For example, an adequate answer to the seemingly simple and well-meaning, but ultimately deeply insulting, question, "Where are you from?" can only be given in the form of a dialogue between concurrently present images, and can never be achieved without revealing one's own contradictions. Perplexity can only be met with complexity. The containers of these contradictory images require an opener; and the process of disclosure, opening up—whether through a physical effort on the part of the messenger, some mechanical device, or, best of all, a sensor that responds to a verbal cue—is the heart of the *Ægis*.

The appearance of the stranger, in this new identity wearing and operating the proposed equipment, resembles that of an angel or prophet. The author of this project believes that contemporary strangers intentionally or unintentionally perform an angelic or prophetic mission in today's migratory and alienating world. They are messengers of a better world to come as well as critics of the unacceptable world in which they live. They announce and denounce the world. They are also discoverers of themselves in the process of disintegration and becoming, and invite others to join them in this self-exploratory process toward a new community of difference. I imagine crowds of strangers presenting themselves in such unsolicited disclosures as they make their way through the city. To help them do so successfully amidst the stormy interferences of the contemporary world of communications and media is the purpose of this special psychocommunications equipment.

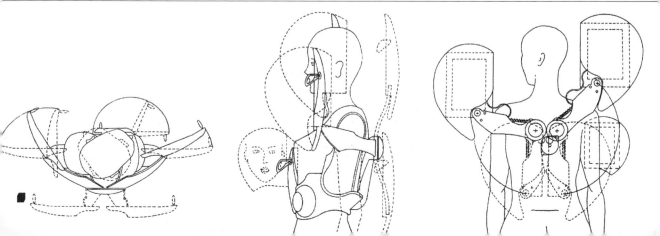

Technical Description

The *Ægis* is composed of a set of two winglike screens enclosed in a backpack hanging from the shoulders of its wearer, to be activated by a staff carried by the wearer. When the wearer is ready to deploy the equipment, the screens will unfold in response to physical, mechanical, or verbal cues (delivered either through pressure on the staff or words spoken into a microphone, for example) and simultaneously play prerecorded video and sound images of the wearer's face driven by a laptop computer.

Each of the many sequences will be activated by a specific cue, a given word or phrase designated in advance by the wearer. A microphone with a voice recognition system is fitted on the tip of the staff carried by the wearer, with a small shield to protect from the intrusion of ambient sound.

A more advanced version of *Ægis* will react to the changing verbal environment at any given place or time. It will respond to words spoken both by the wearer and by interlocutors. It will also react to words detected in conversations occurring around it, as well as any verbal material being disseminated by electronic media in the area. The voice-recognition system, microphones, and power supply will be located in the shieldlike housing covering the shoulders and chest of the wearer. This version will be hypersensitive and hyperresponsive to certain words or sentences, and will "hear" and "overhear" preselected speech without regard to speakers' intentions or the discursive context. In response to detected words, it will unfold its winglike screens and activate their spoken responses automatically, selectively, and without warning. The investigative argument between the faces seen and heard on the screens will explore and expose their perplexed and critical reactions to the word or sentence that triggered the response. The *Ægis* will appear as a device, a prosthesis, or a bodily extension that overreacts and behaves "inappropriately," with no "self-control." In order to calm puzzled, amused, or disturbed interlocutors, the wearer may choose to "explain" to them the "symptomatic" nature of the instrument (as one does on behalf of a unruly child), to switch the device off (folding and silencing the screens), or to let the *Ægis* continue speaking.

Preliminary discussions with potential users suggest that the most favored verbal cues for *Ægis* wearers revolve around the question "Where are you from?"

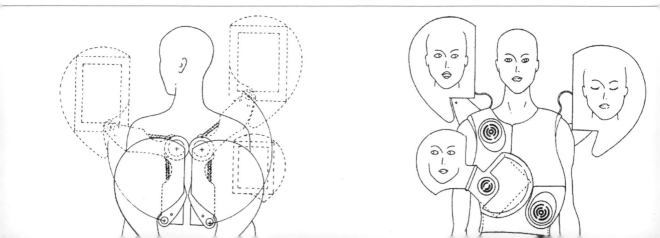

**Transcript of Preliminary Video Recording, to be Played
     Simultaneously on Two Screens of Ægis**

Left screen
Where are you from?
Where are you from?
Where are you from?

Enough!
I don't want to hear that any more!

Fi-gu-red out!

I don't want to be figured out.
Pigeon-holed.
I just don't, that's all.

What if we had met somewhere on a
trip around the world, and you
asked me, Where are you from,
and I asked you, And you?

Fine. Everything in order.
We're in the same boat.

And here
You're on your your own home
    ground,
And me from somewhere else.
From where, then?

Am I to explain how I got to your
    country?
Just a minute—
Can't this country be my country,
    too?
Am I supposed to go back where I
    came from?

You shrug.
You don't understand what I mean.

Right screen
Is that any way to start a
    conversation?
Where are you from?
I'm from here!
I'm me.
Just like you,
You're yourself.
With your own first and last name.

You're so smart—
You figured out my accent.
So quick?

Where am I from?—
I'm from outside.

What good will my answer do you?

Maybe give me a feeling of
    inferiority.

And you a feeling of superiority.

You're from here.

Your Highness.

Settled down.
Pacified.
Feeling at home.
No longer thinking of escaping.
Independent,
   Independent,
      And again, independent.
Reconstructed,
Remodeled,
Strong.
With faith in oneself
Because she proved herself in a
   foreign country.

Is that me?

But there's that tiny nose-tweak.
"Where are you from?"

Is the building already tottering?

You recognized my accent,
And asked where I was from.
Just like that.

So ask, "just like that,"
About anything else.
—My shoe size
—Do I like wild strawberries?
—Do I have goldfish?
But don't ask,

"WHERE ARE YOU FROM?"

Because that question creates an
   abyss between us
And it makes me feel
As tiny
As a dwarf
Next to you.

And I thought
I was grown-up.

Do you really
Want to be
A giant
Next to me?

Previously unpublished proposal. An experimental prototype of the *Ægis* is to be completed in the spring of 1999 with the assistance of Adam Whiton, Sung Ho Kim, and other members and students of the Interrogative Design Group at the Center of Advanced Visual Studies at MIT. Jagoda Przybylak and Jerzy Stypułkowski are consulting *xenologists*. Steve Weiss of Parallel Inc. and John Kuntsch of Brooklyn Model Works will collaborate in the fabrication of the final working models of the *Ægis*. This project is supported by the MIT Council for the Arts and the School of Architecture and Planning.

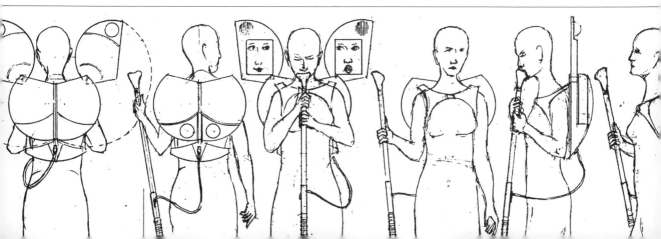

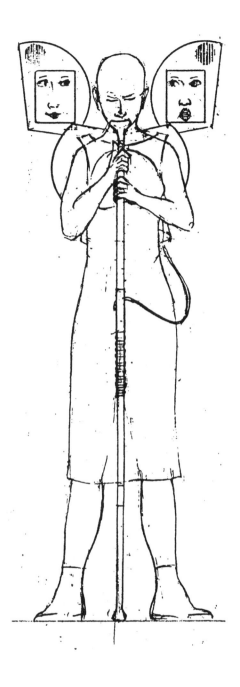

five **Questions**

A Response to the New Museum (1991)

Question: Is your work meant to provide a critical interpretation of the world in general or the world of art? In other words, are its references and concerns independent of art history and art criticism, or do you see your work as being situated in the continuum of art history, in which it relates to art of the past and/or to contemporary art with concerns parallel to yours?

Answer: My work would like to be independent of art history and art criticism, unless it takes as a reference the artistic avant-garde, especially constructivism and situationist aesthetic practices (if one were to assume that the Situationist International has become a part of art history). So, I could say that I feel some affiliations with the artistic avant-garde in terms of its relation to ethics and methods of public address and its relations to popular culture and the communication media. I am definitely not interested in making art which relies on artistic or art history references and formal codes, such as neo-Duchampian or post-pop art which plays sophisticated games with landmark strategies in modern art history. If I see any other relation in my work to situationist or futurist or constructivist or Fluxus work, I see this relation as interesting but superficial. It is only at the points of their interest in addressing audiences outside of the art system, and their disregard for art history as a reference and engagement in interventions within mainstream culture, that I feel connected. For me, then, the relation is more like an anti-continuum, or only an "anti-art" avant-garde continuum. . . .

But, at the same time, I am not really an avant-garde artist. My work only partially overlaps with that tradition since I am not a working member or a leader in a collective group, not do I have any concept of utopia, of a better society, nor do I believe that my work will contribute to revolutionary change. I am concentrating on the possible effect of my work *between* the revolutions, and on making a contribution to the level of critical discourse in the public space, creating alternative public spheres that would, together with the work of popular media artists and others, possibly make a revolution unnecessary. It is not a concept of a permanent revolution. I would like, for example, to see some kind of implosion of criticism in the public life of the city that would prevent us from a bloody social explosion, like the Paris Commune so favored by situationists.

Revised from a response to questions posed by Bruce Ferguson, in *Rhetorical Image,* exh. cat. (New York: New Museum of Contemporary Art, 1991), p. 85.

A Response to Maria Morzuch
(1992)

Morzuch: I would like to make a connection between your work from 1969 titled *Personal Instrument* (presently in the collection of the Muzeum Sztuki in Łódź) and your recent public projections. Despite the fact that your early "equipment" in its direct physicality (as the body, the photo cells, and sound filters) differed from later public projections which engage the larger socio-political sphere, can one see both projects as an examination of the problem of communication and silence, speaking and being mute?

Wodiczko: Since 1969 all of my works, from the *Personal Instrument* to the present projects, refer to the socio-political sphere. The *Personal Instrument's* silence is haunted by its public voice. Mysterious private play with public sound is its socio-political statement. By its very name, the *Personal Instrument* suggests its close association with private rather than public space. The private character of this instrument is made visible, however, only through its use of public space, on which it depends in two ways: first, as an acoustically active environment (it needs the sounds of the city to process), and second, as a socially active environment (it needs passersby who would observe its performance and imagine how it works).

The *Personal Instrument's* private character (privacy) is thus submerged in the public character (publicity) of this space, and this determines its social character (communality). The *Personal Instrument* is a public-private exaltation of the citizen's freedom. It is an art of private countercensorship.

The street presentation of the *Personal Instrument* in use was an attempt to create a public monument to a private human being in a monumental public space, in "state socialism" of the early 1970s, during the epoch of Gierek's liberal technocratic autocracy (comparable in some ways to Franco's late rule in Spain). It was a metaphoric articulation of the boundaries of freedom and of the ways of practicing it, as well as of the individual Polish citizen's reserves of power in relation to the use of public space.

The *Personal Instrument* was the point of departure for all my public projects; it was my first attempt to metaphorically define the situation of a human being as "citizen" in a totally controlled environment. It was also my first test run for tactics of speaking through public space under conditions of the practical deprivation of speech rights. Operating in space that was completely politicized by the state, I abandoned direct speech and proposed instead a technique of indirect but *public* speaking through half-silence/half-truth; a grotesque exaltation of virtuosity in creative listening. My current works (the public projections, the homeless vehicles, and the immigrant instruments) are a continuing investigation of the strategies of communicating through public space, but this time under the conditions of a nonautocratic yet troubling capitalistic system.

Since the days of the French Revolution, the public space of capitalist democracies has been intended to function as a space of communication (a space for the exercise of communicative rights). The Declaration of the Rights of Men and Citizens (France, 1791) assured communicative rights as a fundamental human right. And the active practicing of this right was recognized as the only means of spreading and reinforcing it. Public speech was considered a primary civic responsibility. Democracy and freedom are therefore everyday practices. Rather than something given or guaranteed, as a gift from "good authorities," they should be understood as an obligation to communicate through public space, to insert one's original voice, to voice one's own opinion, to share a public discourse.

It is my opinion that art is an alternative act of speech and an important ingredient of the practice of democracy. Active and critical art helps democracy to preserve its life.

Under the conditions of life in existing public space, democracy as the practice of making oneself heard (instead of passively listening to someone else's voice) is possible almost everywhere, including Poland. However, communicating one's own critical voice through the kind of public space that exists today is a truly difficult political, cultural, and aesthetic undertaking. Poland must learn how to do it "from scratch," just as I was forced to learn it after my departure from Poland in 1977. To make the passage from "speaking through silence" (critical listening) to "speaking through voice" (critical speech), despite and often against the presence of great orators who are speaking too much already and who do not intend to stop speaking, is the real task of the artistic speech act. How is one to speak in or through a space jammed with powerful voices? How is one to treat such a crowded space as an instrument of democracy when this instrument is not in our hands and when public space is barricaded and sealed off by the colossal bodies of the great speakers (demagogues), ringing with the choirs of advertisements, and occupied by armies of heroic memorials?

The strategy of public art, as an art that is critical and not official, is the object of my socio-aesthetic investigations and experiments, while public space is both their terrain and their stake. Today art is one of the voices in the complex discourse of power and freedom taking place within the space of the city. To be silent in such a city would mean to give a sign of agreement and a seal of approval to the disappearance of public space and consequently the disappearance of democracy. Without disturbing voices, such public space would become in the end a private space for the rulers, who would consequently be its owners. It would become a totalitarian work of art, created by real-estate magnates, drug lords, landlords, and city politicians corrupted and coopted by the present-day corporate and industrial action groups.

The public space in Poland would then become a capitalist extension of Stalinism, a stage for a life in the nightmare of "capitalist realism" as the only and official response to the demand for public art. The *Personal Instrument* would once more become the only critical option permitted. And then once more a proletarian revolution, and again a battle for the return of a democratic public space? I would not like this scenario to have to happen again.

Excerpt from Maria Morzuch, "Krzysztof Wodiczko z Instrumentem osobistym/ l'Instrument personnel," in *Krzysztof Wodiczko,* exh. cat. (Łódź: Muzeum Sztuki, 1992); reprinted in *Museum Sztuki w Łodzi, 1931–1992,* exh. cat. (Lyons: Musée d'art contemporain et Espace lyonnais d'art contemporain, 1992).

Deutsche: Last winter you showed *The Homeless Projection* as a proposal in a New York gallery. What procedures would be required to execute the work in its proposed site of Union Square?

Wodiczko: I can only recall for you the procedures required for a work proposed for Washington Square in 1984. It was explained to 49th Parallel, the gallery that helped organize the project, that permission was needed from the New York City Department of Parks and Recreation and from the community board of the area. In that case, the Parks Department had no objections, but the community board, which was asked for approval on short notice, said no. A single individual, the head of the community board, was responsible for the refusal, because the decision had to be made in an interval between board meetings. He explained that the board had refused many other proposals, apparently because they are not interested in organized public events, which they feel would disturb the normal activities of the park. As you know, Washington Square has a very rich life, students, people exercising, drug traffic. I haven't attempted yet to realize *The Homeless Projection,* but I assume the procedures would be the same for Union Square.

Prospect Park, which administers Grand Army Plaza, where I did a projection in 1995, also has an agreement with the local community board. I was told that the agreement states that any cultural or artistic event that would bring politics to the park should be excluded. I was given the impression that my *Grand Army Plaza Projection* should not be politically explicit.

Deutsche: What do you suppose they think public art is?

Wodiczko: I think they want public art to consist of undisturbing but spectacular events or objects that will satisfy the community in an easy and immediate way, which I do not wish to oppose initially. It is essential to be able to take advantage of any administrative desire for art in public places, to "collaborate" in such events and infiltrate them with an unexpected critical element. In this case the main event was the annual Brooklyn New Year's Eve gala, with a fireworks display by the Grucci family, music, and hot cider. My projection was intended as an integral part of the event.

Lajer-Burcharth: What was the reaction of the authorities who contracted you to do the event?

Wodiczko: I was invited to participate by Mariella Bisson, a special officer in the Prospect Park administration for organizing an art-in-the-park program. She is an artist herself and is very knowledgeable about the park's history, a committed "patriot" of the park, devoted to the notion of the park as a space of both historical and contemporary aesthetic experience. She has created a sculpture gallery in the interior—monstrous in its scale—of the Soldiers and Sailors Memorial Arch, and another art gallery in the boathouse in the park. She thought that one of my projections, regardless of its subject, would create an added attraction for the gala, differentiating this year's event from previous ones. But her supervisor was not informed about what I intended to project, even though it was known some two weeks in advance, since we had to do trial runs. Instead, the supervisor learned of the projection from the *New York Times,* whose section on what to do on New Year's Eve mentioned that U.S. and Soviet missiles would be projected on the arch. That must have smelled of politics to the supervisor. Not knowing how my projections function, how they illuminate the relation between image and architecture, the park administration evidently feared they had condoned a work of political propaganda. But once the projection was in place, it didn't have the shock of propaganda; the missiles looked very natural there. The projection lasted for only one hour, from 11:30 to 12:30 the next year, and when the supervisor arrived it was all over. But she still wanted to see it, so even though I was packing up my equipment, I set it up again for her. She was amazed by her own positive reaction to it, seduced by the brightness and glamour of the image, "pleasantly surprised," she said, by the integration of image and architecture. "The customer must be satisfied. Misunderstandings are out of the question!" as Witkiewicz wrote in the epigraph for his "Rules of the Portrait Firm" in the 1930s.[1] I heard that the threatened reputation of the art officer was restored immediately.

Crimp: What about the people who came to see the fireworks?

Wodiczko: That's a different story. Part of the public was disappointed that the slides didn't change. Slide projections mean, for most people, a "slide show," a multi-image spectacle. Because the public had to look for other aspects of the image than those of relationships between different images, they had to try to see the relation between the image and the architectural form. At first, people don't see architectural structures as images in themselves; they see them

as physical surfaces, as screens for the projection. But keeping the image static helps to integrate it with the architecture.

Deutsche: How many people saw the projection?

Wodiczko: I was told that 1,400 people attended the event, but since the Grand Army Plaza is Brooklyn's major vehicular traffic circle and the red lights forced cars to stop exactly in front of the projection, many more hundreds of people must have seen it. Many cars stopped or slowed down despite the green light, and some circled around for a second look. Most of the people who came to the event were from the black and Hispanic community in Brooklyn, many of whom were school children. They were people who had no place else to go to celebrate New Year's Eve. Some members of the cultural intelligentsia, as well as some junior high school students who had seen photographs of my projections shown at the New Museum at that time, made an effort to be there. The projection was on the north side of the arch and therefore could be seen, not from Prospect Park, but from the small adjacent park in front of which the arch stands. Cars drive all around that park, making it a very circumscribed and intimate viewing area. There are no sculptures or reliefs on the north side of the arch. This is a monument to the Northern army, so the south side of the arch is very busy with representations of the army marching south to liberate the South from "wrongdoing." The monument has absolutely nothing to say about the North, because if it did, it would have to reflect on itself. So despite the fact that the arch is symmetrically designed to carry sculptures on both sides, there is no sculpture on the north side.

Lajer-Burcharth: So you were interested in completing the monument symmetrically with images that ironically echoed the structure and the elements on the southern side. For example, you projected a padlock, a sign of constraint and limitation, on the keystone of the arch as a dissonant equivalent of the figure of liberation, the winged victory.

Crimp: It also reinscribes the North/South conflict with an East/West orientation.

Wodiczko: After growing up in the "East" it certainly helps to arrive in the "West" from the north, by which I mean Canada, in order better to see all sides

of the arch, especially the repressed, northern side. Ironically, this arch, which is conceived as receiving the victorious Northern army and which uses a classicizing beaux-arts style, is challenged by two small realist bas-relief sculptures by Eakins placed inside the arch. They are the only two figures actually walking north, coming back from the war, extremely tired. One of the horses is limping. As far as I know, this is the only monument in the world that contains such an internal debate, aesthetically and historically. The fact that a realist was allowed to enter the beaux-arts domain in reverse direction is extraordinary.

Anyway, my reorientation of the arch to an East/West conflict converts the reading of the arch from its commentary on the South to one of left and right, to the weight of the arch's two bases. The people viewing the projection offered their own interpretations. What I liked was that everyone was trying to impose his or her reading upon others. It turned into a political debate based on reading the symbols and referring to the contemporary political situation. It was a time when the public was being prepared for impending peace talks between the U.S. and Soviet governments. There were great expectations about coming back to the conference table and perhaps for a reduction of the arms race. I wanted to respond to this, but, of course, it's impossible today to be optimistic and intelligent at the same time. So I wanted the people to see various possibilities. But since everyone was interested in convincing others of his or her own reading, only a few seemed to realize that the various readings were all simultaneously possible. One reading was that the missiles were two phallic symbols. Another was that the projection was about disarmament, the nuclear freeze, the liberal position. And a third group spoke of the interdependence of the superpowers, the fact that they are locked together, that they cannot exist without each other, and that there is a frightening similarity between them. Because the debate was open and easily heard, all the readings were most likely received by everyone, and hopefully this social and auditory interaction helped the visual projection survive in the public's memory as a complex experience. For a moment at least, this "necro-ideological" monument became alive.

Halfway through the projection, behind and above the arch, there was another audiovisual experience for eight minutes that gave the projection a new, enhanced context. The fireworks—detonations, explosions, aerial illuminations—this display would have had a double meaning for anyone who had experienced bombings of cities or who, growing up in the ruins of cities, had

seen films of those bombings. This was certainly the case for the Polish intellectuals among the spectators, among them the critic Szymon Bojko.

Bojko, who lives in Poland, wrote a popular book on Soviet constructivist graphic design.[2] He is able to address, both popularly and historically, the relation between art and propaganda. Through his connections in the Soviet Union, he knows a lot about Vkhutemas,[3] the Soviet predecessor of the Bauhaus. Working in the '60s in the cultural department of the central committee of the Polish United Workers Party,[4] Bojko managed to influence the committee with very clear ideas on the organization of industrial design education, research, and practice. He came to see my *Grand Army Plaza Projection* with a group of Polish and American friends from New York, so I was very interested to see how they would respond. They were relieved to see that there were both Soviet and U.S. missiles, because they had heard that one of my projections in Stuttgart consisted of only a Pershing II missile and that one in Canada was of only a U.S.-built Cruise missile. So there was probably some talk of my not acknowledging both sides of the problem, which is a very sensitive issue in Poland. They also suggested the reading of the interdependence between the superpowers, and some of them mentioned the ironic relationship between the heroic monumentality of the arch and the new "heroism" and "monumentality" of intercontinental ballistic missiles. Poles are very well educated about public monuments. As the Polish playwright Sławomir Mrożek put it, "Somewhere between the monuments and the memorials lies Poland."

Lajer-Burcharth: Your projections also remind me of an important aspect of Polish May Day parades. The focal point of the parades, the pompous facades of the socialist-realist buildings on the main street in Warsaw, used to be adorned with huge, four-story-high portraits of contemporary Polish heads of state hung side by side with those of Marx and Lenin. This display was obviously a kind of wish fulfillment of the Polish rulers anxious to secure symbolic continuity between themselves and the unquestioned heroes of the communist past. The socialist-realist architecture was made to reinforce this continuity with the authority of its classicizing forms. And the portraits reciprocated as an endorsement by the current leadership of the excessive grandeur of this postwar architecture. Obviously, the effect of your projections is very different. Far from this reciprocal completion, the clashing of image and architecture calls into question the authority of both. But wouldn't you say that the Polish context is relevant to your attitude toward images of authority?

149

Wodiczko: Yes, to the extent that the architecture of the '60s, and even more so that of the '70s, the Gierek era, embodied a new style, a fetishism of progress, a Westernized, technocratic version of progress (echoing Lenin's New Economic Policy), a "state productivism," if I may put it that way. In this period the acquired capitalist, "scientifically exploitative" organization of production was wedded to the state socialist, centrally planned, bureaucratic exploitation of workers' labor; all in the name of achieving a higher, which is to say, closer to Western, standard of living. The environmental evidence of Gierek's new "New Economic Policy" was painfully visible in the form of the rapid development of office towers, gigantic hotels, shopping centers, automobiles, superhighways, and urban vehicular arterials. In this context, the grand official manifestations of the '70s provided an opportunity to see very clearly the propaganda effects of both the earlier, Stalinist architecture, which now looked "romantic," and the new, Western-style, abstract, technocratic architecture.

Lajer-Burcharth: With the advent of Gierek an important change was introduced into the official symbolic practices in order to take account of the new economic order. In the May Day parades, portraits of contemporary Polish leaders were no longer used. Gierek's leadership was represented instead by such signs of technocratic progress as the new Forum Hotel, built by a Swedish contractor, at the site where the parade ends. This building and others built in the '70s became the backdrops for portraits of Marx and Lenin. The architecture itself was intended to testify to the successful continuation of their ideals.

Crimp: Are you saying, then, that this kind of political manifestation was central to your own understanding of the relationship between image and architecture?

Wodiczko: It did help to be able to see the impact of a grand but temporary political decoration on the public's perception of buildings, of the cityscape as whole. It also helped me to understand the effect of the absence of such decorations after they were taken down, to remember the architectural "afterimage" of a political slogan or icon, its lasting but illusive integration with the building. Such an experience suggests, of course, the possibility of a temporary, *unofficial, critical* "decoration," difficult to imagine in Poland, where censorship of the public domain is total, but a little easier to imagine here, where censorship is also strong but less centralized. Generally, Poland was a great laboratory of environmental ideology. But the imagery of official Polish propaganda is so architectural itself, perfect to the point of its own death. The obvious, sloganistic character, the lifeless appearance makes Polish imagery less subversive, less seductive, appearing to be less "natural" than American propaganda imagery, such as advertising or even an official event like the "Liberty Celebration." But Polish propaganda does have a powerful architectural quality which integrates well with the ideological/architectural environment. So I did learn much in Poland, but my education needed to be completed in the context of capitalist consumer culture. It was an advantage that I first went to Canada, where cultural studies of media and communication are very strong. My teaching affiliation with the Cultural Studies Program in Peterborough, Ontario, was important in this regard. Only after several years outside Poland was I able fully to comprehend the degree to which artists and designers in Poland were ideologically trapped by the Westernized, "liberal" state socialism of the '70s. Artists earned their freedom to work with what were called "various means of expression," that is, to exclude official politics from their art, by including those very politics in the work they did on commission for the state propaganda apparatus. So one was political as a collaborator-artist in the morning and apolitical as a "pure" artist in the evening in the confines of one's studio. Only a few artists and designers realized that in such a situation they were really acting as collaborators with the system—not in the morning but in the evening.

Crimp: Was this your experience?

Wodiczko: Not really. I was an industrial designer working full time in the design office of the Polish Optical Works in Warsaw, so I was not working freelance, not vulnerable to the changing desires of the ideological design market, and not needing to work for the propaganda apparatus as most painters, sculptors, and graphic designers did. I worked in a factory designing professional instruments such as microscopes, measuring devices, electronic systems for quality control, scientific research, laboratory, and medical purposes. At one point I was on a design team that was asked to design a geological compass.

Lajer-Burcharth: An ideological compass?!

Wodiczko: You almost spoiled my story, because you understand too quickly. There were all sorts of demands coming from the industrial brass to come up with a less professional, more popular tool in response to Gierek's program for an increase in the production of consumer goods. That was, of course, an idiotic demand for a professional instruments company. So I said publicly, in the design office, that we would design this compass only if there were no member of the Communist Party on the design team, because north is north, not east or west. A compass can only show magnetic north. Somehow, nothing happened to me, perhaps because as an industrial designer, a member of a still-young profession, I was treated as an eccentric in the industrial world. As a graduate of the Academy of Fine Arts, I was also treated as an "artist" even though I did everything I could to counteract that view. This experience taught me how thoroughly design is submerged in politics. I learned a lot about politics even regarding the most innocent measuring instrument, something that can be done only in the most technical manner. Imagine what my designer friends were going through when designing refrigerators!

Deutsche: What was your background before you worked as an industrial designer? Can you tell us something about your education?

Wodiczko: In the Soviet Union in the '20s the educational path led from fine art to design, from analytical constructivism to productivism. For me, in the '60s and '70s, the situation was, of course, different. The period of Gomulka's de-Stalinization in Poland provided an opening for contact with Western design circles, such as the school in Ulm,[5] and with those of prewar avant-garde design, such as Blok, Praesens, a.r.,[6] and the Koluszki school.[7] I studied at the Academy of Fine Arts in Warsaw in the '60s. The graduate program in industrial design, in which I was student, was directed by Jerzy Sołtan, a former assistant of Le Corbusier. At that time Sołtan was directing a similar program at Harvard, teaching the fall term in Warsaw and the spring term in Cambridge. I'm sure that Szymon Bojko's support was crucial to Sołtan's success in Poland. Sołtan, his assistant Andrzej Wroblewski, now president of the academy, and Bojko had devised a post-avant-garde strategy for post-Stalinist Poland. The special education of designers was a key point of their strategy. The program emphasized the development of the students' individual and collective skills for infiltrating the institutional structure while working as common industrial designers, organizers of design offices in all branches of industry, teachers, researchers, and so on. It was a neoproductivist model. This was the period of the creation of the Industrial Design Council, whose head is vice-premier of the

government and whose members are vice-ministers. So industrial design was very highly bureaucratized, much better organized than in the West or in Lenin's Soviet Union. I was trained to be a member of the elite unit of designers, skillful infiltrators who were supposed to transform existing state socialism into an intelligent, complex, and human design project. This positive social program for industrial design, indebted historically to the program of Vkhutemas, unfortunately shifted in the Gierek era to a technocratic, consumerist phase and thus adopted the international constructivist tradition in place of constructivism proper, the latter being the constructivism that developed in the Soviet Union as a means of building a society rather than decorating bourgeois society with objects. The depoliticization of constructivism's history was a very unfortunate part of our experience as artists. There is a famous museum of constructivism in Łódź.[8] In the '70s it was already quite clear that the effect and perhaps even the mission of this museum was to depoliticize the entire constructivist tradition, intellectual and artistic, affiliating it more and more with international, Western constructivism, the de Stijl movement, and neoconstructivism such as op and kinetic art.

Lajer-Burcharth: This tendency to depoliticize Polish constructivism by playing down its links with the Soviet experiment should be situated historically within the liberalization associated with Gierek. The reinterpretation of Polish artistic traditions as independent from Soviet art paralleled the reorientation of the Polish economy toward the West. This view of constructivism was also part of the defensive reaction to the postwar imposition of Soviet art policies in Poland, that is, to socialist realism. The imposition of Zhdanovist orthodoxy stalled any discussion of the alternative forms of culture for the new socialist society until the late '50s.

Wodiczko: Quite openly so. As part of the six-year plan of 1949, the guidelines of the council of architects specifically declared socialist realism a critique of constructivism. This "critique" collapsed the complex history of constructivism into one international bourgeois movement, excoriated as "cosmopolitanism, constructivism, and formalism," whose "abstract forms" were said to be "always foreign to the people." But the Stalinist position, for all its regressive effect, was at least conducted in the name of social responsibility, socialist content, the national cultural heritage, a human form for the environment, and so on. The Stalinist era represented a total politicization of art and design, including a politicization of the war against constructivism. The Gierek era, by contrast, represented a total depoliticization of art and design including a war on constructivism carried out through its depoliticization. This most recent perversion of constructivism, then, resulted in what I call socialist technocratism.

Deutsche: So there was a depoliticization of constructivism in the East that is directly parallel to that in the West.

Lajer-Burcharth: Except that in Poland this process took place in a more overtly political context. In the West the depoliticization of constructivism was effected by the art-historical discourse, while in Poland it was an element of national cultural policy. The attempt to restore to constructivism its real history that is now taking place in the West has also begun in Poland, especially in the work of Andrzej Turowski. His *Polish Constructivism* appeared as late as 1981,[9] but Turowski wrote an earlier, popular analysis of constructivism in a book series devoted to twentieth-century avant-garde movements.

Wodiczko: His title for the earlier book was *The Constructivist Revolution,* which suggests the interplay between aesthetic and political revolution. The editors changed it to *In the Circle of Constructivism.*[10] It is against editorial policy to acknowledge openly anything as political, including constructivism. Turowski's repoliticization and rehistoricization of constructivism was a crucial experience for me. The Foksal Gallery, of which Turowski and Wiesław Borowski were the codirectors, had established itself as a center of criticism of artistic culture. It is a type of alternative gallery not really known here in that it was run collectively by critics, and not by artists. Through the presentation of works of art, critical texts, and debates, the gallery wished to affect the larger context. They applied the avant-garde style of manifestos and interventions, but "post-avant-garde" to the extent that they accepted the limitation of utopia, dealing as they were with a reality that was already organized in the name of utopia.

When Turowski entered the gallery as a young scholar of constructivism, he contributed a Marxist methodology to the gallery's tactics and strategies, which was a very significant change, because at that time the gallery critics and artists were operating with surrealist ideas. Turowski's presence resulted in a fusion of a moral critique of established artistic culture with a social critique, and self-critique, of that culture's institutions. Turowski wrote a very important short text entitled "Gallery, against Gallery." It was the beginning of the concept of the gallery as a self-critical institution, an institution questioning its own place in society in relation to other institutions, and doing so to the extent of putting into question the entire institutional system of culture. Foksal also published texts called "What We Don't Like about Foksal Gallery" and "Documentation," which called for the destruction of all the art documents. The "Living Archive" created the exaggerated idea of an archive that would protect documents by preventing their further circulation and cultural manipulation.

Lajer-Burcharth: This occurred in response to censorship. In Poland, unlike other Soviet bloc countries, a certain independence is granted within the domain of culture so long as culture is willing to contain itself and refrain from interaction with other social activity. Foksal Gallery was one such island of cultural criticism that was allowed to exist. But even this self-imposed marginalization did not guarantee complete freedom of operation. When I was involved with another alternative gallery, founded after Foksal, we managed to publish several issues of a journal about critical aesthetic practices without asking for party approval for our editorial staff. We did this by using the paper allotted us for the publication of exhibition catalogues. Soon, though, we were forced to discontinue publication, not because of any specific contents, but because it is prohibited to put out a serial publication, something that can be distributed and read regularly, without the consent of the centralized apparatus of the state. Seriality itself threatened to spill culture outside its prescribed limits.

Wodiczko: The experience with censorship, with official culture, and with the entire institutional system, the changing meaning of each form of cultural activity in political circumstances, was a central part of my experience in Poland, especially because of my affiliation with Foksal Gallery but also because of my father. Throughout the period of Stalinism and the Gomulka and Gierek eras, my father was involved with serious cultural politics as a conductor and artistic director of city and state orchestras and opera companies. He was famous for introducing the Polish public to the contemporary, artistically ambitious repertoire.[11] People such as my father and those associated with Foksal Gallery learned to cope with the system of restrictions and liberties in order consciously to infiltrate and manipulate the system while also recognizing the extent to which they were being manipulated by the system. So, having close contacts with the mechanisms of censorship and self-censorship and with the politics of official artistic culture and of industry and education (I was teaching at Warsaw's Polytechnic), and having my father's example, I learned very quickly that we must adopt some kind of post-avant-garde strategy in Poland.

Lajer-Burcharth: Since you are speaking of the strategy of manipulating the system from within, of interfering with the codes, so to speak, were you familiar with the writings of Roland Barthes?

Wodiczko: Barthes was not unknown to me and my generation. Most of the French theoreticians, especially those working in the field of culture, were translated into Polish, possibly earlier than into English. Writings, films, plays, and art critical of contemporary bourgeois culture were always welcomed by the Polish censorship apparatus. It was, however, difficult to learn from writers like Barthes how to operate critically within the Polish situation. Once one realized the best strategies for one's own place, though, it was easier to understand what Barthes was suggesting for the West. But we should not forget that the situation during the late '60s and early '70s was in some respects similar in France and Poland. We lost our student battles in 1968, too. We lost faith in our utopian revolutionary approach, and we needed new strategies. Polish students' demands differed from those of the French students, but there were many similarities. Poland and Czechoslovakia were part of the overall movement in the '60s. So after the failure of all of our revolutions, we found ourselves in similar situations, whether we happened to be reading Barthes or not. I wonder, by the way, whether Barthes would have understood the strategies of Foksal Gallery in the context of French cultural politics of the same period. But you know very well that Poland and France have been very closely connected. Many Polish students witnessed what happened in France in 1968. Turowski was one of them. The work of Daniel Buren and the Support-Surface group would not have been clear to me without the conversations with Turowski and some of his friends from Poznań . . .

Lajer-Burcharth: In Poznań there is a dynamic Marxist intellectual milieu, a rarity in Polish academic life.

Wodiczko: I realized that what the Polish constructivists Katarzyna Kobro and Władysław Strzemiński were dreaming about, "the organization of the rhythms of life" as the ultimate aesthetic project, was already organized all around us. So, learning from the constructivists the relationship between society and form among politics, art, and everyday life, by combining this with the knowledge of futurist, dada, and surrealist interventions, we could begin to understand that our aim was not to contribute to the further organization of the "rhythms of life," but to interrupt, interfere, and intervene in the already highly organized "rhythms of life."

Crimp: So this strategy of interruption or interference, which might be said to characterize your work now, is something that you had already developed in the Polish context.

Wodiczko: Yes, seeds of my critical activity here in the public sphere can be found in my early works in Warsaw, especially in the two "de-constructivist" technical "inventions." The first of these was *Instrument,* presented to the public in Warsaw in 1971. I designed it with the help of technicians from the Experimental Music Studio. It was an electro-acoustic instrument/costume that transformed, through my hand gestures, the accidental noise of city traffic into modulated sounds that only I could hear. The second was *Vehicle,* constructed with the help of Foksal Gallery, and shown publicly in Warsaw in 1972. Through a system of gears and cables, the vehicle was propelled forward by perpetually walking back and forth on its tilting top surface. It thus transformed the conventional back-and-forth pacing associated with intellectual reflection or with being stymied into the forward movement associated with the official notion of progress. You can see that my metaphoric vehicle was an ironic reconsideration of such an optimistic, techno-socialist project as Tatlin's *Letatlin.*[12]

Deutsche: If, to some degree, your work still involves the interruption of the official organization of society, how does such a strategy function here, in a different context? In Poland, as you've explained, you had to work within a social organization that includes official and overt censorship, while here censorship functions very differently; the entire organization of the social is much less apparent, much less obvious. How do you transfer the ideas which had formed your strategies in Poland to a different context?

Wodiczko: By trying to intervene in the public sphere as close as possible to the legal and technical limits that are imposed. Acting in the public sphere in the West, I have confronted not only censorship, but a different level of it. There is a greater general possibility for working in public, but this creates a need for more complicated strategies to deal with a complex set of institutional, corporate, state, and community restrictions. But the "transfer of ideas" to the West must be discussed in relation not only to forms and categories of censorship, to different kinds of artistic unfreedom, but also to the applicability of the ideas to the new situation. It is safe to say, however, that, despite all the differences, there are great similarities in our everyday lives in relation to our physical environment, whether in Poland, Canada, the U.S., or the Soviet Union. There are similarities in the ways that architecture functions as an ideological medium, a psychological partner, in the way it educates, orders, participates in the process of socialization, in the way it integrates its "body" with our bodies, in the ways it rapidly changes or even destroys our lives. My public projections developed first in Canada, because in Poland I could not even consider such an art form simply because of technical limitations, and obviously because of the censorship of the public sphere. Even to use images from the press for my gallery projections, which I had done in an exhibition called *References,* I needed to have permission, because individuals don't own images; the state does. The result is that it is impossible to change the context of images, because the state is perfectly aware of the semiotics of the image. In order to use images, one must resort to metaphor rather than direct statement.

Crimp: Do people learn to read metaphors better in such a situation than they do here, to perform a hermeneutic operation on every image?

Lajer-Burcharth: This is, in fact, how culture survives. Filmmakers, writers, and artists who want to comment on social reality usually employ metaphor. Otherwise their possibilities of affecting public opinion are very restricted.

Deutsche: But can't the censors also read those metaphors?

Lajer-Burcharth: Yes, they can, but they are also embarrassed to admit that they can recognize them, because that would imply that they are aware of the shortcomings or problems that the metaphors address. They are afraid to admit to the pertinence of the criticism. This is why the books of the journalist Ryszard Kapuściński, which expose the corruption of such regimes as those in Ethiopia and Iran,[13] are permitted to be published. Otherwise, the censors would implicitly acknowledge their recognition of the analogies of those regimes with the regimes of Eastern bloc countries, of Poland itself.

Wodiczko: One must read Dostoyevsky's *Crime and Punishment* to understand the relationship between censor and censored. You learn the language of the censor in order to communicate, and, to some degree, the censor must also learn your language. There is a final episode to the narrative of *The Grand Army Plaza Projection* that is relevant here. Several months ago I went to Poland and presented Foksal Gallery with a proposal to show a reconstruction of the project in the gallery. The idea was submitted to the censorship board, and the woman in charge explained that it would be impossible to present the work because it would violate article number eight hundred and something or other of the censorship code, which says that under no circumstances are weapons of the U.S. and Soviet Union to be visually depicted as of equal weight, volume, or quantity. An exhibition of documents of my public projections is opening at Foksal Gallery in September this year with *The Grand Army Plaza Projection* and a few others excluded. A catalogue with reproductions of the projections and my theoretical texts is being published. The texts, both in English and in Polish translation, are of course censored. "Public Projection," originally published in the *Canadian Journal of Political and Social Theory* in 1983, attempts to situate my work in the relations among body, architecture, power, and ideology. This was accepted for publication with only one "criticism"; the words *power* and *ideology* must be omitted entirely.

Deutsche: But presumably you knew what would not pass the censorship when you submitted your proposals.

Wodiczko: No, because the laws of censorship have changed. But also the very essence of authoritarian existence is that you never really know what is allowed and what is not. There used to be a "black book" of censorship, a general list of rules and regulations. That has now been replaced by a code of specific regulations, which is changed regularly in response to changing circumstances, so the situation is much worse now. It is much more difficult to fool the system when there are very highly qualified censors immediately interpreting changing conditions and implementing regulations. Some of these people have PhDs; they are "intellectuals." It is a perfect illustration of Marx's definition of censorship, which is that it is centralized criticism. So in Poland there is a kind of centralized art criticism. No one in Poland can complain of the lack of "critical response" to his or her work. Art criticism is democratically guaranteed!

Crimp: Apart from the contents of the images, what is the response in Poland, not only of the censors, but of the intellectuals, to the production mode of your work? Is there any problem of their reading this as aesthetic activity? Are they sufficiently aware of recent developments, albeit marginalized, in the West to understand your mode of working?

Wodiczko: I don't think there is a general problem with understanding my working methods in Poland, nor is there a problem of information about art developments in the West. Information about the West is temporarily limited today, but in the '70s it was quite accessible, and is beginning to improve again. Hans Haacke's and Daniel Buren's work, for example, is well known to Foksal Gallery, Akumulatory 2, Studio, and many other galleries. Foksal showed Lawrence Weiner, Art and Language, Victor Burgin, European and American Fluxus, and so on. Poland is marginalized less by lack of information about art in the West than by the lack of information about art in Poland available in the West.

Lajer-Burcharth: I don't think the political nature of Krzysztof's work would prevent people in Poland from accepting it as aesthetic practice. After all, they are used to looking for political messages coded in art rather than in the political discourse itself, which is considered totally corrupt.

Wodiczko: My work receives an informed response in Poland. If there is any problem, it is related to different perspectives on global politics, between my perspective, which developed just across the border from the U.S., and theirs, which develops across the border from the monstrous presence of the Soviet Union. Polish censorship and Polish intellectuals have similar but opposite doubts about my position with regard, for example, to the question of the equivalence of Soviet and U.S. weapons.

Crimp: What were the circumstances of your leaving Poland?

Wodiczko: I did not really leave Poland in 1977, in the sense that I had the idea of not returning. It's only that I didn't want to lose contact with the outside world. It was extremely crucial for me to see Poland from the outside. Each time I returned to Poland I was more aware of the extent to which social questions were neglected, how thoroughly we were locked into the prison of an Eastern

European perspective. My position was never met with much understanding, even within Foksal Gallery. As long as questions were limited to the politics of culture, things were fine, but when I went beyond that domain, my views were treated as irrelevant. So I wanted to continue to travel back and forth. How naive I was! Obviously there is no such possibility. You might not get your exit visa; then again you might also not get your entry visa to a country in the West. I had to face the typical dilemma. It was set up for me by the Polish police, who began to blackmail my friends, reading all of our correspondence and sometimes quoting telephone conversations verbatim in order to terrorize friends, who also needed to get exit visas. This particularly involved a woman whom the authorities discovered had previously been secretly traveling with me. In the eyes of both the Polish police and the immigration authorities of the Western states, this should never be done, because two people, especially couples, might not return. When one person leaves and the other stays, it's less suspicious to the bureaucracies in both East and West. The result was that my friend was psychologically assaulted by the police, and after a year was warned that she could leave only if I came back. The only answer to this was not to go back, because one should under no circumstances make a deal with the police. Such a deal often means to them that one is weak and frightened enough to accept other deals. I didn't want to lose my critical perspective about both socio-economic systems, I wanted to learn more from being here, but I never planned consciously to stay. But finally a decision was, in effect, made for me because one cannot stay anywhere indefinitely without papers. This is the sort of story that later gets collapsed into the "decision to emigrate."

Crimp: You were then in Canada?

Wodiczko: Yes. I had a number of part-time teaching positions there. The longest was at the Nova Scotia College of Art and Design in Halifax, where I taught for three and a half years. I began teaching in the design program but later moved to the intermedia program, for which I acted as coordinator for one year. It was a very fortunate opportunity, because that program is connected to the visiting artists program, so I was able to meet and work with people such as Martha Rosier, Mary Kelly, Dan Graham, Dara Birnbaum, Allan Sekula, Connie Hatch, Judith Barry. I also coorganized the Cultural Workers Alliance, a short-lived project, first in Toronto, then in Halifax. It was an unaffiliated umbrella organization of the left for members of the cultural intelligentsia, a forum

161 for political and artistic discussion, particularly focused on the labor situation in the cultural sector. I managed to involve a number of the more radical students from the college, which provided them with an opportunity to discuss the relationship between the college and the community, the politics of the province, and of Canada generally, something which could not easily be discussed within the college. Certain people at the college considered it a conflict of interest to give any such support to the radical students, but I thought it my obligation to involve them, to help them to see critically their place not only within the college but within the entire cultural system. It was during this period that I began working with public projections.

Deutsche: Were you invited to do a projection on the New Museum of Contemporary Art in New York, or did you apply for the opportunity? And what was your projection's relationship to the exhibition *Difference: On Representation and Sexuality*?

Wodiczko: I was asked to participate in the "On View" series, smaller exhibitions held in conjunction with major shows, such as the *Difference* exhibition. It was not my primary focus to relate my projection to that exhibition. If there was a relation to the *Difference* show, it was mediated through the relation of my projection to the architecture and to the politics of the entire building. The situation at that time was very dramatic. It was winter and I was living very close to the main shelter for homeless men and quite close to a shelter for women. I saw many people living on the street, trying to survive the bitter-cold temperatures by burning tires. It was therefore shocking to me to see one of the largest buildings in the entire neighborhood empty. It was very evident that the building that houses the New Museum was completely dark. People speaking to me at the time of the projection had no doubts whatsoever about the meaning of it. I learned that the upper floors of the building were awaiting new tenants at a price of nearly one million dollars each and at the same time the New Museum received the basement and ground-floor spaces for free, or at least for a very cheap rent. The very fact that the museum moved into the building creates a certain myth for the building. There are, in fact, two exhibition spaces there. One is for the New Museum exhibitions, and next door there is an exhibition of the former state of the building and how it will look after renovation, a real-estate exhibition. There is obviously a connection between the presence of the museum and the subsequent conversion of the entire surrounding area into one of art galleries and other art-related institutions and businesses. I'm not saying that there is direct responsibility on anyone's part, but this is a mechanism and it's important to recognize and reveal our place within that mechanism, even if we cannot change it at this point.

Crimp: It is my understanding that the Astor Building functions similarly to the Museum of Modern Art Tower; that is to say, the real-estate development of the tower is used to provide the financing of the museum's space and perhaps a portion of its operating costs. Is it not a part of your working methods, as it is of Haacke's, for example, to investigate the particulars of such a situation?

Wodiczko: If I were to project information onto the building about its operations I would certainly undertake systematic research, but what was immediately striking here was the emptiness of this huge structure when all around it people were living on the street. The bottom padlock was decided upon later, when I learned more about the connections between the museum and this art/ real-estate operation. So this was, first, *The Astor Building Projection,* and then, second, *The New Museum Projection.*

Crimp: Since we're on the subject of the New Museum, I wonder if you want to comment on the *Sots Art* exhibition shown there recently, insofar as it is a show of artists from the Eastern bloc, specifically the Soviet Union, working, with one exception, in the American context.

Deutsche: You've already made an interesting comment to me about the exhibition, noting that the museum relegated the critique of bourgeois culture— Connie Hatch's *Serving the Status Quo,* the Group Material work—to the small, back space while giving much greater prominence to the art which purports to be a critique of Soviet society.

Wodiczko: Without in any way taking back that comment, I have to express my enthusiasm for the fact that the New Museum provides so much space and time in its program for critical work, and I'm sure there are many reasons for a political stratification of that space. In order to survive, that institution must deal with a very complex situation, responding to the conflicting demands of its sponsors and supporters, as well as its various curators. If there had been a reversal of critical priorities in this particular case, it would have created a far

greater impact on the community, which I obviously would have preferred, but it is impossible for me to judge the organizers' intentions. So, in spite of many reasons for dissatisfaction, this last season at the New Museum consisted of a fair number of critical exhibitions, including, for example, *The Art of Memory, the Loss of History.*

Crimp: Perhaps I can refocus my question regarding a so-called dissident art by Eastern bloc artists showing in the American context by referring to the event organized for May Day at the Palladium by Komar and Melamid, two of the central figures in the *Sots Art* exhibition. They staged a mock May Day celebration in the discotheque which is partially owned by Roy Cohn, who, as you well know, is one of the most repulsive reactionaries in recent American political history and has recently been disbarred in New York State. Another of the owners, Steve Rubell, was quoted in the newspapers as saying that one of the things he liked about the Palladium was that it was a place were young people could forget about the problems of Nicaragua. The Palladium is also the discotheque that uses art-world celebrity events as the drawing card for its clientele.

Deutsche: In such a context, I don't see how Komar and Melamid's May Day celebration can be seen as anything but cynical.

Wodiczko: Not everything is to be seen from the perspective of the New Yorker. From the vantage point of global relations, I would like to try to see their point, which is not to say that I would support it. Though they have organized this event here, it is possible to imagine that they would prefer a double event, to stage simultaneously a discotheque in Red Square, for example. Perhaps they would like to be able to show the degradation of the Soviet May Day celebration by juxtaposing it with something equally degraded in this context, such as an art-world disco.

Lajer-Burcharth: But what is the purpose of staging this mockery of a Soviet political manifestation in New York in 1986? If Komar and Melamid want to criticize the atrophy of this particular symbolic practice, doing so in New York only diverts our attention from the historically specific factors responsible for this atrophy in the Soviet Union. And, when suggesting that these once spontaneous workers' celebrations ossified into their opposite in the East, do these artists wish to imply that the May Day parade has also lost its meaning in the

West? One of the reasons for the loss of meaning of the May Day parades in the Eastern bloc is constraint: people are forced to participate. But in the West participation is, of course, still voluntary. It was a great surprise to me to see masses of people joyfully celebrating May Day in Denmark, where I lived after leaving Poland. It is Komar and Melamid's glib implication of the cultural and political equivalence of the two that I find problematic.

Wodiczko: It would be interesting if such an event could be extended—not for balance, not to adopt the liberal position—to show the disco as equally ideologically determined, as equally a part of official life as the political manifestations in the Soviet Union. But, in fact, Komar and Melamid are not clearly critical of either system. They submerge themselves with perverse pleasure in the repressive realities of both Soviet and American existence, wallowing in what they see as the equivalent decadence of both empires. They perform art-historical manipulations to support their political nihilism, creating, for example, pop-art versions of socialist realism. I question the political clarity and social effectiveness of adopting pop-art strategies for the critique of Soviet culture. Even though they developed a powerful humor, which would have been a liberating experience in intellectual circles, it would hardly have been so liberating for anyone who did not enjoy the privileges granted to artists in the Soviet Union. There is a similar problem in the reception of their work here in the United States, where people only have the most general notions of socialist realism and of the Soviet reality.

Deutsche: In discussing *The Grand Army Plaza Projection* you mentioned various possible readings of the work. But there are other works, such as the projection of the swastika onto the pediment of the South African embassy in Trafalgar Square, that have very unambiguous meanings. Does the necessity of responding to specific political events suggest a different kind of projection?

Wodiczko: That was a very short-lived dilemma for me because I had to make a decision very quickly. I already had permission for the projection on Nelson's Column, permission to project hands onto the column. I had therefore already committed one violation in not projecting hands but rather a huge intercontinental ballistic missile wrapped in barbed wire, and tank treads underneath the lions at the column's base. But I knew they wouldn't be able to stop me. For one thing, bureaucracy doesn't work at night, even if the media does; BBC televised the projection nationally. I also knew that I had six xenon arc slide projectors concentrated in Trafalgar Square. No one knows when such an opportunity might happen again and it certainly never happened to me before. Many people would have liked the opportunity to affect this building, for example those who were demonstrating in front of it just at that time. The projection on Nelson's Column was to take place on two consecutive evenings. So the first evening, I came prepared with slides with spots of different sizes to test the proper focal length of the projection on the South African embassy. I had a very short negotiation with myself. Artists are so trapped in their own so-called histories. I thought, "Wait a minute, this is not the type of work you do. You do not project swastikas." But the other side of me answered, "So what? Just because you haven't done this sort of thing before doesn't mean that there isn't a reason to do it now. What do you know of your so-called artistic development?" I agree with you, Rosalyn, that this might open up new possibilities for a more specific contextual type of intervention. It's public art, and one must respond to changing circumstances. It was just at this time that a delegation had come from South Africa to ask the British government for more money, which Thatcher actually gave them, a very shameful act. So my little negotiation was quickly resolved and I reproduced the swastika slides of different sizes. All I had to do was to use one of the projectors from the *Nelson's Column Projection* and turn its 400mm. lens ninety degrees. It was projected over the sign in the pediment, which many people knew. There is a relief of a boat, underneath which it says "Good Hope." This building is the most illuminated of all buildings in central London, obsessively illuminated, as if it were afraid to wake up in the morning and not find itself. The projection lasted for two hours. Of course, I consulted a lawyer. The only charge on which they would be able to arrest me was for being a public nuisance, and those were the grounds on which they stopped the projection. After two hours I saw the police sergeant coming. I switched off the projector and removed the slide, so he could do nothing. But he told me that if I were to resume the projection I would be arrested, and he also said, very pompously, "If I might offer my personal opinion, I find your projection in very bad taste." Photographs of the projection appeared in the press the following day in conjunction with condemnations of apartheid, so the South African embassy sent an official letter of protest to the Canadian embassy, which is just across Trafalgar Square, and which was exhibiting documents of my work. The Canadian embassy responded with a letter saying that the views of individual Canadian citizens are not the responsibility of the Canadian government.

Crimp: I'm curious to know more about the legalities of such a situation. Can a slide projection, which is after all immaterial, be considered a means of defacement?

Wodiczko: We should be precise. This is not a clear legal question but a para-legal response of the police based on their own interpretation of regulations. That doesn't mean that what I am doing is illegal, but neither does it mean that I cannot be arrested.

Crimp: Was it especially difficult to get permission from the Swiss government for the projection on the Swiss national parliament building?

Wodiczko: It was a bit difficult, especially for Jean-Hubert Martin, then director of the Kunsthalle in Bern, who was negotiating the permission for me, since my projection was done for a show he was coorganizing called *Alles und noch viel mehr.* I knew that I would have to use an image that would be acceptable to the bureaucracy, and here I think my Polish experience helped. One has to know the psychology of officialdom, which is in many ways similar wherever I work, because it involves the very concept of modern bureaucracy, the kind of bureaucracy which is supposed to be objective, objective in the sense of helping people take advantage of "democracy." I knew I wanted to project onto the pediment, since it was the only free surface on the building. It was a question of what would be acceptable, and then, when accepted, what would make a point. I figured no one would object to the image of an eye, and at the same time they wouldn't have to know that the eye would change the direction of its gaze, looking first in the direction of the national bank, and then at the canton bank, then the city bank of Bern, then down to the ground of Bundes-platz, under which is the national vault containing the Swiss gold, and finally up to the mountains and the sky, the clear, pure, Calvinist sky. It was difficult for them to refuse to cooperate because the work was part of the Kunsthalle show, which had already received the support of the city. Of course, the parlia-ment building belongs not to the city but to the federal government, which would not want to create tension between itself and the city. I had spent a

certain amount of time in bars in Bern and I learned there about the Swiss gold below the parking area in front of the parliament, a fact which most people in Switzerland take for granted. It's not, after all, so bad to be a tourist. Sometimes you learn things that local residents take for granted and are then able to expose the obvious in a critical manner. But of course tourism cannot simply be treated as an individual experience. It is becoming an ever more complex political phenomenon which requires its own analysis. I intend to focus my projectors on this phenomenon in my work for the Venice Biennale this summer.

Notes

1. S. I. Witkiewicz (1885–1939), painter, photographer, playwright, theoretician, created The Portrait Firm in 1925 as an ironic response to bourgeois conditions of art in Poland. "The Rules of the Portrait Firm" were first published in 1928. A translation into French appears in *Présences polonaises* (Paris: Centre Georges Pompidou, 1983), p. 73.

2. Szymon Bojko, *New Graphic Design in Revolutionary Russia* (New York: Praeger, 1972).

3. Vkhutemas, an acronym in Russian for Higher Art and Technical Workshops, was founded in the Soviet Union in 1920. In 1927 it was re-formed and renamed Vkhutein (State Higher Art and Technical Workshops); it was dissolved in 1930. For a brief history, see Szymon Bojko, "Vkhutemas," in *The 1920s in Eastern Europe* (Cologne: Galerie Gmurzynska, 1975), pp. 19–26.

4. Polska Zjednoczona Partia Robotnicza, the official name of the Communist Party in Poland, which was created during World War II from a merger of the Polish Socialist Party and the Polish Workers Party.

5. The Hochschule für Gestaltung was founded in Ulm, West Germany, in 1955. Walter Gropius delivered the inaugural address, saying, "The work once begun in the Bauhaus and the principles formulated there have found a new German home and an opportunity for wider organic development here in Ulm." The school was closed in 1968.

6. Blok (founded 1924), Praesens (founded 1926), and a.r. (Revolutionary Artists, founded 1929) were the major Polish constructivist groups as well as the names of their publications.

7. Katarzyna Kobro and Władysław Strzemiński taught at the industrial school in Koluszki in 1930–31 using a curriculum based on the educational principles of Vkhutemas and the Bauhaus.

8. At the instigation of Strzemiński and the a.r. group, an international collection of modern art was formed in 1931 at the museum of Łódź, now the Muzeum Sztuki.

9. Andrzej Turowski, *Konstruktywizm polski* (Warsaw: Polish Academy of Science, Institute of Art, 1981).

10. Andrzej Turowski, *W kręgu konstruktywizmu* (Warsaw: Wydawnictwa Artystyczne, 1979).

11. Bohdan Wodiczko (1911–1985) was conductor and artistic director of the Baltic Symphony, Łódź Symphony, Kraków Symphony, Polish National Orchestra, Polish Radio Orchestra, Łódź Opera, and Polish National Opera. He was responsible for introducing postwar Polish audiences to Stravinsky, Berg, Nono, and other modern composers, as well as for engaging such avant-garde figures as Tadeusz Kantor as directors of opera productions.

12. Vladimir Tatlin worked on his flying machine *Letatlin* between 1929 and 1932, at which time he attempted to launch it. He called his glider "an everyday object for the Soviet masses, an ordinary object of use."

13. Ryszard Kapuściński, *The Emperor: Downfall of an Autocrat,* trans. William R. Brand and Katarzyna Mroczkowska-Brand (San Diego: Harcourt Brace Jovanovich, 1983), and *Shah of Shahs,* trans. William R. Brand and Katarzyna Mroczkowska-Brand (San Diego: Harcourt Brace Jovanovich, 1985).

Originally published in *October* (New York), no. 38 (Winter 1986), pp. 22–51.

Wodiczko: Listen, isn't it true that the cultural value of all symbolic structures in the city—whether they are statues or buildings (historic or contemporary), whether they were intentional or unintentional, built or adopted as monuments—depends on the city-dwellers' ability and opportunity to project and juxtapose new meanings on those structures? That is, doesn't their value depend upon the ability to place them in present situations, confront them mentally with the contemporary social context, and imagine, for example, what those monuments "see" (or do not see) when they "look" at the homeless people on their steps? What kind of meaning or appearance can these monuments assume—monuments on the federal (not city) territory of the Washington, D.C. Mall—when they "look" at the current presidential election campaign?

Now, the problem is how much we artists and intellectuals of different kinds—activists, urban geographers, ethnographers, community workers—how much can we activate those symbolic sites to help them to operate as places of critical discourse. What activities can we develop in addition to the organization of urban protest and resistance or defense against police-instigated gentrification battles (the Tompkins Square battle is the most recent example)?[1] Yes, those events—as urban actions—are projecting new meaning on those places, but between those events we must be doing something to retain a level of critical discourse. Now a more difficult situation than ever before has developed because of the gentrification of historic buildings—that is, the increasing withdrawal, from historically significant neighborhoods, of different groups representing different social strata, due to evictions and uneven economic development. In this situation, buildings become gentrified monuments—in effect, decorations for condominiums and shopping centers, or a kind of manipulated object of real-estate and architectural firms' PR and advertising agencies. The monuments become a part of real-estate simulation aesthetics, replacing history with a "past." Then the problem is what kind of strategy would be most effective to challenge those urban processes where the public spaces are becoming private properties, or pseudo-public spaces, completely perverted by real-estate manipulators—for example, Battery Park City. I don't know. I cannot provide a clear strategy for it. But I think that my work is at least partially an attempt to maintain attention and focus on these areas and processes—for example, my *Homeless Projection* on the Civil War memorial in Boston last New Year's Day. To do it successfully, one cannot only count on the individual aesthetic acts of public speech by a "heroic" artist. One must also be

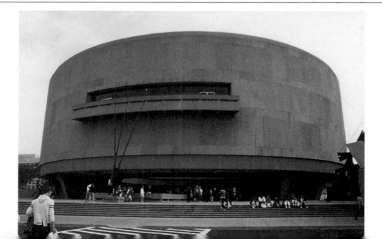

good and precise in working as part of the larger critical urban community, and in working through the city's administrative apparatus, which of course is not disconnected from the political processes which one must criticize.

Gilroy: Who do you think of as your audience? With this site, the literal audience might be some joggers, or occasional strollers on the Mall.

Wodiczko: This is a very unusual situation because I'm trying, in most of these cases, to combine so many things. That is, I must consider the selection of a site in relation to an issue (which can also be understood in a city context, but doesn't specifically have to be an urban issue), referenced to the symbolic structure, while also selecting a site which is physically suitable for projection. Most important, the site must also be accessible to different groups of city-dwellers, not only to one or two groups. In this case, that possibility is limited because the Mall doesn't really function in an organized social fashion at night. I mean, there are people there; we don't know how many. Over the period between 8:30 and midnight for three nights, a cumulatively large number of people will undoubtedly see this work, even if there are no more than ten or twenty people at any particular moment. But it is still not as desirable as situations where there is the possibility of a large concentration of people at a given time, so they could talk to each other and some social relationship could develop, or where they could communicate on a Brechtian scale. It's possible that the event will bring lots of people simply because the media will do a good job in publicizing the event, and also because there are not that many free events like this in Washington. People don't have to be punctual, they're free to come and go. They don't have to like it; they don't have to talk about it, or they can. They can meet each other on their way to somewhere else. They can take a photograph. I can provide instruction or lend a tripod.

Architecture and all symbolic structures of the city often operate as media images, such as postcards and photographs in newspapers; they are also seen on TV news and even described and discussed on the radio. Since the significant context of city events is always city symbolic structures, very often our description of the structure is interconnected with a description of the event. In the cast of my projections, the symbolic structure temporarily becomes an urban event itself. That way, a photograph with a comment and response in the press expands the audience enormously, by bringing more people to the projection. Looking at a picture, they won't see, perhaps, all of the aspects

of the projection—that is, how the images really are related to the three-dimensional form of the building, because they cannot walk around it to see that. But they will get some sense of it. In the case of the projection in London—of a swastika projected on the pediment of the South African embassy—postcards and images of this projection were distributed after the event. Many people told me that even though they hadn't seen the actual projection (i.e., they had only seen media images of it), somehow when they look at the pediment the swastika is seen as missing, as a kind of afterimage.

Gilroy: Do you think there is any way your pieces could become authoritarian given their mass spectacle qualities? What do you make of the guy who walked by while you were testing and aligning the images who said something to the effect of, "Don't point that gun at me. I don't care what you do, but don't point that gun at me."

Wodiczko: Well, this was the only person in all three evenings who responded this way. Bear in mind that the public is subjected daily, by billboards and advertisements, as well as political propaganda, to an enormous amount of manipulative material. In light of these facts, I am skeptical about discussing my work as being somehow "authoritarian," or as having an effect similar to that of an orchestrated mass spectacle. People might be particularly sensitive to specific images or parts of images because of individual experiences. I was hoping the Smith and Wesson revolver would not evoke the memory of the Vietnam War; unfortunately, this was the case with one viewer. He could only see one part of an entire symbolic/iconic arrangement (one of the three projected images), and assigned a particular meaning to it—and then felt threatened by it. I would like to be sure that my work is coherent enough to protect itself from such selected and extreme readings, and I'm always very sensitive about the possibility of making a mistake by not predicting readings that contradict the intention of the work.

I have to compete with the power, drama, and authority of the structure I address and confront. That particular moment, I or someone else might feel a little nervous. But if you think about the same gun, the same image being transmitted daily by the future president of the United States—who is against gun control, who is for a strong military presence as a way of resolving world problems, and who is for the death penalty and against abortion—and if that par-

ticular projection is actually addressing that danger, then I don't think I hold much authority. I only question it.

I can't believe that my work can successfully alter the way things develop. All that the work can do is help those people and groups and institutions, and also larger sections of critical society, to retain a level of criticism and understanding of what's happening. It is a very small contribution. So, to talk about my authority or power in relation to the power and authority addressed by the work is quite inappropriate because that would really suggest too much for the power of the artist as an interventional, temporary, public speaker. As soon as my work reaches the level of power of the forces I question, I will turn my projectors against themselves. At the same time, one must be willing to exercise some power in order to gain access. The fear of gaining access to power is generated by the dominant system of power itself; it is an ideological trap of that system. Those who want to retain total control of the dominant power structure support a kind of religious *fear* of power. One should not moralize as such, but try to gain access to its circulation in order to voice one's critical position.

Gilroy: In your mind, are there multiple interpretations of your work, or is there only one way to really see it?

Wodiczko: There were and are many interpretations, I hope, of most of my projections. But I have to hold responsibility for the initial set of readings which the majority of people would get. But this does not exclude other readings and cannot exclude extreme or partial readings—the man who saw the gun as a threat, for example. One could discuss his reaction in connection to the social relations of the reception of the work, since his comment was discussed by other viewers. Part of the reception process is an exchange of views and responses between the individual members of the viewing public.

Now the work may not be as clear as I want it to be; I'm always dissatisfied in many ways with work, as much as any artist. But the principle is that I seize on these images as symbolic icons taken from their popular context and connected so that the relations between them will correspond with the slogans promoted by the conservative militaristic political platform, and reveal their relations as contradictory and fragmented in terms of their blind aggressiveness. There is a contradiction between them, but also a similarity. Their cool media character is connected with the cool authoritarianism of the Hirshhorn building.

My work is inspired by the media, by photographs. I was inspired by some covers of *Crime Story*. I like this; the microphones, the metallic surface is very striking, the shapes are very cool, very much like the media itself. I like that quality, which is inspired by consumerism, but also by political advertising. Because that's what people will read very quickly, and that's also what interconnects with the building. The building itself is also "media"—a medium. It's a very slick, very precise, and very abstract structure, and easy to remember. So that is why I cannot be that creative in terms of inventing new images. I have to refer to what people can recognize.

There are many entries to this work. One could start responding to one part of this projection, like the candle, and generate possible meaning of that candle; as one point of light, as the hope of some kind of individual act, or some attempt to conquer the darkness, or something which refers to the history of use of this particular sign. There is a history to that symbol. So it might actually be going very far, but I hope it will somehow be arrested or limited by another image; the moral force of the gun, Ku Klux Klan vigilantism against the "terrorist" world. The building itself is the body, so the mind—I hope—will start correcting and working through the relation between one part and another—especially with the left and right hand belonging to the same person—and the building itself and the place where the building is located (between the Washington Monument and the Capitol) and the direction in which the images are facing (the White House and the National Archive), and connect all those things and the similarity of what's projected with the body or shape of the building itself. I would hope they do not read it as one slogan or as some very simple so-called message; rather, viewers would ideally be able to work through it and experience it for themselves, but their experience would be directed and focused, I hope, in a disturbing way. This experience will continue for a while in relation to what's being said, reading newspapers, and coming back and seeing this building without projections at another time. I hope this image will last in the viewer's imagination—as an afterimage—as long as the conservative political platform in the U.S. continues on its present course.

Since this site belongs to the United States, not just to the District of Columbia, it is very important that images of this projection will be reproduced and circulated, juxtaposed with images of the building itself, which are also circulating. As a public artist, I worked closely with people in the curatorial and public relations departments at the Hirshhorn, who were very sensitive to the difference between working on projects "inside" and "outside." They employed their own public relations mechanisms, which are very important in order to transmit and reproduce this work beyond the reach of the normal museumgoing public. The museum took the risk of involving itself in complex curatorial negotiations with the "curators" of the federal pseudo-public space, the Washington Mall.

Gilroy: Does it bother you that the scaffolds which hold the projectors are clearly visible in front of the projection?

Wodiczko: I like that. I don't like too much of mystery attached to the technology. I like that people can ask questions, talk to members of the crew, that they learn there are no "lasers," that it is actually standard equipment that is used, or misused or abused, or pushed to the limit. They see that we are still on the same side and that I am not representing some kind of institutional authority, that I don't run a corporation involved in projecting images.

Note

1. On the night of August 6, 1988, antigentrification demonstrators in Tompkins Square Park (located in the heart of Manhattan's East Village) were attacked by policemen. Until recently, the area has been largely home to poor and working-class people, but, as a result of intense real-estate speculation, a large number of long-time residents have been driven out. See "Cops in Crisis: Police Riot in Tompkins Square Was No Accident," *Village Voice,* August 23, 1988.

Originally published as "Projection as Intervention," *New Art Examiner* (Chicago) 16, no. 6 (February 1989), pp. 29–31.

Royoux: What accounts for your choice of themes? Are the stark dichotomies that appear in your projects justified by the fact that work in a public space must have an immediate impact on the greatest possible number of viewers?

Wodiczko: Claude Lefort has written that public space is an empty space, a space that doesn't belong to anybody and can be used by all who can bring a meaning to it and raise issues of rights. But the homeless are the living proof and the principal victims of its absence. Since it is theoretically linked to the space of communication, people ought to be able to make a statement in this space—especially homeless people, because they actually inhabit it, in a very real way, in the parks and on the steps of monuments to the great heroic figures of constitutional rights, of human rights, figures who in the present context become homeless themselves. Aloïs Riegl would have called these figures "the homeless of history." So my work with public monuments, for example, does not only seek to project the contradiction between reality and the idealism of those who gave their lives for democracy; it also attempts to reawaken those figures, to reactualize them, because they have been subjected to gentrification. In that sense I'm a historical artist, a little like Courbet when he said it's necessary to take history into account as long as it still has something to do with the present. That is what Benjamin, in his "Theses on the Philosophy of History," and Nietzsche, in *On the Advantage and Disadvantage of History for Life,* have called critical history, as opposed to antiquarian or monumental history, or history as a celebration of heritage. Monuments normally convey a monumental history, the glorification of something that "could have been," as Nietzsche puts it. An artist, on the other hand, can propose ways of talking about this history in relation to our present. Critical history consists of a reanimation of what is called public space, with the help of what has been relegated to private space—and reciprocally, it consists of bringing into public space what has been isolated and defended as exclusively private. For example, I invest public monuments with the experience of an absolutely invisible person, a night cleaner from Haiti, a black woman without papers. This person, totally outside the networks of communication, is suddenly put at the center, at the summit of the symbolic structures. But the extremely patriarchal character of these monuments, completely immobile, barricaded within official history, and also their great authority, all make this kind of work very difficult. What I can do in relation to these grand symbolic figures is to project unexpected problems onto them, and thus confront their megalomania, their dreams, their utopias, with very powerful evidence of problems that are of similar categories, because in this way a dialogue or a contradiction can come out. That's a technique of popular theater, of the grotesque. The contradictions only appear if you present the other aspect of the same thing, and that is why there is a limit to this type of work. However, the projections are very specific to each situation. These situations can only be perceived in a very general way by someone who remains outside the context, but I spend a lot of time at the site, talking with all sorts of organizations, with intellectuals, activists, people in coffeehouses, and I gather enormous amounts of information. Everybody tells me everything, because I'm a stranger and therefore maybe the only one who could produce these projections.

Royoux: In his later work *Les frontières de la démocratie,* Etienne Balibar writes: "A human citizen without ownership, a citizen lacking or dispossessed of property, would be a contradiction in terms." Could it be said that your interventions, particularly the homeless vehicle projects, are meant to return citizenship to those most lacking, to those excluded from society?

Wodiczko: I don't think my work bears exactly that kind of relationship to the problem you bring up. For the first time in history, nomads are being born in the city itself. These projects are above all involved in describing or revealing the living conditions of a particular group of inhabitants, people who cannot rent apartments but who still contribute day and night to the quality of the urban environment, by collecting bottles for recycling without being paid for it by the city. To do it they use shopping carts, vehicles that are not considered working tools by the other inhabitants but rather something outside the law, something that has to do with garbage. The homeless have no legitimate identity.

By conceiving an instrument that is specially designed for this particular type of work, I show the homeless as actually being entrepreneurs. In this way I pervert an existing situation by rendering it somehow legitimate, but without legitimating the crisis of homelessness. The "operators" of these vehicles are suddenly taken seriously, by themselves as well. You see this in certain gestures, certain ways of behaving, speaking, dialoguing, of building up stories, narratives: the homeless become actors, orators, workers, all things which they usually are not. The idea is to let them speak and tell their own stories, to let them be legitimate actors on the urban stage.

Another advantage of this vehicle is that it can transgress the boundaries between rich and poor neighborhoods. For example, it seems to fit perfectly in Battery Park City: it ironically mimics the surrounding architecture, but horizontally, at ground level. Coming from Tompkins Square Park, a completely devastated quarter of Manhattan's Lower East Side, it transports the evidence of the problem in a sarcastic way. As a stimulus for dialogue, a functional tool, and an architecture that confuses design as the image of a better world with this object responding to an unacceptable situation in the present, the vehicle absorbs a multitude of unresolved connections between sense and nonsense, between humor, practicality, and tragedy—and then explodes all the questions it raises.

Royoux: Would you define yourself as a political artist?

Wodiczko: This vehicle doesn't point the way out. On the contrary, it shows that it shouldn't exist, that it isn't a solution. In this sense it is critical art rather than political art. But you could also say I am a politician. The Sophists and later the Cynics were politicians when they animated or provoked a certain form of political discourse. By establishing a point of absorption, a point of convergence that concentrates a plethora of embarrassing questions—which, according to the official division of discourses, should *not* meet—I try to oppose one-directional thinking, or the utopian perspective. For me, this is an important aspect of critical practice.

Royoux: Do you trace your work back to the avant-garde efforts, in the first half of this century, to reconstruct a public space?

Wodiczko: My vehicles advance on the ruins of the modern tradition of "Fordism"—which plays an important part in the ideology of the avant-garde, whose vision of society lacked an understanding of social antagonisms. You see this in Poland, for example, in Strzemiński's unism or in Kobro's oeuvre (the attempt to design a form that would bring harmony to tomorrow's world, that would organize the rhythms of life, negotiate the differences and conflicts of forms in something like a communist elimination of conflicts and contradictions). Still, I do uphold certain aspects of this avant-garde tradition in my work, especially through my continued interest in public space. The concept has changed, however. Brecht saw a possibility for communication or communal experience in theater; by breaking down the established divisions between roles, characters, actors, and spectators, he invented a new way to think democracy. This *epic* theater must be continued today in relation to the entire theater of democracy, by breaking down all the borders: it's a kind of dada technique that's still valuable, that has an affinity with popular theater, with forms that question social borders. I'm trying to head in this direction, particularly along certain lines suggested by Henri Lefebvre—who for me is linked to the entire tradition that holds the creation of a public space to be an important part of any aesthetic project. This is a critical program focused on the right to the city and the differences within the city, but extended to the *xenopolis* of today, the city of strangers, of crossed borders and borders that cross people, dividing them from others and within themselves.

Royoux: In what specific way is art, in your view, capable of formulating these problems?

Wodiczko: First of all, I do not believe that artists represent a special discipline. Art contains or straddles all intellectual enterprises, but also the popular discourses, the media. . . . It is not easy for me to say what in this world is inherently specific to art. From architecture to the media and even in our perception of others, we are submerged in aesthetic ways of apprehending the world. For example, CNN during the Gulf War did nothing more than actualize battle scenes by Velázquez. We live in art. The artist should be someone who reorganizes this in one way or the other, by defining his role as a popular artist, which is what critical artists have always done.

Royoux: Could you introduce the project you want to carry out in France, *Alien Staff*?

Wodiczko: There is a very interesting architect in France named Lucien Kroll, who developed a way of involving the users in the elaboration of his projects. I want to further the tradition of this type of design. The first model should only be a metaphor of my ideas, because the principle is that the main contribution comes from the users themselves. This is an instrument of communication, for which, however, I would like to propose a few rules. It would be desirable that the user herself or himself speak through this instrument, in order to create a truly individual act of speech. The user's face should also appear on the screen.

The importance of the face is not only the fact that the immigrants I want to work with are considered "faceless." What is important is the simultaneous presence of the real face and the image, in order to create a situation in proximity with the user. The screen of the video monitor atop the staff will be very small, and the attraction of the object and of what's happening on the screen will incite curiosity. Those who really want to see will have to come up close, and then they'll realize the two faces are the same. Perhaps they'll remain up close for several seconds to hear what's being said, facing the user who won't necessarily speak.

Many questions about this project still remain open. The other aspect of it is the sculpted *xenolog,* which is a second, more symbolic manner for the user to tell his story and to make others acknowledge him as someone who has a history. There is a tradition of such staffs, as symbols of authority, of power.

Royoux: You seem to refuse the term "integration." What is, for you, the truly democratic way to recognize the stranger? Does it involve a rehabilitation of what has been termed "the right to difference"?

Wodiczko: There could be two outlines juxtaposed here: one would be my assimilation, the other my refusal to be assimilated. Who has the right to tell strangers that they are strangers, without admitting that one is also a stranger to herself or himself? When will come the day when the majority recognizes it must assimilate itself to the minorities, or consider itself as a minority? Some people may wish to try to become French, but others cannot. There ought to be a constitutional right allowing them to exercise their differences first. Then there also ought to be a right guaranteeing that those who are different from me will not be privileged.

Royoux: What image of the community does your conception of citizenship imply?

Wodiczko: The right for each of us to be strangers to ourselves, or to be the others, as Julia Kristeva says; going even further, the right to the multiplicity of one's own identities, or othernesses, that are within each one of us. But I'm not trying to put together a laboratory for new metaphors: maybe the important thing is to find a way to *disintegrate* rather than to integrate, to disintegrate

181   each individual a little more, in order to discover more possibilities for points in common, for new and complex relations.

Originally published as "Krzysztof Wodiczko: Nouvelles digressions sur l'étranger," *Galeries Magazine* (Paris), no. 49 (June–July 1992), pp. 56–59, 123–24; reprinted in *Creative Camera* (Manchester), no. 323 (August–September 1993), pp. 38–41. Translated by Brian Holmes.

Ferguson: Krzysztof, what were the circumstances surrounding the original idea of a vehicle for homeless people?

Wodiczko: I began thinking about it in 1983. In the area where I lived, near Union Square in New York, you could see on a monthly, almost daily basis, a growing number of homeless people. But I don't remember exactly when I made the first drawing.

Ferguson: You could have made clothes, or worked in a shelter, or found some other way of dealing with this issue. Was it because you had made or proposed "ironic" vehicles when you were still working as an industrial designer in Poland that this idea occurred to you?

Wodiczko: Yes, I just thought of how I could best contribute from the strength of my professional and artistic background. I saw myself as someone who could come up with something based on my industrial design experience and education. It's not true that a designer can design everything, or that every artist can be or is a designer, and I'm more comfortable with industrial design than with clothing design or social work because of my background and skills.

I was also working on projections or maquettes for projections that dealt with homelessness. Like the proposal for image projections onto statues in Union Square. I was thinking of presenting the first sketches of the vehicle at the gallery 49th Parallel where I had shown those, but I rejected this idea because the drawings were not developed enough.

Ferguson: Is there an implication in what you are saying that the vehicle addresses the limitations or constraints of the projections?

Wodiczko: Yes, definitely. The projections rely on images, existing images. The recognizable, circulating image of the homeless—a romanticized media image—is already an image of a victim. For the projections, I had to rely on those kinds of images which were already carved into the memory of the viewers. And then I would try to carve those images onto the monument in a fitting way. The technique is complicated, but its aim is to question both the contemporary media image and the monument as image—to create an embarrassing or disturbing connection, a contradictory relation between the two.

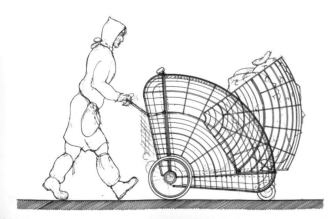
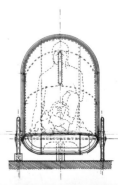

But I knew that a designed vehicle—a "pragmatic" and a symbolic object—could create even more of an intervention in terms of the way in which people perceive the homeless. I believe that there is more for the nonhomeless and for the homeless to think about when they suddenly are confronted with a new architecture and a new space. In other words, I began to build a new kind of monument.

But those thoughts came later. At the time, the real motivation was the urgent need I felt to supply whatever skills and experience I had to this debate. I understood that it would be a critical and aesthetic intervention, but I also hoped that I could get closer, through my own work, to the real situation of homelessness itself. That I could help not only the nonhomeless but the homeless, become a partner or a colleague, not someone who is just looking at them from the other side of the image.

The projections, as spectacles, act as a critique of representation by addressing the image of the homeless in relation to other images, and they are important as such. But the vehicle enters unknown areas as well, and breaks the isolation of myself, the artist, from the situation. The vehicle forces a very real social engagement—discussions of design and compromises introduced by homeless people themselves. I think that there is an ethical complement to my industrial design practice—my history of doing this in Poland and the particular education I had—which recognizes the need for something and, rather than finding a solution, adds a work or supplements reality in a positive and performative way. And only design can do it, really.

Ferguson: Obviously the media representation you mentioned is a voice which speaks as though for society when it actually speaks only for a few vested interests. As does the monument in its present state. They are both pseudo-voices, in effect. How do you feel the artist can speak between those two images, or does the artist speak through them? How can the artist be more authentic?

Wodiczko: I don't have a clear theory on this. I know there are some theories, but for me it's always very important to project onto the monument something that corresponds to life—to something real—to make the monuments pregnant with something real. The irony is that, of course, it is not real, it is only an image, and by necessity it must be recognizable as a media image. In other words, it has to be a quotation, appropriation, or displacement of an image.

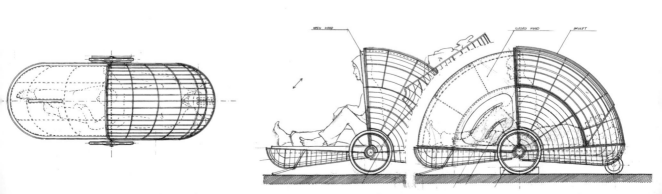

I would prefer to come up with something that isn't a quotation—without any reference to a media image—and I often try for some other icon but one which is as immediately recognizable. I don't work by simply taking a media image and projecting it. I photograph all my images, and I try to rely on something attractive and dramatic, like the cover of a crime novel, for instance. The image has to have those qualities or no one will even see it. I simply eliminate images that won't be recognizable or strong enough, clear or crisp enough, because people have difficulty recognizing icons they haven't seen before—grasping new iconic arrangements in a short time.

But in a sense, art was always doing this anyway—photography, architecture, planning, advertising, painting, sculpture, film, and television rely on existing codes. So, for me, there isn't a big difference, in the end, between the monument and the projected image. However, I do make the image as a counterimage or a countermonument. Only once have I projected a reproduced image from a magazine cover, like the Pershing missile. Mostly, I have made models of missiles to photograph and to clarify certain aspects of them. By doing this, I can prepare them for the photograph in such a way that they will have certain structural qualities of the monument in order to make an organic counterconnection.

Ferguson: Could you talk about an example of a projection in which the monument has a generic quality, and how you married it to an image from a recognizable code?

Wodiczko: The projection of a missile in Stuttgart is the most perfect example. The structure of the monument was a classical column. It is already a missile. And missiles are always displayed as columns. They are neoclassical monuments of slippery powers. In earlier projections I dealt with ideas of the body—an official body which is the body as facade—from images in which the media present people like buildings. I dealt with the way the media turns those photographs and people into monuments. I also dealt with the way buildings are constructed and the facades are often photographed, by emphasizing their symmetrical features to show a human face and the force of the corporate body. Neoclassicism resembles our bodies because it is deliberate morphology. The question was always how far I should go with the similarity between the image and the building—between these two parallel bodies—and how much should I alter them.

With the projections on monuments, I wanted to break the distance from the monument by creating something frighteningly real and living, like a ghost haunting the monument. To achieve something like the statue in *Don Giovanni*, who starts speaking of the terrible things that have happened. There are things the city doesn't want to talk about, and these are meaningful silences, which must be read. My projections are attempts to read and carve those silences into the monuments and spaces which propagate civic and dramatic fictions within the social sphere.

Ferguson: How do the vehicles act as characters in such a narrative?

Wodiczko: With the vehicle, firstly we have users and their relations to the object, and then we have viewers who are potential users, who have to imagine if this is an object for them. They examine it in relation to how it looks as a newly introduced object. So the vehicle is a kind of projection too, a projection into the world of objects. Because its differences from and similarities to other vehicles, such as shopping carts and cars, are discovered quickly and easily.

And there is also a desire to touch it. So there is a close contact through the object to the user—the Other—who owns or operates it. It is an eerie situation. Why is the other person using it? And how can I, the viewer, get permission to touch it and use it, even partially? When we tested it on the streets, no one asked, "Why are you homeless?" or "Who are you?" Instead they asked, "Why is this wheel here?" or "Why is it this color?" or "How much does it cost?" and "How many of these are produced?" There are certain techniques of speaking through the object that I discovered in testing this vehicle. Then the user might become a performer, in answering or not answering, or themselves questioning these questions: become an artist, so to speak. The vehicle becomes a performative operator, a medium, a stage, or a prop, or an occasion. It becomes a forum by being an object—a legitimate object. And the user—a homeless person— develops his or her own talents for public communication and performance by performing with this vehicle.

In fact, the vehicle became a disturbing communications medium and I hadn't predicted the many responses to it. There was a desire for it, a social desire for it, and the question was, what to do with all those desires? I can't produce many vehicles because I don't have the money, and it was never clear, even to me, if it was a good enough prototype anyhow. And if it were to be manufactured in units of thirty or fifty, they could claim a certain territory and social presence, but they would need an organization. And the vehicle itself can't create an organization.

So there were suddenly all these desires and questions in the minds of people on both sides of the vehicle. Through this object, questions and doubts and fears, but also utopian visions, were communicated, and helping people to concentrate. Just about everything that happened in testing the vehicle on the streets is invisible, because even in photographs or written descriptions of this project the object is only seen partially. Because it was really an event, and because of all the inquiries meeting and crossing and reconverging, the description of the vehicle is exhausted too early, so that it becomes a theory of sorts.

But the object was not outside of anyone anymore. It was the center of many things—it became a critical point. Impossible, and in fact undesirable, except to a few, it became too much for many people to take. And the moment of saturation on the street was very revealing to me. After absorbing all the questions, the vehicle became the Explosive Implosion of the Problem.

Maybe I shouldn't have been surprised, because this is what design is. Or what design should be. It is not just something useful, nor is it just an image with certain associations. It is also an event—a social experiment which is also a philosophical experiment. It is something that disrupts reality. It creates questions with no answers, but it is suddenly more real than something written, for example, because of our complex relation to objects. They always seem to be more disturbing in their merciless, naked presence. The vehicle is both there and not there; it is sculpture and not sculpture. It is an object and an idea at all times, which was the most fascinating and insoluble part of its reception.

Ferguson: You talk about the vehicle and objects as "adding to" or "increasing" or "complementing" a debate—expanding it. But it also seems to me that just as it increases, it decreases. Because it seems like a solution, it may raise expectations which can never be met. It starts to take on a kind of pathos or melancholia precisely because it can't be a solution.

Wodiczko: I agree and disagree with you. I don't know if, when I agree, that means it is a failure. It is an answer that is more of a proposition than a solution, or it is an impossible *solution*. But it is true that after all the technical questions which brought people closer through indirect inquiry, people began to close it off and make it into a new monument called *Homeless Vehicle*. Because suspi-

cion remains between the nonhomeless and the homeless; so it is easier to return to naming it, just as *The Homeless* was the name of a monument before the vehicle was on the street.

For the homeless and nonhomeless alike, the vehicle seemed like a beginning. It looked like a weapon—a projectile—and immediately both groups projected onto it the idea of a mass-produced object. It created an impossible image of a solution—the image of an army of masses of people with those vehicles. This could be seen as a criticism of it, but I think it was morally and politically critical as it became infused with critique, and that's why it worked.

Because mass production of it will never happen. It is impossible economically, politically, technically. And I would be the first to make it impossible if anyone wanted to try to produce them. However, it did effectively produce a monumental image of masses of homeless vehicles being everywhere and replacing, or altering substantially, the environment. And this image will stay. And that image, because it is reproduced in newspapers, journals, or on television, and through word of mouth, already makes it seem that hundreds of these vehicles are on the move.

I think it worked for several years. But I cannot take responsibility for the fact that everything acquires a mystique and eventually loses its meaning. You cannot be responsible for the fact that our art raises itself or becomes shallow with time and changing circumstances. What is important is what is actually happening at the very moment of the introduction of the work, between active and passive actors, and how this is reorganized by introducing this vehicle. It was reproduced everywhere and it was discussed. Now it's being dismissed as a failure because it's not being genuinely produced. But I think it was worth doing because I was genuinely surprised by the amount of debate and discussion and exchange it provoked and still arouses. This is the way in which the vehicle is being produced.

Ferguson: Do you think that your projects act as a kind of visible conscience—in the sense that they relentlessly record the idea that someone unofficial is witnessing this process of homelessness as it is being institutionalized, named, and codified within the official circles of media and other authorities of classification?

Wodiczko: The artist as a kind of tower? Or guard? Yes, I think they may be disturbing the kind of confinement of reality through images and concepts, and by reorganizing the connections that people make. Such projects might add to alertness in place of passivity. They help to communicate because they disrupt communications in the city.

Yet we have no clear way to consider design as a critical practice. Even if only a preliminary social experiment, as the vehicle is, we don't know how to discuss such events or designs, and we come back to the shortcomings of theory. And the limitations of language. Because we don't know how design "works," or what happens when design appears.

This is especially true in a situation of such complexity and magnitude as urban crisis. And it is also true because we are talking about individual perception and imagination. And how when a voice occurs through an object we would need a phenomenological approach as a starting point. We would have to enter a world that is very intimate—what is happening to everyone's mind and body in this provoking situation, and how everyone's reactions are voiced.

Thus we enter a world of fantasy, fictions, fears, the unconscious acceptance, false statements, and a variety of other responses. The object begins to collapse under the weight of an incredible load of inquiry, appropriations, and mental, metaphoric use. It might even start to function as a nightmare. Sometimes, when David Lurie and myself write to city departments, we don't even receive an answer. It's almost as though the project description already acts as someone's nightmare or guilt. Lacan might say that the fact that the letter is sent doesn't mean that it is received. Maybe some completely different letter is received or the answer is sent to somebody else.

So what happened with this vehicle? It is not something that can be easily confined in a normal art discourse, although art, too, has its normal—impossible—objects. But this new monument seems very complicated. I can take responsibility for the first reading of it. But I would like everyone to help me to figure out what really happened, so I would consciously know the entire world of responses this project created.

Ferguson: Could you say that, beginning with the projections in Halifax which dealt with gestures and codes of authority, your artistic trajectory has moved more and more toward an admission of the subjective element of both yourself and your audience?

Wodiczko: Well, in the beginning it was not as closed as you describe it. It was open enough. It was still to be completed in the mind—somewhere between those images of officialdom and the architecture. The South African embassy projection perhaps had less latitude and was more so-called political, and my response to the Gulf War in Madrid necessitated a shift from a more open projection to something directly related to the event. By connecting Franco's fascist Arco de la Victoria to the immediacy of the new declaration of war. But it was not I who made this monument, crowded with contemporary politics and the history of politics. It was the events surrounding me and the monument. Otherwise I would be useless, completely. I would be unemployed. Completely.

During the October Revolution, artists would have been unemployed if they didn't find a formal project related to the social project. So those two projections existed in situations which demanded that the projects not seem open to a variety of readings. Everything seemed to be clear-cut. For instance, the CNN battalistic art is actually a direct propaganda work. And I think that the Madrid projection, in contrast to a truly political piece, was actually more of a puzzle for people. At the time, what was most unexpected was the actual inclusion of the fascist monument in this situation. In other words, it is not what I projected as an image that resulted in a variety of readings, but the sight of the projection itself, the monument otherwise usually dark and free from any relation to reality. Suddenly illuminated, it is a partner to those events.

Not only were hundreds of thousands of people killed, electronically, in the name of some redirection, the access to resources and control over political and geographical spheres of influence, but Spanish people were reminded of their own civil war and the very active monuments to Franco throughout the country. And although they seemed not to want to participate in this contemporary war, the monument was still there, in the dark. And because everyone was a part of that extremely prolonged authoritarian culture, it was through their own experience and stories and images that this new war could act to inspire an uncomfortable memory. Without the monument, my projection is in trouble because the relation between present and past is destroyed.

The past must be infused with the present to create critical history, according to Benjamin and Nietzsche. Watching the monuments to Lenin being destroyed made me think there should be a public discussion before any of this is irreversible. The sculptures are witnesses to the past, memorabilia of the monstrous past. In Madrid, for instance, I thought it was good that this monument of Franco existed. But I'm only saying that there was neither any attempt to destroy it nor any debate about it at all. That's what worried me. That such monuments are morally unemployed and kept physically and metaphorically in the dark.

Ferguson: I've always been very moved by the way you discuss statues or monuments in so-called public spaces. You've drawn me to the urban crisis and the idea that witnesses, perhaps more than critics, are the most disturbing and powerful facts for history. Because someone who has witnessed an event always has the potential to change its meaning.

Wodiczko: Standing in the park at Union Square, the Lafayette monument, a revolutionary monument, is completely passive—the homeless of history. He is abandoned because no one wants to think about "him" any more, of what happens around him, because it is too difficult. How, for instance, can we see Lafayette's ideas in the context of the present social, political, and philosophical crisis of democracy? The procedures inscribed in the American Constitution, with their ideas of a guarantee of happiness and freedom, seem not to be working. So Lafayette and others are being erased and repressed, yet they are still physically standing there. I was interested in how to involve them today.

But there is a problem with simply projecting onto them, and I'm not sure I would torture history—or, I mean, this past, not history. Maybe those historic monuments are not only astonished or petrified by what they see. Maybe it is possible to say that they turned a blind eye, a blank eye, on past reality. Or maybe the whole concept of democracy of the modern kind is simply irrelevant or passé. Maybe there is a point when a new situation requires a break from the past. I think, personally, that the process of democracy is only in the preliminary stage.

Nietzsche reflected on history in an essay called *On the Advantage and Disadvantage of History for Life.* And his insight leads me, too, to think that there is a certain point when history is just an illusion. Because things don't repeat themselves. Do we need another Lincoln? Another Lafayette? So my earlier work had these limitations, not only artistic and aesthetic, but philosophical.

The design projects may be a response to that constraint, because they are not actualizing anything past, but simply projecting certain visions of the future—utopian or dystopian—onto the present. To see the present means then to use the device of science fiction. The difficulty with Walter Benjamin's concept of the future and the past finding a home in the present, in a collision, is the actual usefulness of the past. Nietzsche divided history into three categories: critical history, antiquarian history, and monumental history. My projections, supposedly, are works of critical history, not antiquarian since I'm not merely preserving history. But they have to revive monumental history in order to turn it into a critical history. But by illuminating it, no matter what I project, no matter how critical I want to be, I bring it to its former glory, its presence. It still reemerges from the darkness as a glorious symbol, as Nietzsche would say, giving us "a sense that grand things did happen."

So to pervert or act as a parasite on those monuments with some injections, infusions, or actualizations is only possible to a certain degree. Firstly, most of the images hardly fit because of the strange shapes and iconography of the monuments. And secondly, their formal arrangements are difficult because they are not flat screens. And thirdly, and most importantly, is that we should also be able to detach ourselves from them in order to stop continuing that discourse of power which they represent. Or at least interrupt it. But to destroy them, which people do, I cannot entertain because I am not a physical deconstructionist of monuments. At the same time, I may be getting tired of making dead horses come alive, like some necrophiliac. And why should I resurrect them from death? It is very tiring and I can only do it for a short period of time because of course we know that they are dead. I just bring a kind of artificial life to them as an alternative to the artificial character of their lives, and I am a little tired after working with these horrifying structures, these terrible objects, since 1980.

Ferguson: The communications vehicle is both filled with contemporary, up-to-date technologies, and has the look and feel of a medieval object. Even if it tries to avoid the past in some way, is it inevitable that the past explodes into the present in the sense that Walter Benjamin spoke of?

Wodiczko: I think perhaps the communication vehicle (the *Poliscar*) could be understood iconographically as a kind of grotesque, but it is simply a response to the image of the contemporary city, which the uniformed police and the real-estate armies have made a militarized zone. And the image of the city being overtaken by a force of communication vehicles everywhere, an impossible insurrection, accounts for the ridiculous aspect of its appearance. As McLuhan told us, there is not only war but there is a war of icons, and humor might have a liberating effect—help us to recognize this image of revolution and the fear of it differently.

I mean, if I were to respond to the idea that my work is political art, I would say that it is not. I would say, however, that it is a work of the politics of art. The true political art is the official monument, the officially built environment, as well as aesthetically considered works of any political propaganda or ideology. Repeating my disassociation form the label "political artist," I may say that I am perhaps a politician of art, in the sense of a new kind of Sophist in the contemporary polis; an artist-politician revealing the politics of the art of official space. My art must be understood, then, as a form of aesthetic politics; of making space within the space of political art (*polis*). Bringing a set of "political" icons, unwanted and disturbing; bringing issues that are silenced; bringing the private life, so to speak, to this public death; my art, as politics, may then depoliticize this totally political art—this monument—this city and its image.

What I am doing is making monuments less political, because the references I project on them are what people regard as horror. My work attempts to enter and trespass this field of vision, the position of the individual as a subject being constructed, or produced through the urban space in relation to others and in relation to monuments. I try to disrupt this continuous process of reproducing the individual in space.

Now that I am living in Paris, the conditions are different, because Paris has no monuments, in that everything is a monument. There is absolutely no relation between Paris and the present world, except a general feeling of the total lack of correspondence between the modern liberal state and the new Europe, with its problems of xenophobia and reviving symptoms of racist disease. It's a place which successfully detaches me from monuments. There is a lack of a public sphere because the history of a royal court or royal class continues from Louis XIV to Mitterand—a royal cultural project. For instance, the new Bibliothèque, not by accident, is going to be standing on the site of the biggest camp of the homeless, now relocated and dispersed by the authorities. A monument will be placed on the site of the crime. As Bataille said, "Architecture captures society in the trap of the image it offers . . . where the cement of faith confirms religions and kingdoms in their authority." He was paraphrasing Freud, who said, "Society, from then on, is based in the common wrong; but it covers up the site of the crime with discreet monuments to make it be forgotten. Architecture does not express the soul of society, but rather smothers it."

So the new Mitterand monuments are major coverups of crimes of omission and expulsion; of depriving minorities and foreigners of human rights. The major pyramids have a top, and that top is still the state—the "nation" state. The pyramids of modernist liberal vision still silence the elements which do not fit the image of a pyramidal integration of society into "la civilisation française."

Originally published as "A Conversation with Krzysztof Wodiczko," in *Krzysztof Wodiczko: Instruments, Projeccions, Vehicles* (Barcelona: Fundació Antoni Tàpies, 1992), pp. 47–65.

Robbins: A passerby in the street sees someone holding a walking stick with a TV monitor on top like a hooded cobra. There is a moving image, there is the sound of a voice, perhaps an accented voice. The person holding the staff seems to want to make eye contact. What goes through the passerby's head? Another crazy foreigner? Someone who needs help walking? Moses in front of Pharaoh?

Some of the brilliance of this seems to me the play on what Guy Debord calls "the society of the spectacle," on the fact that people will not stop for human beings telling their story but will stop for a televised image of the same human being telling the same story. When the image replaces the person, when there's an obstacle between you and the person, there's a better chance of making contact. Otherwise the operator is likely to be taken as someone asking for spare change. Is this what you had in mind? What sort of public encounter are you hoping to produce?

Wodiczko: It's very hard for me to present a theoretical model for what I hoped would happen, or even what I noticed did happen during these performative presentations. But it was clear that without this object, none of this would happen. Any kind of object held and operated by a stranger can be useful. But if the object performs and is attractive by virtue of being strange, it relates to the tradition of strangers, magicians, performers using instruments that come from somewhere else, to make magic, or just to sell something. In the environment of the contemporary city, too, a new object is always desirable. . . . The *Alien Staff* proved to be very effective because it was recognized as something familiar at the same time as something strange. It's like a cliché. A biblical staff. [Laughter.]

Robbins: Does Emmanuel Levinas laugh when he talks about the face of the Other?

Wodiczko: Comically, the face here is the face of a character and the face of an actor at the same time. The face of a media performer and an actual person. And there is the operator, also an actual immigrant, who is performing in relation to the prerecorded image. The presence of the actual immigrant takes several forms. One of the forms is to embody disagreement with what was prerecorded. Nothing here is very stable. It's quite open for exploration. When

others ask questions about what's in the containers, for example, it brings up things that weren't said in the prerecorded material. But very often the immigrant will also refuse to explain. He or she will say, "It's none of your business. It's there because it's important to me." Other things are explained even if nobody wants to hear. Horrifying descriptions of the immigration department and so on. You ask for it, you get it.

Then there is yet another person, a person from the crowd—the beginning is the gathering of a crowd, and things are already leaking out of this two-person encounter into the crowd—which is listening to all of this and is voicing its own opinion: "Well, excuse me, I'm also an immigrant," or "I'm not an immigrant, but . . .". Levinas's "third" is the person who says, "I am not an immigrant, but . . .". This is the person who sees the whole situation from the point of view of a symmetrical democratic project. In France, which lives the classic democratic Enlightenment, the third is the person who says, "But wait, aren't we all members of one large community?"

This triple relation—me, the Other, the third—can be reversed. Any one of these can be the one who sees the triple relation. But the object helps in this process. It makes a multiple. The possibility of a like artifice, the *Alien Staff,* doesn't really exist for Levinas.

Robbins: I'm really fascinated by one aspect of your work that seems to me unique. It seems to be designed so as to require a kind of narrative completion. To stop and provoke kinds of conversation about it and between people who are involved in it, which is a kind of building block of some new community. It's artistic work that provokes and invites intellectual and communicative activity in a very special way.

Wodiczko: When you say a special way, I can only imagine what you mean. What I've tried to do, that I don't see being done enough, is perhaps the creation of some object or some intermediate form which inspires, becomes a starting point for the openings and exchange, and sharing. And that is something that constitutes a tradition of the need of object or instrument, like a storyteller's instrument. A kind of magic staff that will make miracles. As in the Bible. It is clearly stated in Catholic versions of the Bible that the staff is to make miracles. In Protestant versions, it says to make a sign. But in both cases there is a magic to it. Without the stick, people would not believe the person who was using it. But in this case the object can also become a center, a sacred place. Bataille defines the sacred place like Jean-Luc Nancy, as the place where passions are unleashed, where something can be shared that has not yet been shared or that one has refused to share. It is the place of a birth of some kind. This object is a performative object. I think we need more objects of this sort to come between an unprecedented explosion of communication technologies and a dangerous return to the tragic precedents of complete communication breakdown.

How would you connect the [MIT] Media Lab, the most advanced technological media experiments, with the situation of the ex-Yugoslavia? They are almost irreconcilable events. In the space between these two points of reference, in normal everyday life, there is a need for people to recognize each other and take responsibility for each other, which is a highly difficult mission. Definitely recognize each other, face to face. How to do this and at the same time to create, to take advantage of the global communication networks? It's a very personal, very fragile thing. And very direct contact, with all the resources, the historical documents or past cases, we can bring to it—how to bring forward the whole heritage of accumulated layers of the past and wrestle with it when we are actually facing each other? I'm told that tragedy will not repeat itself, so there may be no more ex-Yugoslavias. I think there is still a reasonable hope. Can artists be part of this larger range of efforts? We need a more concrete hope, a clearer agenda. . . . To bring together communication technologies and interaction, direct contact, aesthetic work needs instruments, equipment, but it also needs to create events, acts, so that in facing those events people will start communicating directly. In a way, the ancient public space.

This arena or stage still exists. In fact it is a bloody scene, the stage of massacres, ethnic cleansing. You cannot simply say the city is passé or the human body is passé. Torture and killing remain the most important and unfortunate performative medium today. What I am saying is that this is a necessary agenda for art. There is a growing number of projects that I really admire done by other artists right now on the Internet (WorldWideWeb) which really are provoking or inspiring interaction and growing kinds of discourse. But what they don't propose is this bodily element; they don't connect electronic communication with the body and its experience, with direct face-to-face contact. I'm not criticizing these projects. Actually I'm saying that the discursive aspect of my work is not so original because of this electronic work already done.

Robbins: But you were just saying that the body must continue to have a place in what we've been calling the public sphere, that bodiliness is something that can't be forgotten. And one thing people appreciate about your work is the way it refuses the idea that the true public in our time is cyberspace.

Wodiczko: But in this case I disagree with those who appreciate my work. Because their conservative reaction against cyberspace or the electronic public unnerves me. I think it is important to connect the most contemporary digital communicative techniques with the ancient bodily and performative know-how in one work. We know the incredible growth of the Internet and World-WideWeb also mimics dangerously the growing division between the poor and the rich, especially in the United States. This means a separation between the way populations communicate, hence a new form of alienation.

Robbins: What about the Greek side? Xenology, and so on?

Wodiczko: The Greek side is definitely Socrates. It's all between Moses and Socrates. If this equipment seems to be prophetic, it's because it puts every immigrant, every operator in the role of a prophet, interrupting history to open up a vision of community. Each one brings his or her own experience, and in this experience is the seed of a new community. Of a world that would not ask the immigrant to integrate, but a world that would *dis*integrate, made of people who have disintegrated.

   This connects with Socrates because Socrates did not tell people what to do. Socrates used an amazing discursive technique: he created situations in which people had to start thinking. What is Socratic about the staff is the position of the performer in what used to be called public space. Maybe a public space is being created in the very moment, the very act of performance, or in the act of dwelling in the polis. Or, in Bataille's terms, a sacred place. Where people face each other's passions.

Robbins: Tell me a little about the science of xenology.

Wodiczko: By "xenology" I mean a field of knowledge which also connects with the field of experience. The field of historical intuition or present intuition. I want to propose an existential knowledge combined with life practice. A struggle of displacement. This has something to do with displacement.

Robbins: Not especially transnational displacement? It could as easily be an internal or domestic displacement?

Wodiczko: As inside of yourself.

Robbins: Oh, I see. Strangers to ourselves, as Julia Kristeva says.

Wodiczko: Yes. This external *and* internal displacement is about crossing the boundaries inside of yourself. Because there are all those different borders one is discovering. Maybe they were there before. But one recognizes this whole incredible world which is normally not recognized by people who stay in one place for too long. One can definitely learn a lot from strangers. Those who move less should listen very carefully to those who move more. And maybe the opposite. But the fact is that xenology would be experiential, theoretical, and artistic. In the further development of my project, xenology could be its aesthetic, not just its cultural or theoretical frame. The xenologist would be someone who is more aware of the field, a kind of prominent scholar or practitioner in the field. Like a doctor. A Talmudic doctor exists as long as Talmud exists. Here we are dealing with an oral history, not written texts. There are cases. Xenology is not centered around sacred literature, but it could assign to certain fragments of this historical material something like the meaning of a sacred text. Maybe it should be more displaced, not fixed in one body like the Torah.

Robbins: In your experiences of displacement, your wanderings, can you think of any discovery that might serve as an example of the sort of knowledge xenology would produce?

Wodiczko: I learned about xenology from a person whom I know well, Jagoda Przybylak. I would call her a xenologist. She runs an informal network of domestic labor for Polish immigrants. She cannot stop, cannot stop lending her experience, exchanging addresses, finding rooms for people, mediating. She spent so many years working and is still working today, despite the fact that she is teaching photography here and is an artist. She is still working in the field of undocumented labor, or half-documented labor, or labor in the process of being documented. This is a rescue mission, part of the Polish culture of resistance and survival. She is an ethical advisor to Polish people. They call her.

And sometimes they leave messages on her answering machine. Recently she started to connect those messages. Now she has a bank of cases, messages left about miserable experiences or comical stories. She is working, so she's not home, but her answering machine is on. And people call, and they cannot stop. There is so much traffic of telephone calls that it is almost impossible to reach her. It is something for which she has not been paid or recognized. There are other people like her. She is not alone. But I've learned that for the immigrant, people like her are the most important figures in every country.

Jagoda needed the *Alien Staff* simply because she had never acknowledged to herself that her experience is something very valuable and something to be proud of. She told me at first that she didn't want to be part of the project. It took one week of my persuasion. I would say, "Why don't you try?" "No! I'm not going to speak about this! This is awful and in fact I don't even want to remember it." Or, "No, I don't even want anyone to know about this because there are all these people in Poland who need to know that immigrants succeed." And when they travel and they immigrate or when they stay, there's an incredible market for such fantasies.

But she eventually started to search for relics. That was the first thing. She was interested to find a photograph of her nighttime cleaning colleagues at IBM. Just to find those great friends from Puerto Rico or from Poland. And she found it but then she had to travel across the whole city to find one of those friends. She of course took a camera, because she's a photographer. She discovered what had happened to this woman. Now there are eight people from Poland with her—actually six children—and something incredible developed around this person. She realized that there was so much to recover. She started to write down her memories about a time when she was enslaved taking care of an elderly German woman who herself had been an immigrant fifty years before. It was a kind of revenge or compensation for her to enslave a new immigrant. So Jagoda started to write it down. This started to connect in her and finally led to videotaping and editing. It became several stories. One is called "Plejsy," another is called "Kompaniony," and another is called "Ofisy"—a Greenpoint language for cleaning apartments, taking care of people, cleaning offices. Then this turned into shorter, more refined stories. And then more objects were found, usually so well hidden that she thought she could never find them. Because they were the most important objects that she had brought from Poland. And photographs and correspondence she received from someone in the immigration department. Finally she put all this together and she started to speak, with an incredible ability to say things, and she grew to like it. She is always a consultant in the development of my projects. I cannot take any new steps without talking to her.

Robbins: I have a larger question about the politics of your work and its trajectory, about what the word "stranger" means to you. If one were unsympathetic, as I'm not, one could say that to focus on immigration is to forget all the people who have not immigrated—to privilege, as we say in our jargon, the metropolis as the center of the story, and to drop out all the people who have not left the countries that immigrants have come from. Is it to deal with an unhappy but somewhat privileged group?

Wodiczko: That brings us back to Benjamin and Levinas. To put emphasis on the stranger is to see ourselves, and to see ourselves as a democracy. It's the only way to know whether this democracy is human or ethical. We badly need strangers. We call ourselves a community, we claim openness, rights, and so on, but we have no way to see that community. So it must be interrupted by strangers (Benjamin), who are more important than we are. (I don't consider myself a stranger, though I am of strange origins; I now have three passports.) For Levinas, the symmetry of democratic process can only be sustained by an asymmetry of ethics. If the stranger to the city and someone born in the city are equal, and democratic equality is guaranteed by human rights and by the Constitution, our obligation is to challenge that symmetry, to open ourselves to those who are less capable of taking advantage of their rights. But it is we who are less capable of recognizing the needs of others, who do not fight for the rights of foreigners to vote. We impose taxation on everybody, but we don't demand that strangers have representation. They are living here, they have children, they have nothing to say about how their children will be educated, and so on. There is a myth of equality, a myth of symmetry between us and them, that needs to be challenged. To make that symmetry possible, one has to act asymmetrically. You have to overexpose people who are underexposed.

This is also an aesthetic effort. There's a need for a bandage to cover the wound. But something at the same time that helps people articulate, recognize the origins of the wound. Most of the designs I've made belong to this category of the bandage. The bandage also shows the location of the pain. It's in between, a communicative device. These instruments prove to be necessary, as the operators tell me. After they go through all the trouble of gathering information and opening it up to everybody, they report that they can manage their pain better. They can cope.

Robbins: Apropos of the bandage, one of the things I like so much about the *Mouthpiece,* your other instrument for immigrants, is the suggestion that it's a monstrous gag. While it's a prosthesis helping people express themselves, it's also expressing the impossibility of speech. It's a sort of bandage over the mouth, blown up to monstrous proportions.

Wodiczko: What I'm hoping to do with the new variant of the *Mouthpiece* is a truly monstrous prosthesis, a cyborgian bandage that overemphasizes the need for equipment, for aid. It allows the mouth of the speaker to be both covered and uncovered. The monitor section of the equipment, showing the lips of the speaker, can now be shifted, so the operator can speak directly as well as with prerecorded speech. Or it can be switched off.

Robbins: What kinds of changes in the *Alien Staff* do you have in mind?

Wodiczko: I'm interested to see to what degree instruments of this sort can be more playful. Inspire more of an artistic or baroque use. In other words, if they can respond better to the gestural and narrative virtuosity of strangers. Of course, instruments of this kind are not for every stranger. Clearly they are for people who are more artists than others in their technology of survival, of insertion into the culture. They are for special agents—or angels.

Robbins: In ancient Greek, "angels" meant messengers.

Wodiczko: Yes, messengers who like to speak, who are angry enough, who are motivated. Sometimes even desperate. Or, say, initially reluctant, yet having an internal need to construct, reveal, or open up their experience and share it. It is very hard to describe the whole process in which people, once they learn about the possibility of this kind of project, select themselves to be part of it. But the person who chooses it is usually either the one who is in the worst trouble, or is in trouble but not as much as he or she has been. They are people who want to be more public than they are despite the fact that what they say, the so-called public doesn't want to hear. With the kind of equipment I am giving them at the moment, these people can do more than what they are expected to do.

But there is also possibility there. I am talking about an instrument that is not yet designed. I am designing a tool or instrument which will create a new situation. That level of the unknown is connected with a kind of intuition of the present, a revolutionary intuition of the present. There's an intuition that those people will be able, for example, to come to terms with their impossible set of experiences, the impossible reconfiguration of their identity or the new forms, new connections, inside of them. As they start recording and reenacting their stories and reinterpreting, rhetorically articulating them in front of others, in interaction with the others, one hopes they will learn more about what they would like to say and also that they will learn to play with this somehow painful, difficult, and maybe tragicomic device, enjoy it in some humorous and baroque or maybe even in a more polite, rococo way.

I emphasize the possibility of modulating the audiovisual recordings with gestures or even allowing the other people around to participate in this replay or reenactment. The Media Lab at MIT is continuing the project that was developed by Theremin, a Russian inventor, and recently perfected an instrument operated by gestures. It connects human electromagnetic fields and the electromagnetic fields which are electronically generated. I would like to test this gestural instrument. I have to build it to see how one could become a virtuoso of his or her own story, also maybe adding new components to the story, discovering more and more aspects of the experience and making it into a more playful act of speech and also, psychologically, an act of self-construction. The playfulness is definitely a psychological need here, for the operator and also for everybody else. In the space between strangers, and between strangers and nonstrangers (if one can describe them this way), this artifice which is already there as a kind of object could become more interactive and more interpretive or performative than it is now. I hope that it may be the birth of some other kind of instrument.

Robbins: Could you say something about the political uses you mentioned—people who want to use instruments like this to represent others? Are there any examples that come to mind of people who want to use this technology less to speak about themselves than to speak on behalf of other people?

Wodiczko: Everyone starts with his own misery. But there's one person in a refugee camp in Poland, for example, who came from a very miserable situation in Algeria [see "Voices of the Mouthpiece"]. He had lost contact with his family and he claimed, probably rightly, that if he returned to Algeria he would be prosecuted because of his antifundamentalist stance. So he contacted his family by phone. This is what he actually started with. But then he brought a seriously prepared speech to be recorded that was about fear, a problem he thought should be addressed. Such a large part of the population of this planet lives in fear. He had a theory of fear, which came out of his own experience, and he proposed the theory to Polish people. He speaks French. He got it translated from French into Polish. He asked Poland to recognize the need to help Algeria in this impossible situation where people live in fear. But he also asked the Poles to rethink the way they think about their own country and their own politics because of the danger of Catholic fundamentalism, which threatens to take over politics and eventually all human rights. Suddenly he was talking on behalf of the Polish population with which he had limited contact. But clearly he had picked up quite a lot about problems in Poland, maybe by listening to the radio or speaking to people. He knows Polish well enough.

Actually, when I think about it, everyone mixes politics in, connecting the personal and the political. But only on occasion does it get dangerously close to using this equipment to address political issues more than their own experience. As Benjamin said, when you transpose the personal into the historical, that is what is revolutionary. They think this is the moment in which history has to be addressed. Because if one doesn't speak about it right now, things can irreversibly turn into catastrophe. Both in their lost land and in their promised land. This is how they are messengers.

Robbins: Could you say something about any of the reactions to the use of these instruments either that you've seen or that you've heard about from people who were using them?

Wodiczko: It has become clear that much more is happening with this stick than I anticipated. The reactions were usually good when there were both immigrants and nonimmigrants around this stick. First of all, there was an attempt to exchange and share experience between the operator and other immigrants, maybe from other countries. There is usually very little connection between immigrants. And then there are the nonimmigrants who, of course, might have imaginary relations to their memories of their own "first place." They might feel that in that sense everyone is an immigrant. Everyone feels strange, everyone is alienated. So what's the problem? But when they start getting into the details of the exchange of experience among immigrants, they realize that they are actually not part of the same conversation. They cannot be. They want to listen. Or, they want to speak more in order to dominate the discourse, to reinterpret the situation of immigrants for them. This was very apparent in France. There were some types who immediately translated fragments of what they heard into a kind of rough theory, making it an act of their own speech, political speech. "Let me tell you what you mean," and "What does it mean from the point of view of democracy in general?" All of those concepts, like egalitarianism, that they carry from the eighteenth century—they truly believe in them in France. But usually it is so ridiculous that they are overwhelmed by the reaction. Or there is silence. A very thorough kind of silence. They are trying to learn based on some sense of ideals or recognized ignorance.

There was one moment I found quite amusing. Conversation developed so well between the immigrants around the stick that they forgot about it. They ended up in a restaurant and the stick was just leaning against the wall. One of the immigrants, from Morocco, was laid off. And as a result of this, she got a job from the operator, who needed a babysitter. Later I took this as an important possibility for new equipment. There's something very pragmatic on occasion that comes out of all of the political and cultural debate, about national policy or legal problems they share, an exchange maybe of some addresses of lawyers, or God knows, some services. There is also the job market which appeared here. So I realized that in some next generation or network of instruments I should design in the legal and economic issues.

The immigrant can become a "case." One could say, "Okay, actually this reminds me that I need to speak with someone because I don't know exactly what the situation is in terms of my legal status, which is changing all the time. And there are rumors. Is there any way I could find a job in this immediate situation? Is there anybody who could help me? Maybe *you* could help me." At that moment, the *Alien Staff* could become a transmitter of this question, and the operator could also receive additional training as a messenger, a more informed messenger. Because they have established trust, they have opened up a concrete case which is in itself public. The person thinks, "It is almost impossible that this person holding this staff would be an immigration agent." There's always this question—is she actually spying on us or trying to report us, our cases, to the immigration office? People who are completely fearful and paranoid will never accept the staff. But there are enough people who will suddenly realize, "No, this person is one of ours." So then she could transmit some problems, saying "I'm not giving your name, this is not televised. I have a lawyer on line." In fact, there could be a legal station on line. It could be transmitted very easily to a satellite and it could go to a computer run in the base of the staff which could very quickly identify all of the options for the stranger. But also the messenger could say, "All right, this reminds me of somebody else in your situation." So something like this could be reported or transmitted and then encoded. The case could be retried and also transmitted back audiovisually if it's within, say, a 100- or 150-meter radius. There is no problem in retransmitting an image. Especially if you use a computer system, not video, not television, but a computer screen. There could be an actual person on the screen or it could be a document, a particular immigration form or some kind of formal petition for immigration. They could say, "Do you have this kind of document? Is this the way your visa looks?" So there's a possibility of a very concrete service.

The equipment would have to be transformed in relation to the growth of an organization or network. I have no idea in what direction this would go in terms of the form of this equipment. I'm in touch right now with legal services in Cambridge who help with immigrants. This group of lawyers (who are fascinated, they told me, by this project) think it will be very helpful to have some agents or angels to encourage these displaced people to find help—free help. If this works and the trust is built, if the immigrants are working with the lawyers, if there are some psychological clinics, some neighborhood clinics, it is possible that eventually this project will find some money if there is any hope to find money for any cultural projects. Or maybe cultural research grants. With the possibility of a larger group and a number of instruments and an electronic network, we'd have to really rethink the whole design part.

Robbins: When you were talking about the new computer technology that you'd like to experiment with, I wondered whether you had recording equipment as part of the *Alien Staff,* as a way of making it more interactive, producing something that would include the people around. And then I thought that, practically, this seems like the worst idea in the world because of the fears people have that it would be used as an instrument of surveillance.

Wodiczko: Yes, even the idea that I presented is doubtful. How do you convince people that the possibility of digital transmission is really there and is not really a trick? How to open this up without scaring people to death? Another possibility would be to eliminate this transmission altogether and rely on live transmission, rely on the possibility of meeting the same person at the same time. The operator could reappear the same time the following week. That is what happened in Greenpoint, on Sunday in front of a church. It is a very important place in Greenpoint because it's a church attended by both Poles and Puerto Ricans as well as some other groups, not as many Polish as maybe one would hope, but some. And it is a sacred place because they share the same religion. And a sacred place could be used as a site for this performance. And as I said, someone asked, "Will you be here next weekend?" In this question there is the possibility of a community, a newly born community. It means I will give myself a week to figure out whether I should trust you enough to bring my uncle or my brother and tell you something more. But now I will ask you a few questions. So I will ask you, "Will you be here next weekend? And by the way, do you know anyplace to go for help? Or in what way are you connected with, say, people who clean apartments or people who take care of elderly women or men, or who clean offices at night?" In this moment, the operator will have to rethink whether this is actually a trustworthy person. Eventually by probing questions they will find each other.

Certain fragments of what Jean-Luc Nancy said about community seem strangely familiar when I observe what's happening around the stick. He proposed a different kind of community, and this helps me to understand my own work. He says that there is a kind of undoing of community, an undoing of ties or preconceived notions of the commonality or communistic or communal. And this immigrant is refusing to accept any imposed notions, or ties, or connections with others. She's saying, "No, no, I'm not part of it. Don't worry." Or, "Please do not think that we all have the same situation or that I speak here on behalf of others. No, this is a unique experience I am opening up. I don't know what others go through. Telling you all the complexity, all of the problems I have with myself, with the way I was and I am no longer, with the things that change in me, it is difficult to accept what I am doing. All of the questions, all of the disagreements inside of me, this is something that you have to listen to. Because this is something that I cannot even say without a certain hesitation and pain." I'd like to connect the *Staff* with this kind of community of unworking and undoing, a community of refusing, of refusal to be fused—I think that is what Nancy says, more or less—and yet also a possibility of community disseminated, contagiously spread by the immigrant, a community of all of those disagreements and problems inside of one person. The person will say, "Join me in this exploration and we will have in common all of our doubts about what is supposed to be our collective or community, what is supposed to be the legitimate bond between us. Let's replace it or let's drop it and talk about what is really happening inside of us and whether we can share it." In this way, I could see this stick as, maybe for a moment or fifteen minutes, the point of a birth of a new community. A community that comes from inside the containers, from all those things that are contained in the video and the relics, but also from the play with them. If I could make it more playful and interactive. . . . Laughter— all the jokes, the disruptions, the changes of topics, all the absurdity and impossibility of talking about identity. This is the new community.

Maybe something else will come out of this. Maybe something with which Jean-Luc Nancy will not agree. But it will also be connected with a kind of Brechtian interruption, with what Benjamin calls the "interruption of history." As I've mentioned on many other occasions, the interruptions of the linear continuity of the history of the victors by this secret tradition of the oppressed which is nonlinear and always negative and always performative. And always trying to recover their own history. Nancy's concept of uncommunity or this community of refusal of being fused could be connected with the Benjaminian concept of interruption.

Robbins: Listening to you talk about Nancy and the notion of community, I thought that in a sense this is something you had already been thinking about from the moment you began playing on words with the *Poliscar.* On the one hand, noting the danger of surveillance, that is *police* car, and on the other, trying to revitalize the notion of the *polis,* the community. It also seems that you are not just now beginning to play with fear. Your consciousness of fear has always been part of the aesthetic element for you, maybe even part of the Brechtian *Verfremdung* you mention—your work shouldn't be too warm and cuddly, it shouldn't be too user-friendly. There should always be an element of fear as part of the experience. Or perhaps you feel that there is an element of fear, hostility, negative feeling, which is inextricably connected with the hope for the building of community?

Wodiczko: Yes, because of the legitimacy of community. The community can only be legitimate when it questions its own legitimacy. This is certainly true in a so-called community of city inhabitants. New York as a community has to question itself immediately. "We New Yorkers." The homeless people can define what they mean by being New Yorkers, and this does not correspond to the others.

Robbins: I hope you know that you've been very important to theorists of space, people like Rosalyn Deutsche and Neil Smith, and they find that your work helps them think about space. Maybe it would also be interesting to think about you as working with time. You've spoken about constructivism as a kind of experimentation with rhythms of life. The way that you use the ephemeral, the knowledge that such and such a projection will not last, won't be there, or the way you were just talking about the "same time next week" theory as a possible way of mobilizing the *Alien Staff*—all of these things make me think that in some way you are doing a kind of art in time. That time is the material you are working with.

Wodiczko: Yes, it has something to do with the life of the city, inserting itself into the existing rhythms of life or ways of perception or interaction between different inhabitants, their relation to changing circumstances. What was good yesterday might be wrong today, and might be idiotic tomorrow. That's probably what Brecht believed. If one disrupts the routine perception of everyday life, one has to be tactical and temporary by principle. And that was definitely endorsed by the situationists. This is not only the beautiful theory of everyday life presented by Henri Lefebvre, but also an extremely humorous kind of surrealist touch. Life is also a kind of popular art, living your patterns and enduring. The disruption of this everyday life makes perfect sense as an aesthetic project because the everyday is already an aesthetic project.

Robbins: Are you aware of being in dialogue with the perceptual rhythms of television advertising, to which you feel in some way you have to offer an alternative?

Wodiczko: I don't think they are necessarily my enemies. On occasion you see some level of risk and innovation and maybe meaningful disruption in advertising. I don't want to be a kind of a straight moralist like many of my colleagues. I still have, even today, certain hopes that more intelligent and critical artists and designers working within the system might be able to, if not challenge the system, at least insert some degree of alertness into it. I would never really give up on extending critical strategies within the population of designers. We need some colleagues, some infiltrators, there. Some artists working in advertising leave and reenter again, perverting, reversing, or appropriating its priorities. In terms of reception (not necessarily intention), the Benetton advertising on some occasions has provoked challenging cultural discourse.

Robbins: Well, one of the reasons I asked you about time, and the work it seemed to me that you are doing in the medium of time, on the materiality of time, is because I'm very curious about the extent to which the question of the public is a question of time as much as it is a question of space. We ask, "What's a public space?" but of course in this speeded-up, speed-it-up rhythm we all know, the public is also very much a question of time.

Wodiczko: I'll make this short. In France, when I started to discuss what benefits the *Alien Staff* could bring to immigrant populations, many of the activists and social workers told me it might be a necessary bridge between the new younger immigrants, people born of immigrant parents, who are still treated as immigrants in France, and their parents, from whom they are often alienated, and their parents' experience of crossing. Their parents are socially segregated, a population which it is hopeless to try to integrate—so the French say—so let's integrate the youth. The *Alien Staff* was understood as a possibility of a parent-children link that was something new. But this might require different equipment, or even a different cultural project than mine.

When Jagoda took the *Alien Staff* to the New York Institute of Technology, she decided bravely to present herself as an immigrant and not as a professor. And most of her students are Long Island children of immigrants. Somehow, electrified or hypnotized by her presence with this *Alien Staff,* they recognized something similar between her and their parents, something that they never really understood. Who are these immigrants? What are those silences? What does it mean? They learned from this so-called class session. There's no definition of what it was. Was this a lecture? Was it a history lesson? Was it a media course or performance? I witnessed it because I had to help get her there. Some people started to take photographs, and it became a spectacle. The students completely changed their normal seating position in relation to her. They created a different space in the classroom. And she thinks that they respected her afterwards much more. Oral history, memory, the transmission of experience: these have something to do with time.

Originally published as "Alien Staff: Krzysztof Wodiczko in Conversation with Bruce Robbins," in *Veiled Histories: The Body, Place, and Public Art,* ed. Anna Novakov (New York: DAP, 1997). Another version appears in *Alphabet City* (Toronto), no. 6 (1998), pp. 134–47.

Jedliński: Let me begin with the question about the relationship of the Polish *Vehicle* from 1973, a replica of which we have here in the Muzeum Sztuki in Łódź, to the *Homeless Vehicle* you created in New York in the late '80s, as well as to the other vehicles you created or designed in the intervening years, like *Vehicle for the Worker, Vehicle-Platform, Vehicle-Podium,* and *Vehicle-Café 1* and *2.*

Wodiczko: It is easier for us to talk about this since we both know how different the context was then, and how hard it is to talk about it here today, in the United States, in Western Europe, or in contemporary Eastern Europe. People cannot possibly imagine the situation of the artist or intellectual in the Poland of the '70s.

We were immersed, if not submerged, in a very "liberal" authoritarian system, if that is possible, a system that allowed artists to work using all means and methods, as long as they stayed away from anything political and didn't make any explicit reference to cultural politics or, above all—and this was very important—to the politics of life in Poland.

In the morning, artists went to the different jobs the State provided for them, since everything was organized by the State—that is, quite often work meant producing State propaganda and reproducing an image of a glorious and well-run society.

The morning work continued in the evening in the name of freedom, where we tried to "experiment with different means of artistic expression," as the media put it, completely cut off from the morning work, and, of course, we liked this separation. But artists forgot that it was less in the morning that they were collaborators with the State than in the evening, when they enjoyed the freedom not to get involved in politics or in any other social problem. Unlike other citizens who had no privileges, they had studios to work in and got more living space, and they took advantage of that freedom. But in fact, their freedom was simply a part of the self-legitimation system of the autocratic machine, which wished to present itself as being open, as offering freedom of creativity, and as "having a human face."

In this way they greatly contributed to the political propaganda by doing nothing that could be called political. The State could then say, "Everything is all right. Artists work where they should be working (during the day), but they are also doing what they all like to do—art (at night)." Artists gradually adopted, without realizing it, a kind of logic—or supposed logic—for living in

that sophisticated authoritarian system, a logic that my friend Andrzej Turowski has called *ideoza*—how shall we translate that?—"ideosis," a compilation of everyday "commonsense" choices and their "philosophical justifications," all with a view to safe navigation through the system. Part of this navigation was the life they led at night.

But I, too, have changed, in the sense of my so-called "artistic development," and independently of the context I work in. All those vehicles have been seen in art exhibitions, and those encounters were planned by me or by the curators of those exhibitions precisely so that such a question would arise. For example, in Warsaw in 1994, where that question was best formulated, this was done very simply by raising all the *Vehicles* off the floor and lining them up along one axis, as if it were a fashion show or automobile showroom. Suddenly they appeared on the same plane or platform, although they weren't originally supposed to. That's because they belonged to completely different contexts. They all had wheels, of roughly the same size, especially the first and latest ones. An absurd resemblance. They were all meant to move. Now that I have seen them all gathered together in one exhibition, I ask myself the same question you asked me. I don't have any clear-cut answer. Actually, I see a lack of relationship among the *Vehicles*.

However, there is one fundamental difference among them. The first vehicles mostly dealt with me and my artist friends, whether as an intellectual milieu of the system of culture within which we functioned, in turn part of a larger ideological mechanism, or as a total work of art and politics—for those vehicles were nothing other than a metaphorical concretization of that one great vehicle that was the technocratic Poland of central planning, the Poland of progress, a progressive movement of the Newtonian type. Every slogan we saw on buildings announced that we were catching up with the West, "on the road of progress," picking up speed on the "highway to a better future." The intelligentsia was to contribute to the rational progress. Progress was guaranteed, on condition that everyone, including artists and intellectuals, devote themselves to that machine and accept it as a given. Within the machine, it was they who would revive and inspire it. Furthermore intellectuals were considered a stratum of the working intelligentsia—an interesting concept, by the way, of the productivist type, the same way productivists dressed in workers' overalls (which they themselves had designed) and wore worker' hats (or caps, to be more precise). We were already a part of that productivist regime. There were all kinds of events where we had to dress everything up in a certain kind of progressivism or

"productivism." You couldn't just go around thinking too much or too critically; you, the artist, also had to function like a poet "creatively" lost in the clouds, for whom there was also allotted a certain amount of room in the machine. A certain part of the intelligentsia had a similar place in the machine, and one could say that the subject who operated the vehicle was in fact an object, a part of this machine. And yet there was, in this vehicle, a certain illusion of freedom, moving back and forth and seeing the world independently, in peripatetic fashion. And for all that the independence was limited by the dimensions of the machine and the manner in which one moved upon it, there emerged a dubious dialectic based on this dual point of view. The thesis and antithesis were to influence the synthesis, but the synthesis had a direction determined in advance. It was not simple locomotion, just moving along the ground—dangerous terrain—but rather involved elevation above it, to the level of the platform of the vehicle, somewhat closer to the clouds. The result was that I gave up every other vehicle project to work on this one for over a year and a half. At the time I was working with Krzysztof Meissner, one of the leading industrial designers in Poland. We were taking part in a design competition for a new vehicle that was being sponsored by some Japanese company. We produced a huge number of proposals for translating the muscle and mechanical power of the human body into forward motion.

At a certain point I saw that despite the fact that I myself had come up with many proposals—one of which was very close to the winning design, which I didn't know at the time—the whole thing had ceased to interest me. The vehicle I had in mind had a totally different dimension. When I discussed it with various artist friends, I constantly had to defend my design. They were always trying to convince me that it should go forward and backward. Like the operator moving back and forth along that tilting platform, they insisted that the vehicle should be designed to move in *both* directions. But I didn't agree. To emphasize that it was a one-way vehicle had, for me, a political character, and not a self-investigative "Wittgensteinian," existential, "conceptual," or "body-art" one.

Jedliński: Your project had a critical basis.

Wodiczko: Yes. And it also had a connection to my emphasis on design. I intuitively understood the convergence between my situation as an industrial designer and the whole system, which was itself operating as such a monstrous

productivist designer. The basic difference between the first *Vehicle* and the others is that other people operate the later ones. They move along the ground. They are not simply prisoners of the vehicles; they have, economically and politically speaking, a much more active, though still undetermined, role.

Jedliński: A role compelled by their social situation, especially with respect to the *Homeless Vehicle*.

Wodiczko: That's true. For it is a machine, the capitalist machine, that forces people, even on the lowest economic level, to operate as entrepreneurs. Their destiny is in their own hands. In the long run, they have the possibility of escaping this. They have some chance of doing so, and they are trying not only to free themselves, but also to be articulate, like people that are free. Of course, this is a different kind of absurdity than the one we were talking about in 1970s Poland.

Jedliński: That first *Vehicle* was in a certain sense conceived as a political metaphor.

Wodiczko: Yes. It was a kind of metaphoric translation, but here we are dealing with a work of a more performative character having to do with aspects of concrete daily life. The *Homeless Vehicle* also has an economic character. These vehicles really look like they might be useful. They superimpose themselves onto concrete conditions of living and the attempts at surviving those conditions.

Jedliński: Do you yourself have an answer to the question as put, that is, the difference, rather than the similarity, between the older vehicles and the more recent ones?

Wodiczko: I'm still looking for the answer. . . . What does the whole absurdity of such a productivist way of life depend on? Under a system of central planning in a caretaker state, they care about people, whether they imprison them, reward them, or simply tolerate them. Everyone is a part of that caring machine. Then I began dealing with the question of that machine in the capitalist jungle, where there are also certain myths and a faith in possibilities. Each person is like a helmsman, the captain of their own ship, even in the most miserable

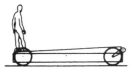

of conditions. But at the same time, there is no way that they can be free. Of course, people have the illusion that they can be free. There were similar illusions in Poland in the '70s, the illusion of artistic and intellectual freedom, for example, but the level of unfreedom was higher.

Jedliński: Yet in lining up the *Vehicles* in a row, you suggest a continuum. One might suspect such a link anyway, just by looking at your work over time.

Wodiczko: Yes, I do think there is one definite continuity. That is the attempt to design a vehicle to articulate the human situation, a kind of existential design. The machine articulates, and at the same time investigates, both people's conditions of being and their interior situation. They are constantly assailed by what is going on outside them; their souls are haunted by the system. But the system is also haunted by individuals, and, in some sense, so are the vehicles. They can only tell of the vicissitudes of our lives in two completely different but symmetrical man-machine systems. In the Polish *Vehicles* there is either a passivity or some illusionary activity on the part of the user; in the American ones there is an incredible activism. They practically become a weapon for survival, a challenging, even provocative, piece of equipment.

Jedliński: At the time of the second Biennale of Contemporary Art in Lyons in 1995, you showed the *Alien Staff,* along with a videotape documenting its use. Here there is also continuity and development.

Wodiczko: Yes, but it was through the creation of something that would be economically feasible, that I could pay for myself—mostly out of my salary as a professor. With help from various organizations and museums I could assure that it would really be produced, and that those who decided to participate in the experiment would be able to use the equipment. Immigrants were the ones who had to formulate—that is, find words for—their experiences as strangers in a way that could not be expressed in normal language. These experiences were first formulated in front of a television camera, since it is easier to talk to a camera than to another person. They then took part in the editing of the visual material. Often they told the same story to the camera in various languages—the story was different each time—so we could grasp both what was most important and what had been forgotten, relegated to the unconscious, or suppressed. Because in order to survive, many of their experiences had been

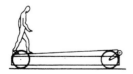

crumpled, smeared, or spit out, in order that they no longer have any clear form. This clarity of form was recovered and readied so that it could be made known to anyone, whether people passing by on the street, at work, even to family members. The greatest accomplishment was that the people who use the *Staff* became surer of themselves, regained confidence. They acquired the possibility of speaking and communicating, along with understanding many aspects of their inner as well as exterior situation.

Jedliński: I'd be curious to hear about your experiences with using these objects in Poland. For years, even decades (even limiting oneself to the postwar period), the Poles were the strangers for the West. Now they are the hosts in a place where lots of foreigners come, whether it's from Romania, Africa, or wherever. Apparently you worked with an Algerian in Poland.

Wodiczko: There is little evidence that emigrant experiences really help people to understand the situation of others in their own country. I saw this very clearly in Spain, in Catalonia. The Spanish were a part of that great emigration, but at home they are unable to acknowledge or understand the situation of their immigrants, whether they come from Africa or from Poland. It seems to me that, for example, bringing the experiences of a Spaniard abroad back to Spain might help, through the superimposition of the experiences of "one of us" abroad onto the experiences of foreigners here. (Incidentally, *Xenobàcul,* the first prototype of the *Alien Staff,* was tested in Barcelona in 1992.)

I wanted to go back to the role of the object itself, the extent to which the role of the object differs between the *Vehicles* and the *Staff. Poliscar* was an intermediate vehicle. There wasn't any relationship between those vehicles as objects and their users, as there was in the case of the *Staff* or the *Mouthpiece.* Here the relation is a more intimate one. These instruments are electronic and physical containers of experience, exposed and vulnerable objects that in turn invite trust and confidence. They become personifications of the users, their doubles. The user can also question what the instrument says. The new version of the *Mouthpiece* is constructed in such a way that the user can move it aside even as it is speaking the user's words, to say something else in his or her own voice. Thus one can always add new narrations, because history is always new. There is a constant arguing with one's own memory or ideology, of today against yesterday or tomorrow. In this regard, these instruments have taken on something of what British psychologist D. W. Winnicott has called the "transi-

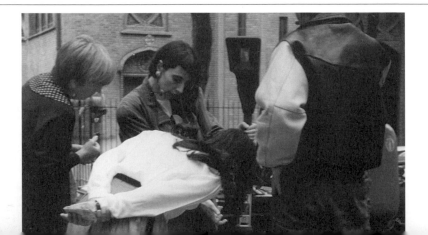

tional object," an object situated between the internal and the external world. The external world, which changes, is something which we do not master. We do not master the internal world, either, but here very complex psychological and biological processes come into play. This object-in-between is something we can play with, and play very creatively. This object is a holy object in the development of the child. Immigrants are in some sense like new children who don't talk yet, who have to acquire self-understanding in a totally new world and, simultaneously, a self-understanding as they transform themselves, as they develop. In my opinion they are people who are prophets of a better world, because they have developed further than others. They reject the world in which they found themselves and propose a world in which the mistakes that have been their experience should not be repeated. They have to use an object which they first must psychically reject as something that I have imparted to them, in order that they may convey their own inner world into it. They begin to play with these objects. There even occurs a dependence on them, which was not the case with the vehicles. The basic function of this object is *healing,* the treatment of the symptoms of a situation, in the sense that Julia Kristeva said that the emigrant is a symptom. At the same time it treats another symptom, that is, of xenophobia, another disease. Thus, on one hand we have the transitional object, and on the other, what Kristeva called a communicative artifact. Those who are horrified reject the other because they are afraid of their own otherness; the presence of the other is a manifestation of something within themselves. In order to see this and acknowledge it at all, something artificial is needed, an artifice—something you devise, as in a bad dream or a story. On one hand it is somewhat unreal, but on the other it refers to reality and is strangely familiar. One can not be afraid of it. There is something of the trickster in the magic of the stranger. Strangers have always communicated through an excess of gestures and accents, assuming, as Kristeva put it, a "baroque personality." These objects bring with them new functions, yet they continue the tradition of the vehicles. But the *Mouthpieces* introduce yet another function that does not exist in the *Staff:* the understanding of the stranger as cyborg, a figure that is part artificial, part natural. This cyborg, he or she, can play on that boundary between the natural and the artificial. There is a certain interior discourse between who I was and who I am becoming or who I am, a state of continual undermining of every stereotype and identity. I propose this kind of playing with the world as play that makes the world better, one where the stranger would no longer be so strange, where we all would play with our

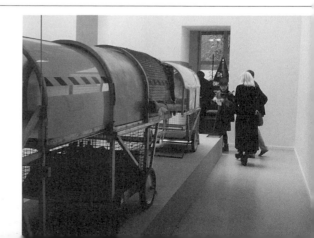

identities. This is obviously a utopia, as it was for Kristeva or Freud. I only refer to that utopia. I don't believe in it, but neither do I deny its importance. One can never attain utopia; I am only saying that contesting the world we live in is our duty. For this reason, I can recognize utopia for its critical value without "believing" in it. Strangers are the agents or messengers of this process, and the instruments that I propose help them become artists, virtuosi of the mission to interrupt and undermine this world and announce another one.

Jedliński: So far we have been talking about the various themes in your work. I would like to ask about the nature of the various objects that have been created in your work, their material and objective nature. I am also directly raising the question about your relation to art institutions, museums, galleries, collections, and exhibitions.

Wodiczko: In the museum I consider them to be an interesting set of relics, reminders which are quite capable of continuing their critical mission even as museum artifacts. In particular, the *Staffs* and *Mouthpieces* in their own way are already a kind of museology, since they are reliquaries and recorded video narratives, as well as being documents which portray the situation of an exchange of views around these objects. I designed these objects above all to be functional in the living world, but I have nothing against their second life as museum objects, since they are witnesses, bearers, and containers of the experiences, and of the existential and cultural situations in which they functioned. They were tools, but now they contain within themselves the memory of the conditions of which they were born, and on their video screens and in their reliquaries the photographs, films, and other documents display all the artisticality and virtuosity brought to the interpersonal situations which were created thanks to their existence. Compared to painting and sculpture, which themselves contain a certain number of references to their original situation in the world, my instruments may be more charged as museum objects. They bring with them experience and exchange with respect to the totality of the external and internal situation of the people involved during the time of their use.

Jedliński: In addition to being reliquaries, as you put it, at the same time they are relicts, remains and documents of your actions or the actions transpiring between you and other individuals or society.

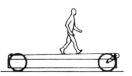

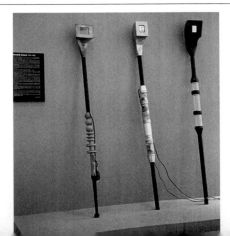

219   **Wodiczko:** But the hope is that they will become useless in the world outside museum walls, that they will someday concern a time long past. Then they will truly be relicts, which is also somewhat utopian. My hope is that they will one day only be a part of the ancient history of art or of culture, that they will be truly passé.

Jedliński: They'll be like those displays of medieval instruments of torture, which show some misery from the distant past.

Wodiczko: Let's hope so.

Recorded at Krzysztof Wodiczko's studio in New York on April 20, 1997; first published in the journal *Odra,* 1998.

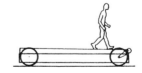

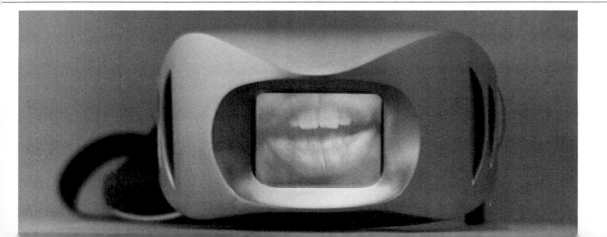

Bookshelf

Allison, David B., ed. *The New Nietzsche: Contemporary Styles of Interpretation.* New York: Dell, 1977.

Althusser, Louis. "Ideology and Ideological State Apparatuses (Notes toward an Investigation)." In *Lenin and Philosophy and Other Essays.* New York: Monthly Review Press, 1971.

Arendt, Hannah. *The Human Condition.* Chicago: University of Chicago Press, 1958. Especially chapter 2, "The Public and the Private Realm."

Arendt, Hannah. *The Origins of Totalitarianism.* London: George Allen and Unwin, 1963.

Bakhtin, Mikhail M. *The Dialogic Imagination: Four Essays,* ed. Michael Holquist. Austin: University of Texas Press, 1981.

Balibar, Etienne. "Rights of Man and Rights of Citizen: The Modern Dialectics of Equality and Freedom" and "Fichte and the Internal Border: An Address to the German Nation." In *Masses, Classes, Ideas: Studies on Politics and Philosophy before and after Marx.* London: Routledge, 1994.

Barthes, Roland. "The Eiffel Tower." In *The Eiffel Tower and Other Mythologies.* Berkeley: University of California Press, 1997.

Barthes, Roland. "Semiology and the Urban." In *The City and the Sign: An Introduction to Urban Semiotics,* ed. Mark Gottdiener and Alexandros Ph. Lagopoulos. New York: Columbia University Press, 1986.

Bataille, Georges. *The Bataille Reader,* ed. Fred Botting and Scott Wilson. Oxford: Blackwell, 1997.

Benjamin, Walter. *Illuminations,* ed. Hannah Arendt. New York: Schocken, 1969. Especially "What Is Epic Theater?," "The Storyteller," and "Theses on the Philosophy of History."

Benjamin, Walter. *Reflections,* ed. Peter Demetz. New York: Schocken, 1986. Especially "The Author as Producer" and "Critique of Violence."

221   Bhabha, Homi K. *Nation and Narration.* London: Routledge, 1990. Especially "DissemiNation."

Bourdieu, Pierre, and Hans Haacke. *Free Exchange.* Stanford: Stanford University Press, 1995.

Brecht, Bertolt. *Antigone,* trans. Judith Malina. Harwood Academic Publishers, 1991.

Brecht, Bertolt. *Brecht on Theatre: The Development of an Aesthetic,* ed. and trans. John Willet. London: Methuen, 1964. Especially "The Modern Theatre Is the Epic Theatre," "Theatre for Pleasure or Theatre for Instruction," and "Short Description of a New Technique of Acting Which Proposes an Alienation Effect."

Brusati, Franco. *Bread and Chocolate.* 1974. Verona Cinematografia.

Buckley, Cheryl. "Made in Patriarchy: Toward a Feminist Analysis of Women and Design." *Design Issues* 3, no. 2 (1986).

Bürger, Peter. *Theory of the Avant-Garde.* Minneapolis: University of Minnesota Press, 1984.

Castells, Manuel. *The City and the Grassroots: A Cross-Cultural Theory of Urban Social Movements.* Berkeley: University of California Press, 1984.

Castells, Manuel. *The Information Age: Economy, Society and Culture.* 3 vols. Oxford: Blackwell, 1996–1998.

Castells, Manuel. *The Urban Question: A Marxist Approach.* Cambridge: MIT Press, 1977.

Certeau, Michel de. *The Practice of Everyday Life.* Berkeley: University of California Press, 1984. Especially Part 3, "Spatial Practices."

Chambers, Iain. *Migrancy, Culture, Identity.* London: Routledge, 1994. Especially chapter 7, "The Wound and the Shadow."

222   Chaplin, Charlie. *City Lights.* 1931. Roy Export Company Establishment. Opening scene titled "To the People of This City We Donate This Monument: Peace and Prosperity."

Chaplin, Charlie. *My Autobiography.* New York: Simon and Schuster, 1964.

Chaplin, Charlie. *The Pilgrim.* 1923. First National Company.

Chaplin, Charlie. "What People Laugh At." In *Focus on Chaplin,* ed. Donald W. McCaffrey. Englewood Cliffs, N.J.: Prentice-Hall, 1971.

Critchley, Simon. *The Ethics of Deconstruction: Derrida and Levinas.* Oxford: Blackwell, 1992.

Deleuze, Gilles, and Félix Guattari. *Nomadology: The War Machine,* trans. Brian Massumi. New York: Semiotext(e), 1986.

Derrida, Jacques. *Of Grammatology,* trans. Gayatri Chakravorty Spivak. Baltimore: Johns Hopkins University Press, 1976. Especially part I, "Writing before the Letter."

Deutsche, Rosalyn. *Evictions: Art and Spatial Politics.* Cambridge: MIT Press, 1996. Especially "Men in Space" and "Agoraphobia."

Engels, Friedrich. *The Housing Question.* Moscow: Progress Publishers, 1970.

Erlich, Victor. *Russian Formalism: History, Doctrine.* 3d ed. New Haven: Yale University Press, 1981.

Foucault, Michel. *The Foucault Reader,* ed. Paul Rabinow. New York: Pantheon, 1984.

Foucault, Michel. "Method." In *The History of Sexuality,* vol. 1: *An Introduction.* New York: Vintage, 1980.

Foucault, Michel. "Panopticism." In *Discipline and Punish: The Birth of the Prison,* trans. Alan Sheridan. New York: Pantheon, 1977.

223 Freud, Sigmund. "The Uncanny" (1919). In *The Pelican Freud Library,* vol. 14, ed. Albert Dickson. Harmondsworth: Penguin, 1985.

Gray, Chris Hables. *The Cyborg Handbook.* London: Routledge, 1995. Especially part 6, "The Politics of Cyborgs."

Grosz, George, John Heartfield, and Wieland Herzfelde. *Art Is in Danger!* Willimantic, Conn.: Curbstone Press, 1987.

Haraway, Donna. "A Manifesto for Cyborgs: Science, Technology, and Socialist Feminism in the 1980s." *Socialist Review* 80 (1985).

Hatab, J. Lawrence. *A Nietzschean Defense of Democracy: An Experiment in Postmodern Politics.* Chicago and LaSalle: Open Court, 1995.

Heartfield, John. *AIZ, Arbeiter-Illustrierte Zeitung.* David Evans; ed. Anna Lundgren. New York: Kent Fine Art, 1992.

Hoffman, Eva. *Lost in Translation: A Life in a New Language.* New York: Dutton, 1989.

Hollier, Denis. *Against Architecture: The Writings of Georges Bataille.* Cambridge: MIT Press, 1989.

Hombs, Mary Ellen, and Mitch Snyder. *Homelessness in America: A Forced March to Nowhere.* Washington: Community for Creative Non-Violence, 1982.

Kafka, Franz. *The Castle.* New York: Schocken, 1998.

Kafka, Franz. *The Trial.* New York: Schocken, 1995.

Kluge, Alexander. "On Film and the Public Sphere." *New German Critique* 24–25 (1981–1982).

Knabb, Ken, ed. and trans. *Situationist International Anthology.* Berkeley: Bureau of Public Secrets, 1981. Especially Guy Debord, "Introduction to a Critique of Urban Geography" and "Perspectives for Conscious Alterations in

Everyday Life"; Attila Kotanyi and Raoul Vaneigem, "Elementary Program of the Bureau of Unitary Urbanism."

Kristeva, Julia. *Strangers to Ourselves.* New York: Columbia University Press, 1991. Especially chapter 8, "Might Not Universality Be . . . Our Own Foreignness?"

Kroll, Lucien. *The Architecture of Complexity.* London: B. T. Batsford, 1986.

Lacan, Jacques. *The Four Fundamental Concepts of Psychoanalysis,* ed. Jacques-Alain Miller, trans. Alan Sheridan. New York: Norton, 1978. Especially "Of the Gaze as Objet Petit a."

Laclau, Ernesto, and Chantal Mouffe. *Hegemony and Socialist Strategy: Towards a Radical Democratic Politics.* London: Verso, 1985.

Lefebvre, Henri. *Critique of Everyday Life.* Vol. 1. London: Verso, 1991.

Lefebvre, Henri. "The Everyday and Everydayness." (Translation of an entry in *Encyclopedia Universalis.*) *Yale French Studies* 73 (1988).

Lefebvre, Henri. *The Production of Space.* Oxford: Blackwell, 1991.

Lefebvre, Henri. "Space: Social Product and Use Value." In *Critical Sociology: European Perspectives,* ed. J. W. Freiberg. New York: Irvington Publishers, 1979.

Lefebvre, Henri. *Writings on Cities,* ed. and trans. Eleonore Kofman and Elizabeth Lebos. Oxford: Blackwell, 1996.

Lefort, Claude. *Democracy and Political Theory.* Minneapolis: University of Minnesota Press, 1988.

Lefort, Claude. *The Political Forms of Modern Society: Bureaucracy, Democracy, Totalitarianism.* Cambridge: MIT Press, 1986. Especially "Politics and Human Rights."

Levinas, Emmanuel. *The Levinas Reader,* ed. Seán Hand. Oxford: Blackwell, 1989. Especially "Substitution" and "Reality and Its Shadow."

225   Lichtenberg Ettinger, Bracha. "Metramorphic Borderlinks and Matrixial Borderspace." In *Rethinking Borders,* ed. John Welchman. London: Macmillan, 1995.

Mahler, Sarah J. *American Dreaming: Immigrant Life on the Margins.* Princeton: Princeton University Press, 1995.

Mannheim, Karl. *Ideology and Utopia: An Introduction to the Sociology of Knowledge.* San Diego: Harcourt Brace Jovanovich, 1985.

Marcuse, Herbert. *Eros and Civilization.* Boston: Beacon Press, 1955.

McLuhan, Marshall. *Understanding Media: The Extensions of Man.* Cambridge: MIT Press, 1994.

Merleau-Ponty, Maurice. *The Visible and the Invisible.* Evanston: Northwestern University Press, 1968.

Mickiewicz, Adam. *Pan Tadeusz,* trans. Kenneth Mackenzie. London: Polish Cultural Foundation, 1964. Chapter 12, section on Jankiel's concert ("Koncert nad Koncertami").

Missac, Pierre. *Walter Benjamin's Passages.* Cambridge: MIT Press, 1995.

Mitchell, William J. *City of Bits: Space, Place, and the Infobahn.* Cambridge: MIT Press, 1995.

Mosès, Stéphane. *L'ange de l'histoire: Rosenzweig, Benjamin, Scholem.* Paris: Seuil, 1992.

Mosès, Stéphane. "The Theological-Political Model of History." *History and Memory* 1 (Tel Aviv, 1989).

Mouffe, Chantal, ed. *Deconstruction and Pragmatism: Simon Critchley, Jacques Derrida, Ernesto Laclau and Richard Rorty.* London: Routledge, 1996.

Mouffe, Chantal, ed. *Dimensions of Radical Democracy: Pluralism, Citizenship, Community.* London: Verso, 1992.

226   Muschamp, Herbert. *File under Architecture*. Cambridge: MIT Press, 1974.

Nancy, Jean-Luc. *The Inoperative Community,* ed. Peter Connor. Minneapolis: University of Minnesota Press, 1991.

Negt, Oskar, and Alexander Kluge. *Public Sphere and Experience: Toward an Analysis of the Bourgeois and Proletarian Public Sphere,* trans. Peter Labanyi, Jamie Owen Daniel, and Assenka Oksiloff. Minneapolis: University of Minnesota Press, 1993.

Nietzsche, Friedrich. "On the Uses and Disadvantages of History for Life." In *Untimely Meditations.* New York: Cambridge University Press, 1983.

Nietzsche, Friedrich. *The Portable Nietzsche,* ed. Walter Kaufmann. New York: Viking, 1954.

Papanek, Victor. *Design for the Real World: Human Ecology and Social Change.* Chicago: Academy Publications, 1972.

Plato. *Early Socratic Dialogues,* ed. Trevor J. Saunders. Harmondsworth: Penguin, 1987. Especially *Phaedrus.*

Rakatansky, Mark. "A/Partments." *Assemblage* 35 (1998).

Rakatansky, Mark. "Prototype Handrail." *Progressive Architecture,* January 1992.

Riegl, Alois. "The Modern Cult of Monuments: Its Character and Its Origin," trans. Kurt Forster. *Oppositions* 25 (1982).

Robbins, Bruce, ed. *The Phantom Public Sphere*. Minneapolis: University of Minnesota Press, 1993. Especially "Introduction: The Public as Phantom," and Nancy Fraser, "Rethinking the Public Sphere: A Contribution to the Critique of Actually Existing Democracy."

Ronell, Avital. *The Telephone Book: Technology, Schizophrenia, Electric Speech.* Lincoln: University of Nebraska Press, 1992.

227   Rose, Jacqueline. "Sexuality in the Field of Vision." In *Sexuality in the Field of Vision.* London: Verso, 1986.

Schutz, Alfred. "The Stranger." In *The Psychology of Society: An Anthology,* ed. Richard Sennett. New York: Vintage, 1977.

Simmel, Georg. "The Metropolis and Mental Life." In *The Sociology of Georg Simmel,* ed. Kurt H. Wolff. New York: Free Press, 1964.

Stone, Rosanne Allucquère. *The War of Desire and Technology at the Close of the Mechanical Age.* Cambridge: MIT Press, 1996.

Tafuri, Manfredo. *Architecture and Utopia: Design and Capitalist Development.* Cambridge: MIT Press, 1976.

Tocqueville, Alexis de. *Democracy in America.* New York: Knopf, 1994.

Turowski, Andrzej. *Wielka utopia awangardy: artystyczne i społeczne utopie w sztuce rosyjskiej 1910–1930.* Summary in English and Russian: Great Utopias of the Avant-Garde: Artistic and Social Utopias in Russian Art 1910–1930. Warsaw: P.W.N., 1990.

Vertov, Dziga. *Kino-Eye: The Writings of Dziga Vertov,* ed. Annette Michelson. Berkeley: University of California Press, 1995.

Vertov, Dziga. *Man with a Movie Camera.* 1929. Moscow: VUFKU.

Winnicott, D. W. "On the Use of an Object" and "Psychosomatic Dosorder." In *Psychoanalytic Explorations.* Cambridge: Harvard University Press, 1992.

Winnicott, D. W. *Playing and Reality.* London: Tavistock, 1971.

Žižek, Slavoj. "Fantasy, Bureaucracy, Democracy." In *Looking Awry: An Introduction to Jacques Lacan through Popular Culture.* Cambridge: MIT Press, 1991.

Žižek, Slavoj. *The Sublime Object of Ideology.* London: Verso, 1989.

XOSX-94MIT

Cinema 2 S.00 7544 1

XOSX-94MIT